# Vengeance!

## The Vultee Vengeance Dive Bomber

# Vengeance!
## The Vultee Vengeance Dive Bomber

## Peter C. Smith

Smithsonian Institution Press
Washington, D.C.

Copyright © 1986 Peter C. Smith

First published in the United States 1987 by
Smithsonian Institution Press

First published in the United Kingdom 1986
by Airlife Publishing Ltd.

Library of Congress Catalog Number 87-61974

ISBN 0-87474-866-6

Printed in England

# Contents

# Acknowledgements

The story of the Vultee Vengeance, the 'Forgotten' dive-bomber of World War II, has long needed telling. Although over the years there have been several articles written about this plane, many assumptions and conclusions have merely been copied from one to another without the true facts being verified in any way. Thus many myths have grown up about the aircraft and it is widely vilified in print by historians who should know better.

The reason that so much incorrect information has hitherto been written about this aircraft is because the men who designed, built, tested or flew the Vengeance in combat were hardly ever asked for *their* opinions. I have rectified this, and any merit this book has as a factual account is due to the many people who have responded to my requests for information. The author would therefore like to thank the following persons for their kindness and patience in answering his many questions and explaining many hitherto unrevealed facets of the Vengeance story. In allowing me into their homes for interviews, for allowing me to use their logbooks, memoirs, photographs and notes, and for their encouragement in finally presenting the true story of this misrepresented dive-bomber, my grateful and sincerest thanks. Simply for convenience sake and lack of space only, they are listed in alphabetical order with their main Vengeance connection of the period listed in brackets. Their actual ranks or titles at the time concerned are given in the text of the book for the same reasons:

BERGEL, Hugh (Ferry Pilot)
BERTAGNA, Victor B. (Designer, Vultee — Downey)
BOWMAN, Ken (Pilot, RAAF Central Training School, Williamstown,)
BROWN, Eric M. (Royal Navy Test Pilot)
BROWNING, Bob (Navigator, 8 Indian Squadron)
BRYANT, Jack (T.A.G., 791 Squadron, Fleet Air Arm)
COLEMAN, Theodore (Vice-President, Northrop Corporation, Hawthorne)
COOKE, Mrs M. R. (Widow of Corporal Fitter E. L. Cooke, 110 (H) Squadron)
CROSLEY, Wing Commander Mike (RAF Test Pilot)
CUMING, D. R. (RAAF Test Pilot)
DALLOSSO, Peter R. (FAA Pilot, 733 Squadron)
DAVIS, Frank W. (Test Pilot, Vultee — Downey)
DYER, F. R. (Pilot, 84 Squadron, RAF)
FYFE, Air Commodore E. G. (Commanding Officer, 4 OTU and 77 Wing, RAAF)
GABRIELSON, Ron (Navigator, RAAF, 84 Squadron)
GERBER, John E. (Navigation Officer, 4 OTU and 21 Squadron, RAAF)
GIBBS, Dennis. (Commanding Officer, 82 Squadron, RAF)
GILL, Arthur Murland (Commanding Officer, 84 Squadron, RAF)
HALL, Brian (Sgt. Motor Transport, 12 Squadron, RAAF)
HANSFORTH, T. G. (MT Driver, 84 Squadron, RAF)
HOLT, Walter E. (Production Line Operative, Northrop, Hawthorne)
IRVINE, Charles R. (Project Engineer, Vultee — Downey)
JOHNSTONE, Douglas (Instructor and Pilot, 4 OTU and 12 Squadron, RAAF)
LAMBERT, Freddie F. (Commanding Officer, 110 Squadron, RAF)
LATCHAM, Dr Peter (M.O., 110 Squadron, RAF)
LIMBRICK, George A. (Pilot, 4 OTU, 23 Squadron and 1 WAGS, RAAF)

McINNES, Bud 'Red' (Pilot, RCAF, 110 Squadron, and 1340 Gas Warfare Flight)

McMICHAEL, J. (Commanding Officer, 82 Squadron, RAF)

McPHERSON, Cyril J. B. (Pilot, 12 Squadron, 4 and 7 OTUs RAAF)

MORRIS, Douglas (Navigator, 84 Squadron, RAF)

PEDEN, Edward D. (Production Group Leader, Northrop — Hawthorne)

PEDLER, Aubrey W. (Pilot, RAAF, 84 Squadron)

PIDDUCK, E. L. (Ground Engineer, 45 Squadron)

RAMSDEN, John (Chief Engineering Officer, 84 Squadron, RAF)

RAVENSCROFT, G. (Pilot, 84 Squadron, RAF)

RITCHIE, Donald J. (Pilot, RAAF and CO 110 and 82 Squadrons)

SETON, Hugh W. (Pilot, RCAF, 8 Squadron, Indian Air Force)

SMITH, Richard L. (Pilot, USAAF 8th Air Force)

STEPHENS, Moye W. (Test Pilot, Northrop — Hawthorne)

TIBBLE, L. R. M. (Pilot, 152 OTU and Target Towing Units, India)

TONKIN, Ken (RAAF, Pilot, 84 Squadron)

WIDDOP, H (Ground Staff, 84 Squadron, RAF)

WORTH, Stanley J. (Power Plant Design Engineer, Vultee — Nashville)

In additional to those directly involved with the Vultee Vengeance many other individuals and organisations gave unstinted help and enabled me to track down leads, sources and unculled data to complete the story fully. My thanks therefore to the following:

BALZER, Gerald H. (Archivist, American Historical Aviation Society)

BELL, Dana M. (National Air & Space Museum, Washington, D.C.)

BLACKWOOD, I. D. (RAF Personnel Management Centre)

BROWN, Charles A. (Historian, General Dynamics, Convair Division, San Diego)

BROWN, Wayne (77 Squadron Engineering Section, RAAF — Preserving the Kogarth Vengeance)

BUTLER, Bryan R. (Senior Curator, Audio-Visual Records, Australian War Memorial)

CARTER, Dustin W. (Draftsman, Vultee — Downey)

CHART, Dr Ira E. (Historian, Western Museum of Flight, Hawthorne and Northrop Corporation, Hawthorne)

COOKE, Mrs M. R. (Widow of E. L. Cooke, Pilot, 110 Squadron)

CUNY, M. Jean (Historian, French Air Force)

DEMPSEY, V. M. (Naval Secretary, Ministry of Defence)

DONAHUE, Jim (American Aviation Historical Society)

DOU, Colonel Gilbert, (Director, *Service Historique De L' Armée De L'Air* Vincennes, France.)

HAQ, Group Captain Qazi Mahboobul (Air Attaché, Pakistan Air Force)

HOWARD, L. R. (Air Historical Branch 3, RAF)

JACOB, H. G. (Terminal Manager, Perth International Airport)

LAWRENCE, Lt Cdr H. J. M. (Fleet Air Arm Officers Association)

LYLE, Mrs Virginia R. (Metro Archivist, Nashville Public Library)

MACK, R. W. (Photographic Section, RAF Museum)

MEGGS, Keith (Aviation Historical Society of Australia)

MULLIGAN, N. A. (Air Force Office, Department of Defence, RAAF)

NARANG, Wing Commander N. P. (Air Adviser, Indian Air Force)

NOWLAND, Mrs Betty (Widow of Pilot Officer Raymond Nowland, RAAF, 84 Squadron)

ODGERS, George (Historian, Garran, ACT, Australia)

PIPER, Robert K. (Historical Officer, RAAF, Department of Defence (Air Force)

POLLANEN, Flt Lt R. K. (Central Photographic Establishment, RAAF)

POTTINGER, L. (Australian War Memorial)

PURSER, F. (Curator, Air Force Memorial Estate, Bull Creek, WA)

RAVESTEIN, Charles (Historian, USAF Historical Research Center, Maxwell AFB)

RAYMOND, Stanley (Manager, *Northrop News,* Hawthorne)

SEAGRAVES, Atha (Communications Department, AVCO Aerostructures Division, Nashville)

SAUNDERS, David A. (Restoring second Vengeance at Bull Creek, WA)

SHORES, Christopher (Aviation Historian)

SLITER, Major Lester A. (Historian, USAF Historical Research Center, Maxwell AFB)

WILLIAMS, Mrs P. A. (RAF Personnel Management Centre)

WILSON, David (Air Force Office, Department of Defence, RAAF)

Extensive use has been made of photographs from private collections in order to present the complete pictorial history of the Vengeance, from contract signature to final days in museums. Most of these photographs, and indeed all the colour photography and the combat sequences, are unique and have not been seen before. From over 350 photographs the best quality pictures have been selected in the main, but where particularly rare shots are needed some lesser quality of print has had to be accepted in order that every facet is given pictorial coverage. Acknowledgements and credits are given under each photograph. The drawings and diagrams also add much that is new to the Vengeance history and my thanks go especially to Mr Tibble, Miss Parker, Mr Donahue and Mr Peden for their personal contributions.

Peter C. Smith
*Riseley, Bedford.*
*November, 1985*

# Chapter 1
# Innovation

When considering bomber aircraft as weapons of war the major prerequisite should be that the aircraft is capable of hitting the target it is aiming for. It is pointless for aircraft to fly higher, go faster, carry more bombs, have heavier defences against fighters or longer range if, when they arrive, the bombs they release fail to hit anything! The whole point of their being is negated, no matter what their merits purely as aircraft.

It was the dive-bomber that proved able to hit most consistently what it aimed at, thus fulfilling the prerequisite. In the Pacific War it was the American Navy's Douglas Dauntless that practically won it in the period 1942-43. On the Eastern Front it was the Soviet Petlyakov Pe-2 Peshka, flying at speeds many fighters could not match, that dive-bombed its way from the banks of the Volga all the way to the streets of Berlin, paving the way for the Soviet Army. There was another Allied dive-bomber that proved equally as accurate and precise as these two aircraft, when it was allowed to be; one, moreover, that carried out its function with the *maximum* number of direct hits and in reply took the *minimum* number of losses from enemy action than almost any other aircraft of World War II. And yet it is completely unknown. That aircraft was the Vultee Vengeance. This book is the forgotten dive-bomber's full story, told in depth for the first time.

Between the wars the dive-bomber had been revived and was being perfected by the Naval Air Arms of the United States, Sweden and Japan, and was featuring largely in the build-up of the new German *Luftwaffe*, the RAF's face remained firmly against such types. By 1940 the Germans, wedded to tactical air power, had conquered most of Western Europe in campaigns that lasted weeks rather than years and only the twenty-odd miles of the English Channel prevented their total victory.

With the victorious German army poised ready to invade at any time the bewildered leaders of Britain turned their thoughts to how to hit back at the German tanks and soldiers once they had come ashore, and they belatedly found that twenty years of neglect and derision had left them without the means. What was wanted was the British equivalent of the Ju 87, to do to the Germans what they had been doing to everyone else with such success, but it was not there!

Even now the whole concept of helping the army fight battles was resisted. 'The aeroplane is NOT a battlefield weapon', Wing Commander Slessor had proclaimed in 1934 and, as an Air Marshal, he was still reiterating this opinion in 1941, after Yugoslavia, Greece, Crete and large hunks of Russia had gone down to the *Stukas* in the same way as had Poland, Norway, Holland, Belgium and France. But Slessor, even with invasion still imminent in the spring of 1941, was still protesting, '. . . we don't want aircraft skidding around over Kent looking for enemy tanks, that is the job of the anti-tank gun.'

It needed someone with a fresh insight, someone who stood outside the blinkered blindness of the 'Bomb Berlin' school of thought, to break through this attitude. Luckily, the time produced the man in the dynamic shape of Lord Beaverbrook, the Canadian press baron, hastily brought into the wartime government to cut through red tape and get vital aircraft delivered in quantities. He was appointed by the Premier, Winston Churchill, to get the job done as Minister of Aircraft Production.

Beaverbrook, wrote A. J. P. Taylor, '. . . had no faith that independent, or as it was called, strategical bombing, would win the

1

war by itself. This faith was uncritically held at the Air Ministry, and it provided the underlying reason for the ceaseless carping which flowed from the Air Marshals.'

Despite this resistance Beaverbrook insisted on getting dive-bombers for the army from wherever he could. But where to get dive-bombers, even in America, there was the rub. Fortunately, almost immediately an answer was found. In California was found a small but innovative and go-ahead company of whom most Britons had never heard, the Vultee Aircraft Corporation. And on their drawing boards was the very aircraft for which Beaverbrook and Britain were so frantically searching!

In the 1930s the evolution of aircraft had taken massive strides in a relatively short period. Despite the Depression and a lack of large markets there was room for bright young aircraft engineers and designers to make their mark in this new industry, and the special 'get-up-and-go' always associated with America, and the West Coast in

particular, was conducive to the emergence of a whole succession of brilliant young innovators during this period.

Lockheed's team at Burbank, California, brought out the single-engined *Vega, Air Express, Sirius, Altair* and *Orion* designs. Then developed the twin-engined *Electra* and *Lodestar* with similar features, in response to the Boeing team's Model 247 which followed that company's *Monomail* and B-9 concepts. The Project Engineer at Burbank in the early 1930s was one Richard W. 'Dick' Palmer, a 1925 graduate of the California Institute of Technology (CALTECH), a Bachelor of Science in Engineering and Physics. He also had a Master's degree in Mechanical Engineering from the University of Minnesota. He had worked for the Douglas organisation in 1926/27 before moving to Lockheed in 1929. At Lockheed he was responsible for the retractable gears on the *Altair* and the *Orion,* among others.

John K. Northrop, another former Douglas engineer, founded a dynamic young company at El Segundo in 1932 and found

The historic signing of a Vengeance contract for the V-72 dive-bomber by Eric Roper of the BAC at Nashville. *(AVCO)*

fame with his *Alpha, Beta and Gamma* mailplanes. Designer Ed Heinemann joined his team and from them came the BT-1 dive-bomber with the perforated split-wing dive flaps that became the hallmark of the Douglas SBD when they took over the El Segundo plant in January 1938.

The Chief Engineer at Lockheed when John Northrop resigned in 1928 was his young former assistant, 27-year-old Gerald F. Vultee. (Although some contemporary documents also spell his name as Gerard, the records at the California Institute of Technology, where he was a student in 1921-23, give Gerald — he was known more often as 'Jerry'.) He had worked under Northrop at Douglas in 1926, and followed him to Lockheed the following year.

Jerry Vultee engineered improvements to Lockheed's *Vega* transport and designed the low-wing *Sirius* monoplane. He remained when Lockheed was taken over by the Detroit Aircraft Corporation in 1929 and became the Lockheed Division, but when the cold economic climate forced DAC into receivership in 1931 both Gerald and his chief test pilot, Vance Breese, after temporary employment with the Curtiss-Wright Technical Institute at Glendale, decided it was time to go it alone in order to develop their own concepts, principal of which was a single-engined, six-passenger transport plane on which they had already begun design work. With interest shown by American Airlines in the aircraft, E. L. Cord, President of the Cord Corporation, which already owned the Stinson Aircraft Corporation, put up the money to set up the Aircraft Development Corporation. In 1932 Vultee and Breese accordingly commenced work at Grand Central Air Terminal, Glendale, on what was to become the Vultee V-1 which first flew in February 1933. Orders for ten planes followed.

Meanwhile, Richard Palmer had joined the Vultee team in 1933 and became their Chief Engineer. He had brought with him a host of expertise in the forefront of aerial development and was credited with the design of the special retractable landing gear of the V-1A. At the height of the bad days at Lockheed he had been approached by Howard Hughes who wanted his expertise to pep up his Boeing Model 100 racer into something special. Between November 1931 and March 1933, Palmer's quiet work enabled the Boeing to clock 212.39 mph. Suitably impressed, Hughes called upon Palmer again in February 1934 to help him with his latest idea, to design and engineer for the young eccentric the 'fastest plane in the world . . .'.

This was quite a compliment, and also quite a headache, for Palmer was working at full-stretch for the ADC at this time to bolster the V-11 and he had to devote his spare time to Hughes. Gerald Vultee finally had to ask him to choose which project he wanted to work on, as her clearly could not give 100 per cent to both. Palmer chose the Hughes Racer and left Vultee for the first time.

Vance Breese, the impulsive and tempestuous young test pilot, had meantime

Cockpit of the Vengeance. Vultee's layout was designed in conjunction with RAF pilots to provide the maximum ease and accessibility of operational functions. When the USAAF took over they found it did not fit their standard specifications and altered much of it, to the detriment of the Vengeance unfortunately!
*(Gerald H. Balzer)*

also moved on. He was later to join Douglas to test-dive the embryo SBD. Continued problems saw Cords pull out of the ADC which Vultee reinstituted as the Aviation Manufacturing Corporation in 1934. In April 1936 the company moved to larger accommodation at the former Emsco plant at Downey but it had become the Vultee subsidiary part of the Aviation Manufacturing Corporation and Gerald was concentrating his efforts on an attack bomber variant, the V-11, which he demonstrated to the US Army Air Corps in 1935 but they ultimately chose the Northrop A-17.

Then came disaster. On 29 January 1938, Jerry Vultee and his wife took off from Winslow, Arizona, on their way home from a sales trip in which he had hoped to interest the Air Corps in the XA-19. Shortly afterwards their Stinson cabin plane flew into a snowstorm and crashed on the slopes of Mount Wilson. Both were killed in this tragic accident.

In order to replace his engineering skills

Twin rear .303 calibre machine-guns operated by the navigator. Note armour plate, hand grips and sight. Thought adequate in 1940, this rear gun was actually almost immediately replaced by the RAF in Burma due to unreliability, and in the USAAF A-35s by a single .5 calibre weapon. *(Gerald H. Balzer)*

and expertise the company turned again to their former employee and thus it was that Richard Palmer reappeared on the scene. In the interim period he had utilised some of the Vultee V-1A concepts on Howard Hughes's special 'Racer' for his assault on the world speed record. In particular, he made use of flat narrow sheets of aluminium traversely butt-joined to form the contour of the fuselage itself. Palmer also initiated his own form of retractable aluminium landing gear with spring dampening shock absorbers in the bottom of the strut. It was controlled hydraulically. On 13 September 1935 Palmer was among those who witnessed Hughes achieving his ambition when their plane hit 352.388 mph at Santa Ana airport. But army orders did not follow this impressive demonstration. Vance Breese was among pilots who test flew a later variant in 1940.

The Emanuel-Girdler syndicate had acquired Cord's stock late in 1937 for over $2.5 million, and during the next few years a team of industrial executives were brought in to run the company. The first was Richard W. Millar, a West Coast investment banker and private pilot who had also been a director of Douglas Aircraft. When Vultee was incorporated on 14 November 1939 he was installed as President.

In his new position as Chief Engineer with Vultee, Palmer headed the new design team of the 'Four-in-One' concept initiated at that time. Although his earlier work on the V-1A and V-11 was recognised this radical innovation was a fresh look at the company's future. Despite what has been published previously, there was absolutely no direct line of descent development from the V-11 to the V-72.

Dustin 'Dusty' Carter was working for Vultee as a draughtsman at this time. He explains: 'I spent twelve of my forty-two years in Aerospace Engineering as a draughtsman/designer for Vultee. When I started I was making new drawings for the V-1A, V-11 and YA-19. There was *no* evolution from the V-11/V-12 types into the V-72 at all. The V-11 was a military adaptation of the V-1A transport and its concept and construction was totally different from that used on the V-72, the latter being designed by a totally different group of designers.'

The Downey plant had 133,000 square feet of space early in 1938 (and at one time the working capital showed a deficit of $157,000) but with these successes the plant had expanded by May 1940 to 325,000 square feet, and this was to triple in the next year to 1,008,000 square feet. When the Stinson plant at Nashville was acquired in late 1940, it too mushroomed from 180,000 to 817,000 square feet.

While the young company was still in its relative infancy a totally new factor entered into Vultee's and Palmer's environment. The Aviation Corporation had rapidly grown from its origins in 1929 to become by 1930 the holding company for the largest air transportation system in the United States. The beginnings of two present-day major domestic and international trunk airlines (Pan American and American Airlines) began within Avco Corporation in that year. The Corporation continued to evolve and in the major reorganisation in 1940 Richard Palmer became Vice-President in charge of engineering. 'It was while he was in this role that the V-72 was designed and built,' Dusty Carter told me.

This is true, but the V-72's trigger came somewhat earlier in the form of the 1938-40 series of purchasing visits to the American aircraft industry's leading firms by a mission of French Army Air Force officers, men of *L'Armée de l'Air,* who were urgently seeking new designs to supplement their ailing military aircraft programme, and freshly converted to the desirability of dive-bombers by the example of the Ju 87s in Spain.

Convair's house magazine, the *Vultee Volunteer,* confirmed the origins of the Vengeance in their 9 June 1944 edition. They wrote that the V-72 was 'Originally conceived as a result of negotiations with the French Government' and was engineered 'at the Vultee Field Division'.

Noted French historian Jean Cuny has given this author further details of these

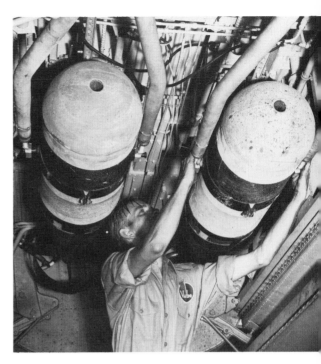

A pair of practice bombs are fixed on the twin side-by-side bomb cradles by a Vultee mechanic. The twin crutches swung out and down so the bomb cleared the propeller arc in true dive-bombing tradition but they could be operated independently of one another on the Vengeance. *(AVCO)*

origins, which have hitherto been totally ignored by writers on the Vengeance. Chief of the French mission was one Lieutenant-Colonel Paul Jacquin, who unfortunately died on 24 June 1984. Also directly involved in the French mission was Lieutenant-Colonel Chemidlin, also unfortunately now deceased, but later to play a further part in our story. This officer was in fact a passenger aboard an early Douglas DB-7 prototype when the aircraft crashed. He survived, but the accident badly injured the French pilot and led to severe political repercussions in the States since he was flying in a secret American aircraft! In later years Chemidlin was questioned about the Vengeance and his reply included the following: 'This aircraft was commenced at the beginning of 1940. It had been designed on behalf of, and along the specifications of, this French mission.'

These two sources seem conclusive enough, but yet a third French source is the clincher. This takes the form of an official telegram from Colonel Jacquin to M Thouvenot, the official in charge of French Military Aircraft Planning at this time, informing him of an order to be placed in the USA for 300 dive-bombers, equipped with Wright 2600 engines. Delivery from the Vultee plant to *L'Armée de l'Air* was specified as follows:

| October 1940 | 3 aircraft |
| November | 5 ,, |
| December | 5 ,, |
| January 1941 | 7 ,, |
| February | 10 ,, |
| March | 10 ,, |
| April | 10 ,, |
| May | 30 ,, |
| June | 40 ,, |
| July | 50 ,, |
| August | 60 ,, |
| September | 70 ,, |

Loading the wing guns in a Northrop V-72 at Hawthorne. *(Gerald H. Balzer)*

The text confirmed the projected delivery of 50 aircraft from October 1940 to April 1941. Cuny adds, 'Absence of more detail (and even any mention in France) probably indicates that events prevented this order being finally officially confirmed before the collapse of the French Government in June 1940.' It make interesting comparison with the delivery dates required by the British when they almost immediately took over the order.

Although Palmer and his team set about producing a specification on the drawing board to meet the urgent French requirement no firm production orders ever came from France. No doubt the French would have taken the V-72 later also had time permitted, but the rout and defeat of June 1940 instantly removed them from the scene as potential customers for the concept they had originated.

Vultee's expansion saw the arrival from Truscon Steel, a Republic Steel subsidiary, of Harry Woodhead. He had taken the presidency of AVCO in April 1940, and the following August became chairman of the Vultee board. (He was later to become President of Consolidated in December 1941 and of Vultee in 1942). The General Manager at the Downey plant was Charles W. Perelle, formerly Boeing Aircraft production manager. G. M. 'Monte' Williams, former General Manager of the Dayton-Wright Airplane Co in World War I, was elected vice-chairman of the Vultee board. Under Richard Millar, Palmer was busy assembling a strong team, all full of new and exciting ideas to translate the French requirement into a viable and effective weapon. Directly under Palmer was Assistant Chief Engineer Bruce, with Dick Harwood as Chief Structural Analyst. Rockefeller, Bossard and De Armond were Aerodynamics, Stress Engineer on the V-72 and Senior Stress Engineer respectively. Chief of Design was Fred Heryer, with John Weaver as Project Engineer. Later, Albert Anslan and Jack Hazard became Senior Stress Engineer and Senior Engineer respectively, with Vance Breese the contract test pilot.

Wright *Cyclone* engines at Northrop's Inspection Department in readiness for fitting to V-72s. *(Gerald H. Balzer)*

Luckily for Vultee and the members of this team the rapid exit of their only dive-bomber customer coincided exactly with the arrival of the British seeking the same type of aircraft, and the French ideas were modified as Hugh Fenwick, the Vultee vice-president in charge of sales, sent back information from the Air Ministry in London that incorporated their wartime evaluations and findings.

These were not all that advanced of course. British experts were still making statements like 'it is doubtful whether satisfactory bomb ejection would be obtained for steep dive-bombing without some form of assister which would add complications'.

Little wonder then that the V-72 design, which already incorporated in it as standard equipment the answers to these outmoded reservations, was so eagerly taken up by the British Purchasing Commission.

The true origins of the Vengeance have rarely been recorded before, although speculation abounds. One source stated that the Vengeance had been 'especially commissioned from US industry in 1940'. Another said that it was 'designed to British specifications and requirements which were established after the British had analyzed the most effective German methods and machines.' A third stated that 'the British Air Ministry hurriedly prepared a specification which received little or no response from the British aircraft industry, already badly straining under the pressure of war production.' But, in truth, as we have seen, the design work was already proceeding at the behest of the French.

What is true is that the British Purchasing Commission fell upon the Vultee design with relief during its search for dive-bombers, confirmed by hitherto secret British official documents of the period. In a letter to the Air Minister, Beaverbrook's successor, J. J. ('Jay') Llewellyn, CBE, MC, MP, wrote that: 'We ordered in the United States as you know because prior to July 1940 no one at the Air Ministry had included dive-bombers in their requisitions, nor had anyone ordered even a prototype. So we had none on the stocks and the quickest way of getting them was in the U.S.A.'

Beaverbrook's biographer recorded the behind-the-scenes in-fighting as follows. 'Beaverbrook also wished to meet the needs of the Army. In July,1940 he placed a large order for dive-bombers in Canada [sic] and the United States. Eden (then Secretary of State for War) was enthusiastic. The Air Ministry protested and refused "to supply or train pilots.'

The original first contract was actually signed on 3 July 1940, following detailed discussion earlier. On behalf of the British Purchasing Commission of 15 Broad Street, New York, N.Y., Mr. A. H. Self signed. For Vultee Aircraft Inc., of Vultee Field, California, the contract was signed by Vice-President V. C. Schorlemmer. This contract was for 200 Vultee Model 72 Dive-Bombers (less engines, propellers, propeller governors, starters, generators, control boxes, radios and armament) and for spare parts, exclusive of tyres and tubes, to be selected from the Sellers's recommended list.

This was a significant order for the young company, and one it would have difficulty meeting working from its existing site. Large-scale expansion was necessary, and the original contracts contained funds sufficient to begin that expansion with a view to future orders. One of the first results was the purchase by AVCO of the brand-new Stinson aircraft plant built between 1939 and 1940 at Nashville, Tennessee. This was bought for Vultee on 8 August 1940 and production facilities were immediately established there to meet further orders. Meanwhile the original design work and testing continued at Downey.

The initial contract called for quick deliveries as the situation was considered critical. The first test plane was to be readied within six months of signature (January 1941). Further production deliveries were specified as:

| 3 aircraft within | 8½ months | |
|---|---|---|
| 10 | ,, ,, | 9½ ,, |
| 18 | ,, ,, | 10½ ,, |
| 25 | ,, ,, | 11½ ,, |
| 30 | ,, ,, | 12½ ,, |
| 33 | ,, ,, | 13½ ,, |
| 38 | ,, ,, | 14½ ,, |
| 42 | ,, ,, | 15½ ,, |

These aircraft had to have successfully passed all inspection and tests, other than flight tests, with all equipment installed and with an Inspection Certificate. The planes were to be delivered boxed for export shipment F.A.S. Hoboken, N.J., or Weehawken, N.J., or flown to Newark, N.J. along with boxed spares.

The contract price was given as $14,202,200 for the aircraft and $2,840,440 for the spares, giving a total contract price for the 200 aircraft of $17,042,640. An additional $800 per airplane boxed for export was also to be paid. Payment itself was 20 per cent $3,408,528) within ten days of contract, with six further payments of five per cent ($852,132) following at monthly intervals thereafter, via the Chase National Bank at Pine and Nassau Street, New York, N.Y. There was also an option clause to increase the total to 400 machines within thirty days. Total price for these would be $25,204,400, with $5,040,880 for the spares, and numbers of deliveries would be increased pro rata up to a period of 18½ months for the final aircraft. A Vignette attached to the contract stipulated that the size of the aircrafts wheels was to be increased from 33 inches to 38 inches at a price of $552.25 per aircraft and that self-sealing fuel tank liners were to be included at a cost of $485 per machine.

Photostats of the first Vultee contract, as well as those of subsequent Northrop contracts, have been made available to the author by Dr Ira Chart and from them a very clear and detailed picture of the original Vengeance design can be seen.

The original Model 72 was a two-seater, single-engined, full-cantilever, low-winged monoplane with *twin* tail surfaces like the Liberator only smaller, or the P-38 *Lightning* or Palmer's ill-fated XP-54 which followed. It was specifically designed as a dive-bomber and built fully stressed and load-adjusted for that purpose alone. It was provided with modified NACA slotted-type wing flaps and also special dive-brakes. It had retractable main landing gear and tailwheel. Except for the steel-tube engine mount, the fuselage was

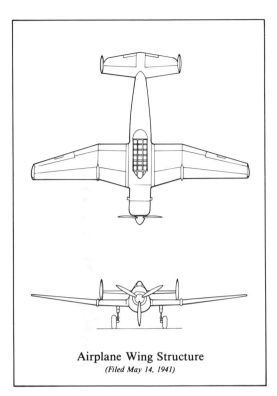

**Airplane Wing Structure**
*(Filed May 14, 1941)*

of semi-monocoque, stressed-skin construction, of substantially elliptical cross-section, which gave less drag. At a time when curved outlines, as typified by the Spitfire, appeared the norm, the Vengeance showed an uncompromising 'squareness', associated with strength and durability rather than speed. The initial estimated performance figures were based upon the normal loading weights. These allowed 360 lb for the two aircrew, 1200 lb for 200 gallons of fuel and 94 lb for 12½ gallons of oil; 232 lb for the forward-firing guns and 152 lb for the rear guns and ammunition; a single 1000 lb bomb; 35 lb for the displacing gear; 130 lb for the communications gear; 35 lb for the glass gunner's shield; and 190 lb for armoured plate, a total load weight of 3428 lb, to which was added the aircraft's empty weight of 7894 lb, giving an all-up weight of 11,322 lb. As can be seen from these figures, the V-72 was a big aircraft for a dive-bomber, designed to the usual US military standard to fit a 6-ft plus 'All-American boy' type aircrew. The resulting generous dimensions were much appreciated by Allied combat aircrews operating them later in jungle warfare conditions.

The first power-plant was the Wright Cyclone-14 Model GR-2600-A5B, an 18-cylinder, single-stage, supercharged radial, with a two-speed blower which drove a 12 ft, three-bladed Hamilton Standard non-feathering hydromatic propeller with governor and controls. The blade was Model No. 6153-A-12, the hub Model No. 23E50 and the governor Model No. 4L13. This type of engine had been developed for civilian aircraft like the Boeing 314 *Clipper* of 1938 and had also been fitted in standard medium bombers like the North American B-25 and the Douglas B-23. One recent historian described this engine as 'thoroughly reliable', a description that would bring tears to the eyes of the engineering personnel of the five nations that tried to keep the original Vengeance airborne!

This engine was mounted in a welded, steel-tube cantilever structure and was enclosed by a NACA ring-type nose-cowl separated from the engine-accessory compartment with a stainless-steel diaphragm. Ease of access was stressed and this was another positive feature of the aircraft favourably commented upon by all ground personnel interviewed by this writer. The gear ratio was 16:9. The high-speed military rating was 289 mph at 3000 ft L.B. and 298 mph at 12,000 ft H.B. Normal rating was 280 mph at 7000 ft L.B. and 290 mph at 13,500 ft H.B. Cruising speed was given as 248 mph at 14,000 ft. Height climbed in 5 minutes, military rating, was 8900 ft and

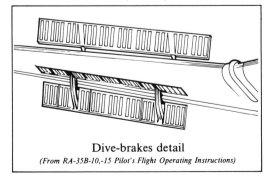

**Dive-brakes detail**
*(From RA-35B-10,-15 Pilot's Flight Operating Instructions)*

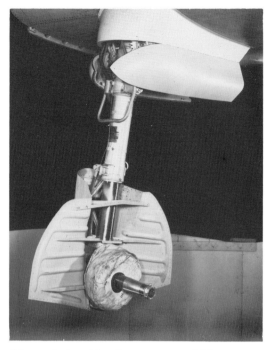

The re-designed landing gear strut fairing assembly as fitted to the A-31. This photograph gives a very good view of this complicated landing gear. *(Gerald H. Balzer)*

the time to climb to 19,680 ft altitude $15\frac{1}{2}$ minutes. The service ceiling was given as 25,500 ft.

The V-72 was designed specifically as a close-support weapon to blast the way forward for ground forces and thus long range was never a high-priority requirement. The Vengeance was *never* intended to fly to Berlin and back from England. Maximum range (with a 1000 lb bomb load dropped half-way and with normal 200 gallon fuel supply) was estimated at 950 miles. With full 400 gallon tanks this could be extended to 1800 miles. As the distance from London to the Kent, Sussex or East Anglian invasion beaches was less than 150 miles this appeared more than adequate for the task on hand! Estimated endurance was given as one hour 20 minutes at normal rated power. Landing speed was 75 mph.

The engine exhaust system comprised corrosion-resistant steel 'stacks' (pipes) led aft from the exhaust ports to connect with a collector ring, which was separated from the other accessories by a stainless-steel shroud, from which an exhaust pipe discharged the gases into the airstream. The engine starter

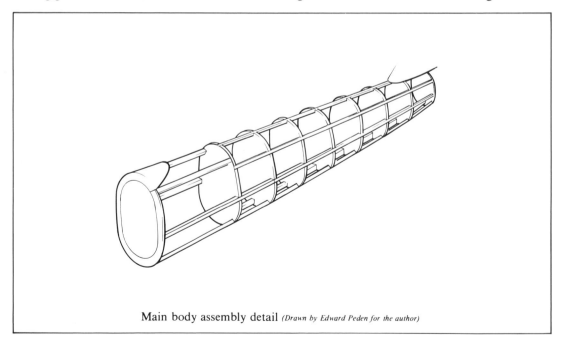

Main body assembly detail *(Drawn by Edward Peden for the author)*

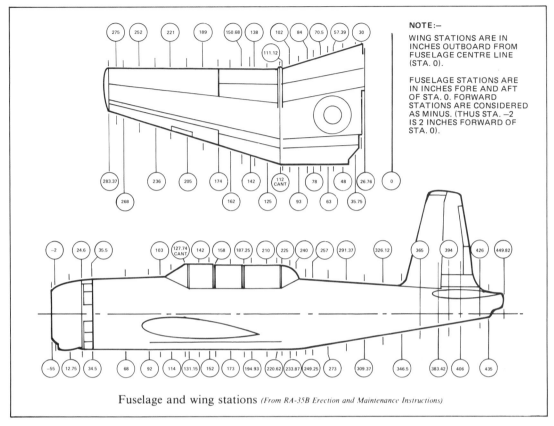

**NOTE:—**

WING STATIONS ARE IN INCHES OUTBOARD FROM FUSELAGE CENTRE LINE (STA. 0).

FUSELAGE STATIONS ARE IN INCHES FORE AND AFT OF STA. 0. FORWARD STATIONS ARE CONSIDERED AS MINUS. (THUS STA. —2 IS 2 INCHES FORWARD OF STA. 0).

Fuselage and wing stations *(From RA-35B Erection and Maintenance Instructions)*

was an electric-inertia type with an Eclipse Type 447, Model 10 solenoid.

The defensive armament comprised four .30 calibre (two in each wing panel outboard of the propeller arc) Colt, wing-mounted, fixed, forward-firing machine-guns with 500 rounds per gun in spanwise-mounted boxes which were released by a special crank. Each gun was individually adjustable and equipped with ejection chutes leading through the bottom surface of the wing. Round indicators were provided in the forward cockpit. They were also fitted with blast tubes and cool air inlets. There was a master-switch for selection and a simple N2 optical gunsight.

The rear defence was provided by a twin Colt .30 flexible machine-gun on a Bell (QA 476) hydraulic-type mount on a fixed pivot, with 500 rounds. The gunner's seat was rotatable and folded up to one side. It was a neat arrangement, though far from comfortable. This allowed him to face forward as emergency pilot, if need be. He had a ring-and-bead sight, and the field of fire aft on the original twin-tail design was excellent of course, being 15 degrees each side of centre aft down to tail interference, and up to 60 degrees above the thrust line.

The bomb load could vary and could comprise either one 1000 lb demolition bomb or two 500 lb demolition bombs. These were carried in an internal bomb-bay. A special displacing gear consisted of special side-by-side Y-yoke trunnions, which swung the bombs clear of the propeller arc in the dive. The very long and roomy bomb-bay had hydraulically operated double-folding doors that were most efficient. They were interlocked with the bomb-release control in the front cockpit to prevent premature release before the doors were opened and had return springs for retraction. There was also electric

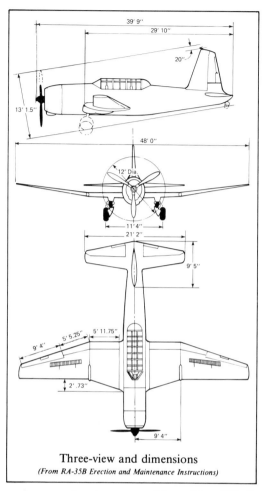

Three-view and dimensions
*(From RA-35B Erection and Maintenance Instructions)*

and manual release provision. The 500 lb load could be released singly or in salvo.

There was also basic provision to carry wing bombs, originally 100 lb, but inked-in modifications on the first contract specified that two British-type 250 lb bombs should be able to be carried under the wings on the standard carriers.

The communications equipment consisted of a radio system, two-position Bendix interphone and a Bendix type radio direction finder. Electrical equipment was on the 24 volt single-conductor system with a master switch in the cockpit.

Without doubt the unique 'crank-wing' shape of the Vengeance was its most obvious distinguishing point. The wings were at first

designed with a straight leading edge and a tapered trailing edge but, as we shall see later, design changes brought about the most pronounced sweepback of the leading edge of the inner wing panels and the straight trailing edge, which were unmistakable. Although its wing form was novel to say the least, its construction also merits praise on several counts. It was an all-metal, full cantilever, stressed-skin type, tapering in plan form and in thickness ratio. Built on two heavy I-beam spars with firewall located at the leading edge of the wing, it comprised a centre section within the fuselage with intermediate, outer panels and wingtip. Its framing was a front beam or shear web at 35 per cent chord, a formed channel beam at 70 per cent chord, pressed metal chordwise ribs and bulkheads and hat-section spanwise stringers.

Built into these wings were the fuel tanks, six in all, the four wing-mounted guns, the main landing gear, the attachments of ailerons and flaps and their operating mechanisms. The centre section was constructed of short sections of the front and aft beams, with strong ribs or bulkheads, reinforced to constitute a torsion box for transmitting wing loads to the fuselage structure. The fuel system was radical and comprised two tanks of 100 gallon capacity on each side of the wing adjacent to the fuselage, one of which was the reserve tank. Outboard of these on each side were 55 gallon capacity tanks in the inner panels inboard from the break and, beyond them in the outer

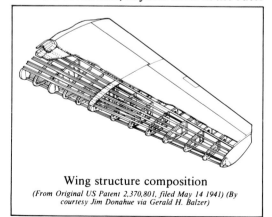

Wing structure composition
*(From Original US Patent 2,370,801, filed May 14 1941) (By courtesy Jim Donahue via Gerald H. Balzer)*

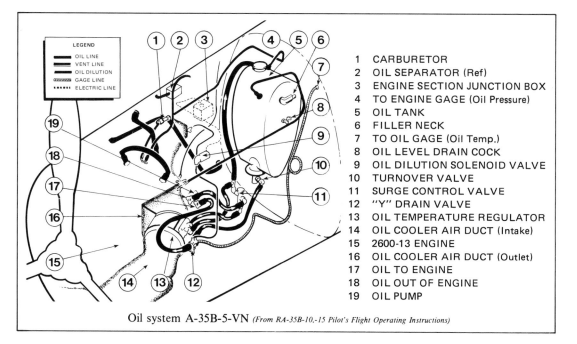

| | |
|---|---|
| LEGEND | |
| ▬▬ | OIL LINE |
| ▬▬ | VENT LINE |
| ▬▬ | OIL DILUTION |
| ▭▭▭ | GAGE LINE |
| •••• | ELECTRIC LINE |

1   CARBURETOR
2   OIL SEPARATOR (Ref)
3   ENGINE SECTION JUNCTION BOX
4   TO ENGINE GAGE (Oil Pressure)
5   OIL TANK
6   FILLER NECK
7   TO OIL GAGE (Oil Temp.)
8   OIL LEVEL DRAIN COCK
9   OIL DILUTION SOLENOID VALVE
10  TURNOVER VALVE
11  SURGE CONTROL VALVE
12  "Y" DRAIN VALVE
13  OIL TEMPERATURE REGULATOR
14  OIL COOLER AIR DUCT (Intake)
15  2600-13 ENGINE
16  OIL COOLER AIR DUCT (Outlet)
17  OIL TO ENGINE
18  OIL OUT OF ENGINE
19  OIL PUMP

Oil system A-35B-5-VN *(From RA-35B-10,-15 Pilot's Flight Operating Instructions)*

panels, 45 gallon tanks, giving a total capacity of 400 US gallons. Immersion pumps connected these tanks in sequence and were to give endless trouble initially. The fuel system had an engine-driven pump, an electrically driven centrifugal booster pump with submerged inlet, a hand-operated priming pump and, thankfully, an emergency fuel pump operable from both cockpits, soon to be known to sweating Allied aircrew as the 'Wobble-pump'. The booster pumps were connected to the fuel selector valve in such a way that only the tanks selected were in operation, the rest of the fuel pumps being idle. The system could in theory eliminate the engine-driven fuel pump with its possible source of failure due to drive-shaft breakage. Unfortunately it led to other problems just as severe.

Each intermediate and outer panel included a box-beam at the leading edge, comprising a formed-sheet nose and a spanwise shear web to which it was riveted at the edges. Chordwise strips extended between and were riveted to this web and to the aft beam. Spanwise stringers replaced ribs at the junctions of the wing sections and at each end

On 'The Merry-go-Round' at Vultee's Nashville plant. The engine section is being put up to the finished main body sections with tailplane (already camouflaged and with British insignia marked up) already in place. Note the neat connecting apertures for bolting on the inner wing sections and the man working in the bomb-bay aperture *(Smithsonian)*

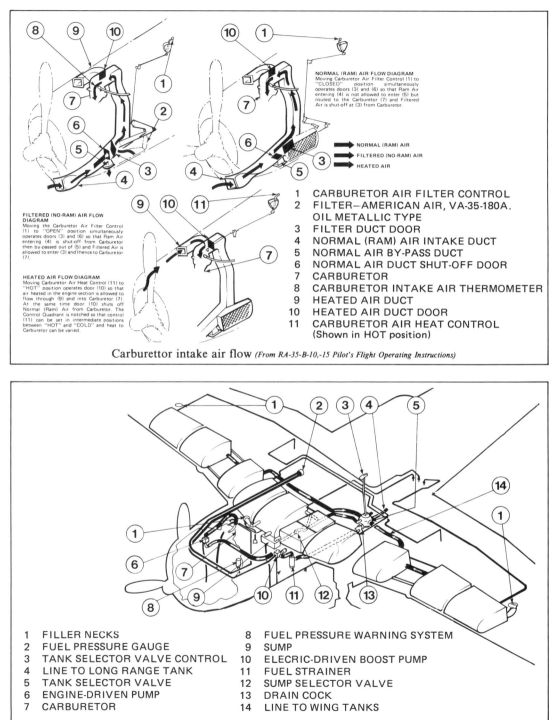

NORMAL (RAM) AIR FLOW DIAGRAM
Moving Carburetor Air Filter Control (1) to "CLOSED" position simultaneously operates doors (3) and (6) so that Ram Air entering (4) is not allowed to enter (5) but routed to the Carburetor (7) and Filtered Air is shut-off at (3) from Carburetor.

➡ NORMAL (RAM) AIR
➡ FILTERED (NO-RAM) AIR
➡ HEATED AIR

FILTERED (NO-RAM) AIR FLOW DIAGRAM
Moving the Carburetor Air Filter Control (1) to "OPEN" position simultaneously operates doors (3) and (6) so that Ram Air entering (4) is shut-off from Carburetor then by-passed out of (5) and Filtered Air is allowed to enter (3) and thence to Carburetor (7).

HEATED AIR FLOW DIAGRAM
Moving Carburetor Air Heat Control (11) to "HOT" position operates door (10) so that air heated in the engine section is allowed to flow through (9) and into Carburetor (7). At the same time door (10) shuts off Normal (Ram) Air from Carburetor. The Control Quadrant is notched so that control (11) can be set in intermediate positions between "HOT" and "COLD" and heat to Carburetor can be varied.

1 CARBURETOR AIR FILTER CONTROL
2 FILTER—AMERICAN AIR, VA-35-180A. OIL METALLIC TYPE
3 FILTER DUCT DOOR
4 NORMAL (RAM) AIR INTAKE DUCT
5 NORMAL AIR BY-PASS DUCT
6 NORMAL AIR DUCT SHUT-OFF DOOR
7 CARBURETOR
8 CARBURETOR INTAKE AIR THERMOMETER
9 HEATED AIR DUCT
10 HEATED AIR DUCT DOOR
11 CARBURETOR AIR HEAT CONTROL (Shown in HOT position)

Carburettor intake air flow *(From RA-35-B-10,-15 Pilot's Flight Operating Instructions)*

1 FILLER NECKS
2 FUEL PRESSURE GAUGE
3 TANK SELECTOR VALVE CONTROL
4 LINE TO LONG RANGE TANK
5 TANK SELECTOR VALVE
6 ENGINE-DRIVEN PUMP
7 CARBURETOR
8 FUEL PRESSURE WARNING SYSTEM
9 SUMP
10 ELECRIC-DRIVEN BOOST PUMP
11 FUEL STRAINER
12 SUMP SELECTOR VALVE
13 DRAIN COCK
14 LINE TO WING TANKS

Fuel-tank layout *(From RA-35B-10,15 Pilot's Flight Operating Instructions)* of each fuel tank. Ribs were reinforced by attached angles and other stiffeners, and by flanging the lightening holes.

The attachment between wing sections was by closely spaced bolting through extruded angles riveted to the skin sheet and stringers at the end of each section. The junction between the centre and the intermediate panels was covered by fairing strips and the junction at the break in the wing was covered by a streamlined 'bump' or cover strip.

In the words of a British pilot, 'She was built like a tank'. Whatever the evaluation, there is no doubt she was a strong, tough baby! Total wing area on the original design was 332 sq ft, with a span of 48 ft. The root chord (theoretical) was 126 ins., the tip chord 42 ins. The taper ratio of the centre section was 1.35, of the outer panel, 2.22. A nil angle of incidence was thus achieved, which made for perfect dive-bombing but resulted, in early models, in a 'nose-up' stance in level flight. The dihedral of the leading edge at the centre section was also zero, with 7 degrees on the outer panel. Aspect ratio was 7.15 and the M.A.C. length was 91.2 ins. The actual wing loading was 34.1 lb/sq in.

The control surfaces were fabric-covered and, save for the tabs, were balanced both statically and dynamically. The ailerons had

Girls making final fittings of tabs and trims on the outer wing sections at Vultee before they are joined to the mainframe on the final assembly line. *(Smithsonian)*

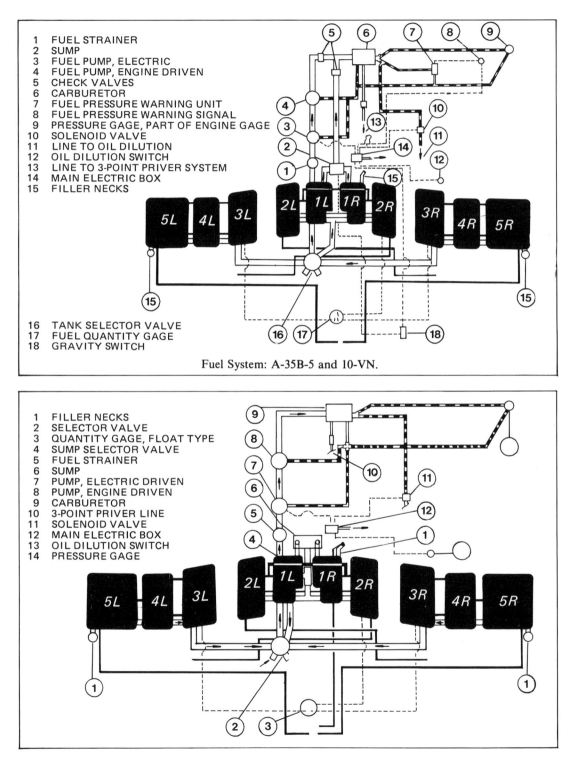

1  FUEL STRAINER
2  SUMP
3  FUEL PUMP, ELECTRIC
4  FUEL PUMP, ENGINE DRIVEN
5  CHECK VALVES
6  CARBURETOR
7  FUEL PRESSURE WARNING UNIT
8  FUEL PRESSURE WARNING SIGNAL
9  PRESSURE GAGE, PART OF ENGINE GAGE
10 SOLENOID VALVE
11 LINE TO OIL DILUTION
12 OIL DILUTION SWITCH
13 LINE TO 3-POINT PRIVER SYSTEM
14 MAIN ELECTRIC BOX
15 FILLER NECKS

16 TANK SELECTOR VALVE
17 FUEL QUANTITY GAGE
18 GRAVITY SWITCH

Fuel System: A-35B-5 and 10-VN.

1  FILLER NECKS
2  SELECTOR VALVE
3  QUANTITY GAGE, FLOAT TYPE
4  SUMP SELECTOR VALVE
5  FUEL STRAINER
6  SUMP
7  PUMP, ELECTRIC DRIVEN
8  PUMP, ENGINE DRIVEN
9  CARBURETOR
10 3-POINT PRIVER LINE
11 SOLENOID VALVE
12 MAIN ELECTRIC BOX
13 OIL DILUTION SWITCH
14 PRESSURE GAGE

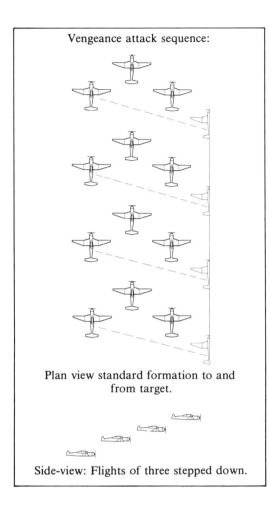

Vengeance attack sequence:

Plan view standard formation to and from target.

Side-view: Flights of three stepped down.

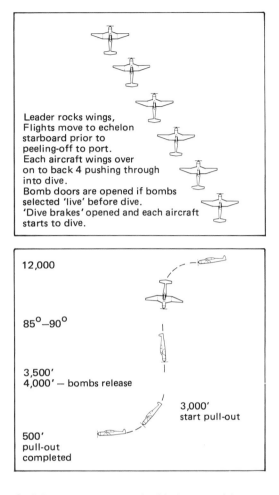

Leader rocks wings,
Flights move to echelon
starboard prior to
peeling-off to port.
Each aircraft wings over
on to back 4 pushing through
into dive.
Bomb doors are opened if bombs
selected 'live' before dive.
'Dive brakes' opened and each aircraft
starts to dive.

12,000

85°–90°

3,500'
4,000' — bombs release

3,000'
start pull-out

500'
pull-out
completed

a total area of 20 sq ft on the original twin-boom design, with angular movements of 30 degrees up and 10 degrees downward. The tabs—trim and balance—had a total area of 1 sq ft. The left aileron tab was controllable from the cockpit, but the right tab was only adjustable from the ground, with movement 30 degrees either up or down.

The horizontal tail surfaces had a total area, including fuselage, of 80 sq ft, with a span of 17 ft and a maximum chord of 68 ins. The total area of the stabiliser was 44 sq ft and of the elevator 36 sq ft, with angular movements of 35 degrees upward and 25 degrees downward. The tabs here—trim and balance—on each elevator, were controlled from the cockpit and had a total area of 3 sq

ft. Movement was again 30 degrees either up or down.

The vertical tail surfaces had a total area of 40 sq ft and the fins 20 sq ft. The rudders totalled 20 sq ft in area with angular movements left or right of 35 degrees. The tab area was 1.6 sq ft and the balance was full static and dynamic. Each elevator unit comprised a formed sheet torsion box ahead of the hinge line, and a stamped sheet frame aft, covered with fabric by the Vultee method with flush joints. Each of the rudder units and their tabs were of substantially the same construction. Each of the ailerons was fitted with a servo-balanced tab.

The original NACA slotted-type trailing edge flaps were installed in four sections,

17

extending over about 45 per cent of the wing span with total area of 41.8 sq ft and a nil-60 degrees movement downward. The dive brakes were of the DFS 'spoiler' type initially and each consisted of parallel slats mounted on curved hinge arms. They were extended and retracted by hydraulic action. The diving speed with brakes fully extended was estimated at 313 mph. The strength of these dive brakes was to be investigated for all deflections up to the maximum terminal dive speed for each angular deflection.

The fuselage of the V-72 was built in three sections, with crew and bomb-bay in the deep forward section, gunner's compartment to tail as the centre section, and the empennage sufaces aft. These were riveted together on final assembly. It had a maximum cross-section height of 82 ins and a width of 53 ins. The cockpit was of the elongated 'greenhouse' type, similar to the BT-13 *Valiant* trainer which was being built concurrently. It was in four sections of light-alloy framing transparent flat Plexiglass panels with the centre section and windshield, formed as a single curvature shatterproof glass segment, fixed, and the forward section telescoping over, and the after section under, the centre section. There were emergency quick-release panels in both sides of the front section with a 'roll-bar' for ground-looping. Armoured plate $\frac{5}{16}$ ins thick was originally specified to protect the pilot from fire from aft and a similar plate protected the rear gunner. Total area of armour was 14.5 sq ft and the flexible guns had bullet-proof glass shields. In the front cockpit were the engine contols for ignition, throttle, mixture, blower, propeller blade angle, oil-cooler air supply and carburettor air temperature. There were two Type A-8 flares on racks and a signal pistol with ten cartridges. Also a special bit of

British Army Liaison Officer seated on the prototype V-72 after initial test flight at Downey. The British Army was at this time desperate for a dive-bomber to do to the German Army what the *Stukas* were repeatedly doing to them in Norway, Belgium, France, Greece, Crete and North Africa. Alas, it came too late. Note absence of armament and of any paint scheme other than metallic silver finish and black anti-glare strip on top of engine cowling. *(Smithsonian)*

American foresight, there was a stainless-steel 'Pilot's relief tube' for real emergencies, as well as fire extinguishers, and of course map and data cases built in. In the back cockpit was a spare stick and throttle for emergencies.

The landing gear was of course one of Richard W. Palmer's specialities and was again novel. Both main wheels and tailwheel were retractable and hydraulically controlled. The single-strut main gear swung backward and upward, rotating 90 degrees in the process, and when fully retracted seated into wells within the wings. The struts then lay close to the lower wing surface in a chordwise direction and were covered with a streamlined cowl fairing into the wing contour. The bevel gear mechanism was covered with clam-shell doors.

Each unit consisted of a semi-cantilever strut containing a hydraulic shock absorber, stub shaft attached to the piston and the wheel unit. Torsion arms connected plunger and cylinder to prevent rotation. The upper ends of the strut mounted to a pin fitting attached to the wing framing. The brakes were hydraulic with the multiple disk system. The tyres, which a current Vignette to the main contract specified were to be changed from 33 ins to 38 ins diameter at a cost of $552.25 per airplane, were smooth contour and mounted on magnesium alloy wheels.

The hydraulic system extended to the landing gear, cowl flaps, landing flaps, dive brakes and bomb doors. It comprised an engine-driven hydraulic pump, a hand-operated pump for emergency use operable from the front cockpit, an automatic pressure regulator, a tank with filler and strainer units, hydraulic power cylinders, control valves, lines and fittings. The lubrication system included an oil radiator, thermostatic relief valve and oil tank with 25 US gallon capacity. This large elliptical tank was mounted in the upper portion of the power plant compartment and strapped to the firewall for ease of access and removal. Cooling air was taken in through a slot in the face of the nose ring near its bottom, ducted to the radiator, controlled by shutters in a valve box behind the radiator and then discharged through a duct to the orifice in the bottom skin of the engine accessory compartment. The oil tank was protected by a self-sealing liner against .30 and .50 calibre machine-gun fire, as were the two main inboard wing fuel tanks. These latter had also been contained in the Vignette and were to be fitted at an additional cost of $485 per airplane.

Already then, even before the first signatures, changes were being penned-in. This process was to accelerate vastly in the months that followed and to lead to a highly complicated series of modifications, which in turn led to delays, which in turn led to political upheaval, and which again led to the production of not only a very different aircraft from that first specified, but indeed to two completely seperate types of Vengeance.

# Chapter 2
# Conception

The actual order for the first V-72s (or A-31 as they were designated soon afterwards) was placed by the Ministry of Aircraft Production on 21 June 1940, after the Air Staff had been consulted. The contract also specified flight testing to severe limits by Vultee's own test pilots as well as by the RAF's own Resident Technical Officers. The latter's brief was comprehensive for he was to 'investigate, give decisions on and advise on matters of design, give technical advice on the installation of equipment, control the introduction and preparation changes or modifications to the Specifications or to airplanes, advise the Seller on all descriptive and technical documents, define in detail the flight tests on the first airplane and (in conjunction with another RAF officer, the RAF Representative) to accept the Seller's flight tests on such prototype airplanes.' The Representative was to 'advise on the location and operation of all equipment, to check operational requirements and to be present at and conduct flight tests on the first and any subsequent airplanes.'

Vultee test pilot Frank Davis recalls: 'The experimental aircraft (two of them) were designed and built at Vultee Field while Vultee's production aircraft were built at Nashville. Group Captain Bulman, RAF, came to Vultee Field at Downey to evaluate the airplane during the development programme and Wing Commander Mike Crosley, RAF, a multiple ace from the Battle of Britain, came to fly the accelerated service testing.'

There were ultimately two prototype aircraft under order A.557, serial numbers AF 745 and AF 746. The reason for a second prototype was that demand promised to far outstrip Vultee's ability to supply, and subcontracting had to be undertaken to another new specialist California aircraft company whose name was indelibly associated with building dive-bombers and which had spare capacity to meet Britain's needs. This was the reconstituted Northrop Company, Jack Northrop's original company having been swallowed up by Douglas a few years beforehand but whose SBD design was destined to be one of the most renowned dive-bombers of all time.

When the first Vultee contract was signed on 3 July, it contained within it an Option Clause which the BPC had to exercise within thirty days. This clause would double the size of the original order to 400 machines, with final delivery of the last to be within $18\frac{1}{2}$ months of contract. Total price to be paid was $25,204,400 for the aircraft and $5,040,880 for the spares. This, in effect, reduced the unit cost per aircraft from $71,011 to $63,011. This option was soon exercised. At 1050 hours on 2 August 1940, Mr Hildred of the Ministry of Aircraft Production telephoned the Air Ministry and informed them that the option was due to expire the next day. Under it, a further 200 Vultee dive-bombers could be purchased with hoped-for delivery dates between March 1941 and February 1942.

Moreover, *further* orders *were* placed for dive-bombers by the MAP. The first of these was placed, for yet another 200 machines, on 26 September 1940.

Theodore C. Coleman, who had attended Caltech in Pasadena with Dick Palmer, was the original vice president in charge of sales at the Hawthorne, California, plant when the opportunity for Northrops to build the Vengeance dive-bomber for Great Britain occurred. He explained to me just how this came about:

'In August, 1940, I was in Washington D.C. on company business and was advised by Dr Albert Lombard of the U.S. Defense Commission [which was later renamed the War Production Board] to contact the British Purchasing Commission office on Lexington Avenue in New York City. There, I was introduced to a Mr Ord, a civilian civil service buyer of the British War Ministry, who was in charge of negotiating contracts with American aircraft manufacturing firms for airplanes for the RAF.

'Northrop Aircraft Inc. had just been incorporated as a new manufacturing firm under the direction of John K. Northrop, a well-known designer of early airplanes for Lockheed (the *Vega*) and Douglas (*Dauntless*) and was anxious to get production started in its new California plant without waiting to have a new Northrop airplane designed and tested.

'Mr Ord told me that he had been negotiating with the Vultee Aircraft Company of California to purchase 200 dive-bombers which the company had recently designed and tested. He said the airplane, which they had named the Vengeance, met their requirements; however, Vultee had advised him that delivery could not commence for two years because their Downey, California, plant was working to its capacity in producing the basic trainers for the U.S. Army Air Corps. They proposed building a new plant at Nashville, Tennessee, where the Vengeance could be produced. This would take a minimum of eighteen months. Mr Ord told me they were unable to wait that long, as the Battle of Britain was depleting their older airplanes and new airplanes were desperately needed as soon as possible.

'I contacted our Chairman and General Manager, La Motte T. Cohu, and asked him to contact Richard Millar, President of Vultee, and negotiate a contract with them to acquire the manufacturing rights to build 200 Vengeance dive-bombers, with delivery to the British scheduled for the earliest practical date. He found Mr Millar very agreeable to the idea, and the Northrop Corporation paid Vultee $1,000,000 for the engineering drawings and rights to build 200 Vengeance dive-bombers with delivery to commence as soon as possible.

'Mr Millar sent a Vultee official, Charles Schorlemmer, to join me in New York and we negotiated a new Northrop contract for 200 airplanes for $17,000,000. I was introduced to C. R. Fairey, Director-General of the British Air Commission in Washington, and we arranged to receive a down-payment of 50 per cent in order to supply the needed working capital to commence production as soon as possible with the balance to be paid upon delivery of the airplanes.

'This represented the first production contract which the present Northrop Corporation had received.'

'A Proposal in the form of a Letter of Agreement to this effect was drafted and signed at Jersey City, N.J., on 16 September 1940 by L. Hartmeyer, Vice President of Vultee, and Ted Coleman for Northrop, and accepted as binding by the British Purchasing Commission on 19 September. Delivery from Northrop's Hawthorne plant at monthly intervals was to commence with three aircraft by 31 July 1941 and to be followed at monthly intervals of 8,12,18,24,35,35,35 and a final 28 machines by 31 March 1942. The aircraft to be built at both plants, Hawthorne and Nashville, were to be interchangeable, of course, once Downey had got the prototypes perfected. The Licence Fee of 500 dollars per plane was agreed to. Northrop's unit price per plane came out at $73,220 per aircraft as against Vultee's $66,863 and $69,860 for the second.

On 30 September 1940 a further addition to contract A-557 was signed by all three parties which agreed to the supply and fitting of the radio equipment to all 600 dive-bombers at a total cost of $3,079.56. The equipment specified the Bendix TA-12B Transmitter and the RA-10 Receiver, together with ancillary items like the MP-28B Dynamotor modulator unit, telegraph keys, cables, amplifiers, station, junction and control boxes and the like.

While the young Northrop firm geared itself up for producing the Vengeance and

21

A rare in-flight study of the second prototype, AF746, being air-tested by Frank Davis over Downey in the summer of 1941. Although Vultee were earlier into design and construction, actual production was first achieved by the subcontractor, Northrop at Hawthorne, due to the decision by Vultee themselves to concentrate their production at their new plant at Nashville, Tennessee. *(AVCO)*

work went on apace in converting the purchased Stinson factory in Nashville into a modern plant, the hard work of translating the many brilliant ideas for the new aircraft into a flyable and working fighting ship began back at Downey. This was no easy task as a later USAAF Statement summarised:

'The problems of giving the A-31 adequate engineering attention, under these conditions, was serious and plagued the production of the airplane to a considerable extent throughout its life. The first year of the production of an airplane is difficult under the most favourable circumstances. Corrections in design must be made, production tooling must be provided and proven, and, where more than one producer is involved, interchangeability must be maintained. Vultee, Nashville, was a new organisation and 2,000 miles from Vultee headquarters.'

With all of which we can but ruefully agree. The very fact that so many new ideas were being worked into the A-31 compounded all the above mentioned problems and those special difficulties peculiar to dive-bombing with its high-stress factor. Among the many 'firsts' the V-72 generated among the skilled team assembled under Vultee's President,

Richard W. Millar (later to become a Chairman at Northrop) is that recalled by Victor B. Bertagna, one of the principal designers there in 1940. He came up with a bolting design (where the outer wing panel was bolted to the centre wing structure) that did away with the customary metal fairing strip; the two assemblies neatly came together with no open places.

'When I first joined Vultee in October 1940,' Victor told me, 'the design of the Vengeance was nearly completed. My first assignment was to design the wing outer panel to centre panel attach joint.

'Since we were considering a Navy version of the V-72 [this became the TBV-1, or *Georgia* concept] with folding wings, the conventional wing joint, with attach angles on the outer surfaces with a series of attach bolts and a fairing stretched over the attach angle, was not considered appropriate.

'Our solution required placing the outer wing to the centre wing attach angles *within* the wing structure and submerging the attach bolts. The long horizontal leg of the rib cap angle provided a good attachment to the wing spars and skin. The thick vertical leg of the rib cap was designed to provide attachment of the wing panel with concealed bolts at each spar location.

'Slotted holes were required on the inboard panel for bolt insertion and a hole in the outer panel for a barrel nut insertion. Cover plates were placed over the slotted openings. This design provided a more efficient flush-wing joint.'

It became known in Vengeance contracts as 'the Vultee Method' but their originality did not survive for long, as Victor recalls: 'This method of flush wing attachment appeared in aircraft trade journals and it wasn't long before all military aircraft started using the V–72 method of wing attachment.'

Vernon Cunningham, a power plant design engineer at Vultee between 1940 and 1943, recalled trouble with the *Cyclone* almost at once: 'too rapid throttle with a cold engine produced an undesirable spluttering situation.'

Stanley Worth was among those who joined the Vultee team at this time. 'I joined Vultee Aircraft in early 1940 and was assigned to the Power Plant design section prior to being transferred to the Sales Department under Vice President Hugh Fenwick. I recall that the engine mounting was either lengthened or shortened as the centre of gravity (CG) went up and down the scales as the weight increased almost daily, causing the

'Cy' Younglove (back to camera) and Robert McCulloch discuss a problem on the final stage of the Vengeance assembly line at Nashville. *(AVCO)*

British Purchasing Commission [later the British Air Commission] at one point to consider cancellation of the project. Another part of the production delay was due to the late decision by the Ministry of Aircraft Production to incorporate self-sealing fuel tanks which also added to the empty weight.'

The distinctive sweepback of the centre wing section was not in the original design at all. Originally the whole wing form had a straight leading edge with a tapering trailing edge. During construction it was found that, due to other modifications required, the initial weight calculations had been changed so radically that the aircraft's centre of gravity (CG) was further aft than had been estimated. Radical correction was necessary and the moving of the whole wing section back was contemplated. However, the idea of cranking back the centre section only was hit upon, as this caused the minimum design change and time delay. Thus the unique Vengeance shape came into being.

Late in 1940 and early in 1941, with preliminary work still under way, further order were placed. This was shortly before the United States Government passed the historic Lend-Lease Act. The further orders were made as follow:

2 December 1940:
   100 aircraft — Vultee (Supplement to Contract A.557)
25 February 1941:
   200 aircraft — Northrop (Contract A.1555)
9 April 1941:
   300 aircraft — Vultee (Contract BSC.145)
17 June 1941:
   100 aircraft — Vultee (Contract BSC.2647)
17 June 1941:
   200 aircraft — Northrop (Contract BSC.2648)

After the passing of the Act the United States Army Air Corps undertook to procure airplanes for foreign governments and Wright Field gave out Defence Aid contracts to both Vultee (DA-119) at a unit price of $64,775 and to Northrop (DA-120) at a unit price of

23

'Cy' Younglove pilots AF746 as she revs up on the field at Nashville under threatening skies. *(AVCO)*

$66,945 on 28 June 1941. These Lend-Lease contracts covered the final 600 aircraft contained in British contracts BSC. 145, BSC. 2647 and BSC. 2648 respectively, and gave a total A-31 production figure of 900 machines from Vultee (400 of them Lend-Lease and including the two prototypes) and 400 machines from Northrop (200 of them Lend-Lease); or 1,300 machines, 700 under direct British contracts and 600 Lend-Lease. But the first aircraft did not actually fly until July 1941, almost on the eve of the Pearl Harbor attack which brought America into the war and caused further problems for the troubled aircraft.

The twin rudder design survived as part of the basic design until almost the first test flight. Its deletion from the aircraft and its replacement by the large single fin, set well forward, was a dramatic, last-minute alteration as Stanley Worth recalled for me.

'The prototype had a twin tail, not unlike the Hudson, but of course much smaller. It is etched in my memory! The day came when Vance Breese, the contract test pilot, climbed aboard to conduct the initial taxi tests and first flight. He taxied out and performed one run to the west, shut off the engine and started to walk back to where we all stood. At this point I was told to take a car and pick him up. When he got in the car he exploded all over me! Apparently he had repeatedly told Dick Palmer and Ernie Bruce, the two heads of Engineering, that the twin tail would result in very poor ground control — if any — and they rejected his experience, which was considerable. I quickly realised why the Vice President and other dignitaries had disappeared when we got back to the experimental hangar!

'The next day—still mad—Breese attended an engineering meeting which resulted in the single tail design and about four weeks later he conducted the first flight and performed some of the initial flight testing.'

A postscript to this affair, and on Vance Breese, is supplied by Dr Ira Chart who told me: 'I did hear, but have not been able to verify, that he was "fired" by Vultee Aircraft shortly after, or at least after this incident. The alleged reason—he didn't live up to their image of what an engineering test pilot should be! Some of these things we'll never know. But I can only gather the V-72 as a twin-tail never flew.'

It is an ironical fact that the German Junkers Ju 87 also started life as a twin rudder designed prototype and later had to be converted to a single-tail aircraft in exactly the same way. Perhaps it is no coincidence that, as Victor Bertagna remembers, there was a German aircraft at the Vultee plant at this time.

'During the development of the V-72, we had a fully intact Messerschmitt 110 aircraft, including machine-guns (with one round of ammo in the breech!). This aircraft helped us in the initial design of the V-72. It was quite obvious that the German design requirements were not as stringent as our design requirements. They used many mass-produced techniques but their structure seemed to be very marginal.'

The new single tail fin (which was not shown as such on the contracts until new orders in February 1941) bore a marked resemblance to that fitted to the Vultee Vanguard fighter and it was obviously 'adopted' almost as it stood, to fill the bill quickly. The new vertical tail surfaces had a new, and reduced, total area of 35.45 sq ft, of which the fin itself was 18.35 sq ft and the rudder 17.10 sq ft. It had a 35 degree right and left angular movement. The tab area was 1.88 sq ft and its type of balance was 'full static and dynamic and adequate aerodynamic'. The new horizontal tail surfaces came out at 91.5 sq ft with a span of 254 ins. The stabiliser area was now 44 sq ft and the elevator 42 sq ft, with angular movements of 26 degrees up and 24 degrees down, and with trim and balance tabs on each totalling 3.3 sq ft.

With the new tail assembly switch carried out at top speed, AF 745 was wheeled out of the experimental hanger in July 1941, with only silver primer paint over its metal skin and with no other markings than its serial numbers on the after fuselage and a black anti-glare coating along the long nose from cowl tip to cockpit. Frank Davis told me: 'The initial flight was made by Vance Breese. I made the second flight and did most of the development flying from that point on. After the usual engine performance and cooling work was done the more interesting aspects of the flight test programme began.'

But before this began there was an elaborate 'christening' ceremony carried out at Vultee Field. With its metallic finish painted over in a somewhat garish version of standard British green/brown mottled upper surface, separated with a wavy border from the light blue undersurfaces and given RAF roundels with a large white circular border, the prototype was wheeled to the centre of the field on Wednesday 22 July 1941 and a flag-bedecked rostrum was erected in front of it. Guests of honour were Lord Halifax, the smooth and urbane British Ambassador, and his wife. With Richard Millar at her side, Lady Halifax made a speech praising 'A new "V" in Britain's campaign for victory', and broke a wand of pure oxygen over the propeller cap. As publicity it was first-class, as propaganda excellent, but there was a great deal more work and heartbreak ahead before the Vengeance was able to live up to its name.

Test flying started in earnest and the first A-31 was soon joined by AF 746, which had also been completed in basic silver dope primer initially. The volatile Vance Breese soon found more at fault, in the dive-brakes. He recommended that Vultee put perforated holes—as John Northrop had done on the A–17 and the BT-1 (forerunner of the SBD *Dauntless*) earlier—in the dive flaps. Having flown the SBD, which featured these 'perforated' or 'Swiss-cheese' flaps, and found them superior, Breese tried to communicate this fact to his superiors but the new type of slotted dive-brakes were installed instead.

Victor Bertagna also recalls that: 'During the initial flight test phase of the V-72 prototype, Vance Breese was not satisfied with the effectiveness of the horizontal stabiliser elevators. I was assigned to work with Vance Breese and our Aerodynamic group had to solve the problem. This was accomplished by enlarging the upper mouldline surface of the elevator approximately one-half inch above the contour in the forward area, from the nose to about the 25 per cent chord section. The problem was resolved through a series of flight tests using fairings of varying thickness until the most effective combination was established. The production elevators were redesigned to include the humped shape.'

Stanley Worth makes the following points: 'With regard the vertical tailplane Vultee extended it by about two feet for more directional stability before any production aircraft were delivered, if my memory serves me right.'

Test pilot Frank Davis remembers that: 'The wing-mounted, hydraulically operated dive-brakes, opening both top and bottom of the wing, originally consisted of horizontal slats three or four inches wide and several feet

At Hawthorne, Northrop's plant was soon in full swing turning out the standard A-31 basic model with few modifications to the original design. Here an almost complete body is on jacks for work underneath to be carried out. In background is the tail section of a Navy PBY-5 flying-boat which Northrop was subcontracting for Consolidated Vultee. *(Northrop)*

This photograph of Northrop-built AN838, taken from the roof of the Hawthorne factory, shows off to good effect the V-72's wing form, engine assembly and flaps, as well as the roominess of the cockpit. *(Northrop)*

long. These caused too much buffeting and were finally replaced with a "picket-fence" configuration, which was quite smooth and had no adverse effect on the stall characteristics.

'The 1G stall characteristic of the airplane was excellent. A gentle pre-stall build-up of gentle buffeting and a straight and level nose drop at the stall with excellent aileron control throughout. Stalls at higher accelerations caused enough buffeting to give concern for tail stress. So strain gauges were installed to measure stress, and what may well have been the first airborne telemetering system was devised to record on the ground the stresses in the air as they took place.

'The signals were transmitted in the audible range and I could hear them in my earphones. With a bit of practice I could tell quite well what the stress was by the tone I heard being transmitted. I would make one stall for each reading of each strain gauge and manually switch to the next gauge. It took several hundred stalls between 1G and 6G to complete the programme. The tail stresses came out O.K.'

Davis, by now, with Breese's departure, Vultee's premier test pilot, recounted another difficulty they had to overcome. 'Another interesting problem, common to single-engine dive-bombers, was achieving light enough rudder pedal forces to allow the pilot to easily control the directional trim change between climb speed and diving speed without having to adjust the trim control. It was eventually solved by a spring-tab, which I thought I had invented, only to find in the Patent Office search that someone in England had tried it back in 1916 or thereabouts.

'The next difficult problem in the development programme was achieving satisfactory control forces during recovery from a high-speed dive. At the higher speeds the airplane wanted to nose down and the stick forces to recover became unreasonably high. Many things were tried, hinge line adjustments, contour adjustments, etc.,etc., but nothing seemed to work.

'Then one day I was diving to test an oil system valve for negative G. Rudder flutter

Another view of the same aircraft shows test pilot Vance Breese clambering aboard while talking to assembled Northrop managers. The smooth tail appendages are also shown to good advantage from this angle with flaps lowered. *(Northrop)*

An almost complete V-72 is swung into position at Hawthorne for some final engine adjustments by Northrop engineers. Note trailing edge of wingtip form. *(Northrop)*

suddenly developed and I lost all of the rudder aft of the hinge line. Fortunately, enough directional stability remained from the fin to keep the airplane going reasonably straight and I was able to maintain control, although it was not until I got slowed down that I was able to force the rudder pedal to neutral. The metal leading edge of the rudder ahead of the hinge line was still intact and it of course wanted to go hard over one way or the other, producing more yaw than I wanted for landing. I was able to hold the rudder pedal in neutral and an uneventful landing was made.

'Our subsequent conclusion was that the rudder had fluttered because the fabric-covered aft part of it was too tender. The original A-frame rib construction was therefore replaced by a much stiffer sheet metal formed rib construction. Because the elevator was built the same way its ribs were also changed. Much to our pleasant surprise this solved the problem of high stick forces in recovery from high-speed dives.'

The horizontal control surfaces became 'fabricated spanwise beams, stamped sheets intercostals supporting spanwise stringers and skin sheet laid flush and smooth' and

were shown on the new Specification Reports duly issued to Northrop's.

That delays in delivery were to be expected from Downey had already been recognised in Great Britain. As early as 13 December 1940 the War Office was urging the speeding up of dive-bomber supply during a heated meeting with the Air Ministry.

Wing-Commander Mike Crosley had this to say to me about his experience with the Vengeance in the States at this time: "A party of us was sent to the U.S.A., having just come off ops, in 1941, to conduct what the Air Ministry called Accelerated Service Tests on new machines that we were getting on the Lend-Lease Scheme. My first machine was the North American Mustang, on which I did about 100 hours of testing. When I had finished that, I was told to go over to Vultee and 'do' the Vengeance. I said, 'What is a Vengeance?'. 'Oh,' they said, 'it is a dive-bomber!' Being a single-seater fighter pilot all my time, I couldn't quite see the connection, but supposed that as the R.A.F. had no dive-bombers at all, I was as qualified to give an opinion on dive-bombing as the next man!"

"Anyway off I went, and found a gigantic

single-engined machine with an observer's cockpit and all. I am ashamed to say that I cannot remember the name of my trusty and trusting observer who flew with me, but I remember Frank Davis well. They were a splendid bunch of fellows at Vultees, and were very, very helpful."

"My logbook tells me that I completed just over ninety hours in her, doing all manner of tests, ostensibly to find out if the machine in its then present form was suitable for the job it would have to do. I used to call the Vengeance the good old 'Flying Cow'—but not without affection! She was fun to fly. Being so big she was a bit heavy on the controls, but she did what she was designed to do extremely well, namely it dived splendidly and wholly controllably. Its best gadget was a set of dive brakes which came out of the top and the bottom surfaces of the wings, and slowed you up to such an extent that however much you stood on your head you could not induce it to go more than just about 300 mph (if my memory serves me right)."

Beaverbrook immediately telephoned Morris Wilson in the States, who responded on the next day by secret telegram to the effect that 'the designing of the new Brewster and Vultee dive-bombers in specific response to this need must take time. Moreover the progress of the designs has inevitably been delayed by the incorporation of successive modifications to meet developments of air technique in the interval.'

Wilfred Freeman wrote to Lt-General Sir Robert Haining at the War Office on 16 December: 'The delay in the production of the dive-bombers has been made necessary owing to the introduction of essential modifications. I have asked Mr Purvis to do all he can to urge forward the delivery of these types and I think it would be best now for us to wait until Mr Purvis has gone back to America and had an opportunity of seeing what can be done. He fully understands the importance of this matter.' On 18 December 1940 Sir Archibald Sinclair duly passed this on to Anthony Eden with the comment, 'I'm afraid it is depressing.'

A report to the Air Ministry dated 3 May 1941 noted: 'Flight tests on prototype Vengeance airplane have revealed faults in design. Present delivery schedule cannot be assumed to hold.'

Nor did the fact that the company went on strike in July 1941 help much. As well as the disruption they also lost many of their most able staff. Victor Bertagna was among those who moved on, first to another company designing full-span flaps for Navy aircraft, and later, in November 1942, to Northrop where he worked on the B-35 'Flying Wing' project.

On 29 August 1941, the two V-72 prototypes were flown by Vance Breese and Frank Davis respectively to the production plants at Nashville and Hawthorne, to give the new workers their first glimpse of the airplane they were waiting to construct.

Darrell McNeal, then working at Northrop, remembers Vance Breese flying in the first airplane from Downey to Hawthorne and commenting adversely on the aircraft's forward heaviness. 'A "fix" was made by changing the engine mount, thus moving the CG back a few inches.'

Waiting at the Nashville Division for Davis was a large assembly of VIPs. After an overnight stop at El Paso, and with no problems *en route*, Davis brought his ship into a perfect landing at Berry Field and taxied up to the service hangar to be welcomed by fellow test pilot Graydon 'Cy' (for Cyclone) Younglove, who was then Chief of Flight Test and Field Service at Nashville.

A National Guard, Flying School and test flyer with the Davis Aircraft Company of Richmond, Indiana, and later stuntman with the Wright Exhibition Corps, Younglove had joined Stinson in Wayne, Michigan, where he became a salesman. He had moved to Nashville with them and stayed on when AVCO took the new plant over for Vultee, where he test flew the 0-49 *Vigilant*. Now the Vengeance was to be his 'baby'.

Vultee's vice president in charge of operations, D. I. Carroll, made an announcement that a $300,000 mechanised assembly plant similar to that at Downey was to be installed to produce the V-72, commencing that October. Considerable subcontracting was also announced and, perhaps inevitably, this was to cause problems. When Stinson had been taken over, among the sites had been the then inoperable Barkley-Grow Aircraft Corporation in Detroit, Michigan, and they were therefore to be modernised in order to construct subassemblies.

Next day, Tuesday, Davis laid on a demonstration flight for the 3000-strong workforce at the behest of the new works manager, Robert McCulloch, recently recruited from North American.

This optimistic, or perhaps naive, feeling also prevailed on the production line at Hawthorne. The tone was set by John Northrop himself in one of his 'noontime chats' and recorded in the company magazine in December 1941, soon after the initial production machine had rolled off the assembly line and had made its maiden flight on 30 November. 'The Vengeance,' he said, 'was one of the best ships designed for a specific purpose.' Coming from one with such a respected track record in this specialised field this statement carried considerable weight. 'The Vengeance was designed by Vultee engineers who threw traditional procedure overboard to telescope into a few months of intense activity the long time usually required in the development of high performance aircraft,' continued the statement.

C. V. J. Childs headed the British Commission at the Northrop plant at this time and he was quoted as saying, 'in working on this bomber, we have embodied not only the advances in design developed by Vultee engineers, but we have used every bit of experience gained through the use of dive-bombers in the war.'

One Northrop engineer, Edward Peden, remembers: 'I worked on the V-72 Vengeance during World War II at Northrop, and at the time had every reason to think that this aircraft was destined for great accomplishments in defeating the enemy.' For Peden, and others, this early enchantment was to fade.

There were still a great many design and production snags along the way that were still to come to light. These were to slow down the two production lines, especially Nashville, and were to take the edge off the early enthusiasm. Because of the need to get aircraft quickly, and the special provisions of the Northrop contract, most of the alterations and changes, either thrown up during development testing or asked for by the RAF, were worked on by Vultee. Despite this it was somehow hoped that the highly desirable quality of interchangeability between the products of the two firms would be maintained. However, Northrop continued to press ahead with the basic model, while Vultee's plant, already behind schedule on the production side anyway, followed up with the modified machines. They became, in effect, two different machines and the British acknowledged this fact by classing the Northrop product (the A–31-NO) the Vengeance I and the Vultee product (the A-31-VN), although this order was placed first, the Vengeance II.

This, of course, is why the subcontractor was to beat the parent firm into the air with the first flight of a *production* aircraft. For a time, lip-service continued to be paid to the principle of interchangeability. *The Northrop News* for June 1941 exclaimed: 'Tools and jigs were ordered jointly by both Northrop and Vultee, assuring 100 per cent interchangeability of all parts.'

Even as late as 30 March 1942, for example, the British Air Commission were sending Letter of Amendment Number 35 to Northrop stating that: 'In order to demonstrate interchangeability between certain components of Vengeance airplanes being manufactured by you and being manufactured by Vultee Aircraft, Inc., you are hereby authorised to transfer immediately to Vultee Aircraft, Inc. Berry Field, Nashville, Tennessee, one set of the components listed in Exhibit "G" of the above contract with the exception of the fuselage, engine mount and cowling of the Body Group, Landing Gear and Tail Wheel Group, Hydraulic system, Fuel Tanks, Gun Mounts, Exhaust Manifold assembly and Ammunition Boxes. A corresponding set of components will be furnished you concurrently by Vultee Aircraft, Inc., in replacement.'

On 28 May 1942, Letter of Amendment No. 43 stated that: 'It is hereby agreed that Vengeance Airplane RAF Serial No. AN868, shall be retained at your plant as a resident airplane until delivery of the last airplane off the Contract unless otherwise agreed, for the purpose of development tests and verification of the functioning of accessories and equipment.'

They were to add, on 19 June, 'the desirability of incorporating in the airplane certain A-31 installations which you are prepared to do without cost to us.'

Well before this, problems continued to be encountered at Downey, as another British report, dated 9 October 1941, spelt out: 'Mr Fenwick of Vultee was completely frank . . . that delays involved were the fault of their own management and teething troubles associated with the prototype and in no way sought to attribute them to modifications emanating from BAC'

But it cannot be denied that the many alterations insisted upon by the British did not ease the situation. A highly detailed Development Statement was made on the Vengeance I by the BAC on 9 February 1942, in which 'Present Position and Operational Fitness' were analysed.

'One aircraft has completed 60 hours of accelerated service trials at Downey, California, flown by RAF pilots of the BAC,' it recorded. 'Production aircraft will be delivered in a few days from Northrop, Los Angeles and Vultee, Nashville.

'This aircraft is very easy to fly and land and gives the pilot a feeling of confidence. It has a fair perfomance but the take-off and the initial rate of climb are sluggish. The controls, with the exception of the ailerons, are on the heavy side but the aircraft has no vices and the dive brakes are particularly good. These are spanwise, slotted slats which swing up vertically both above and below the wing at mid-chord, and reduce the diving speed to a little over three hundred miles per hour. They

do not cause changes in longitudinal trim and have no adverse affect on the flying controls.

'The aircraft is otherwise conventional. Having a large diameter radial engine the forward view is inferior to the comparable German type and this is more of a handicap during take-off and landing than in dive-bombing. Greater accuracy in dive-bombing would result were the flying controls improved. The ailerons are light and effective, but directional control, once the aircraft is committed to a dive and has gathered speed, requires adjustment of the rudder tab.'

It commented: 'This aircraft should prove a useful dive-bomber.'

Tests still outstanding or not completed at this date included: 'Elevator and aileron modifications and adjustments in hand on first production aircraft. The oil dilution system has only been tested in California weather. The Air Cleaner has not been tested. Carbon monoxide tests not yet made. No satisfactory flame-damping exhausts have been designed.'

The tare weight of the prototype was given as 9425 lb, normal gross weight as 12,815 lb and overload, with 274 Imperial gallons of fuel, as 14,226 lb. The C.G. range tested from 20.2 per cent to 30.4 per cent M.A.C. and equivalent to 25.7 ins to 35 ins aft of datum. The fuel consumption was given as 62 Imp gallons per hour at 9500 ft at 200 mph. Careful use of mixture control was stressed at high powers at altitude to avoid excessive fuel consumption. At 200 mph and normal fuel load (166 gallons) endurance and range were 2.7 hours and 540 miles respectively. With maximum fuel (217 gallons), 4.9 hours and 1000 miles. These figures were a combination of Vultee's and the BAC's respective figures. It was noted that the company's corrections 'might be slightly on the generous side.'

On handling, it was noted that: 'There is a tendency to swing to the left during the take-off and the initial rate of climb is poor until the chassis is retracted (flaps depressed 40 degrees). The brakes judder at low speed without any apparent ill effects. The tail-wheel lock will not stand violent turns and should be released after landing. Damage to

Moye Stephens 'guns' the first Northrop production Vengeance in readiness for her maiden flight from Hawthorne. *(Northrop)*

the lower cylinders will result from overdoping, when starting. The electric fuel pumps should be tested before flight.'

No spinning was permitted as tests had not then yet been made. In high blower, generous use of the mixture control at all throttle openings was recommended to avoid loss of power and rough running due to richness. The new equipment listed the dive brakes on both upper and lower surfaces of the wing which, it was stated, 'may be extended before diving and will limit the speed to 320 ASI at moderate heights. If extended at high speeds (over 250 ASI) the deceleration is violent.'

Modifications due to be introduced later included the replacement of heavy elevators (i.e. heavy in flight) and ailerons with a slight

tendency to overbalance at 50 per cent of the stick travel, with elevators incorporating a thickened section forward of the hinge and contra-servo balance tabs. The report concluded: ' . . . these aircraft are being made at two factories whose deliveries are roughly level. Certain modifications will appear on the 56th aircraft from Vultee's but we have not yet got the aircraft number on which these same modifications will appear from the Northrop factory.'

Another report went into more detail of the difference between the machines being produced at the two plants. The Vengeance I being built by Northrop had no provision for an air cleaner or an armoured fire-wall. These requirements were being incorporated in all the Vultee Vengeance IIs from about the one-hundredth production aircraft onward. Other features that were to be standard on the Vultee, but not on the Northrop, were fittings for F.24 camera gun; heating for the fixed wing guns; long-range fuel tanks, reconnaissance flares; and windshield de-icing. In view of the ultimate deployment of these aircraft, heating and de-icing seem farcical in retrospect, but at the time an allocation to the Royal Canadian Air Force was still part of the A-31's future deployment plans. Later, desert gear—filters etc—was also added into extra British requirements, with obvious North African usage contemplated despite a recent assertion to the contrary.

It was ultimately planned to equip the following services with the Vengeance: RAF and Indian Air Force, six squadrons; RCAF, two squadrons; RAAF, nine squadrons; South African Air Force, one squadron. But the allocations to Canada and South Africa were subsequently held back at low priority in order to get what aircraft there were to the fighting fronts in South-East Asia.

Vultee were also reported as encountering problems with the subcontracting firm producing the stub panels, and these had eventually to be made at the main plant. Other parts were proceeding on schedule. Among British suggestions that were sought to be incorporated following the prototype flight trials and before combat duties were the following:

'(i) Strengthened undercarriage fittings, involving retrospective modification.
(ii) Redesign of elevators to give a better pull-out of a dive with flaps on.
(iii) Change of propeller blade specification to give better take-off.
(iv) Investigation into the fuel system which incorporates novel features and has not proved altogether satisfactory.'

Just about the time the first production models flew from Nashville in December 1941, and America's entry into the conflict, Vultee was involved in further reorganisation plans which were to result in more disturbance at all levels from boardroom to factory floor. Manipulation was by AVCO of Delaware, which owned 71 per cent of Vultee Aircraft and was also the holding company for Consolidated. Tom M. Girdler was granted part-time leave from Republic Steel to serve as Board Chairman and Chief Executive Officer of both companies. Under him, Harry Woodhead was President of both. I. M. Laddon became Executive Vice-President and General Manager of Consolidated, San Diego, and was also elected Vice-President of Vultee. Major David G. Fleet, son of Consolidated's founder and Director, later moved to Downey as Executive Vice-President of Vultee.

To finance the purchase of David Fleet's holdings Vultee sold 240,000 shares of preferred stock to underwriters for $5,430,000 and 150,000 shares of common stock to the parent AVCO for $1,500,000. The company obtained an additional $2,350,000 from current funds or increased bank loans, and gave Fleet a promissory 3 per cent note for the remainder: $1,665,000 dollars to be payable in cash or stock by 30 June 1942.

Thus a controlling interest was purchased in the Consolidated Aircraft Company of San Diego. This company was probably best known at the time for its Liberator long-range bomber and the Catalina long-range flying boat. This deal was to result in dramatic changes at Vultee. Harry Woodhead and T. M. Girdler became President and Chairman of the Board respectively, of both Vultee and Consolidated, after a concentrated effort to have both top managements work together failed. The ultimate merger of the two into the Consolidated-Vultee Aircraft Corporation (CONVAIR) did not finally take place until 14 March 1943, but a year earlier, as a result of their differences over the new policy, the three principal executives of Vultee previous to the purchase, resigned. These were Richard W. Millar, President of Vultee; 'Dick' Palmer, Vice-President and Chief Engineer; and D. I. Carroll, Vice-President in charge of Manufacturing. With Richard's departure went a large part of the V-72's original design team.

Charles Irvine describes these early days thus: 'My part in the Vengeance program was that of Project Engineer, doing the prototype development phase at Downey. I was not involved in the preliminary design as I was busy as Project Engineer on the P-48 fighter at that time. I am sure the twin-boom tail configuration was considered because this was a popular concept at that time, which as far as Vultee was concerned surfaced again in the XP-54 configuration a year later. Vance Breese was making known his own thoughts on this design as he had been employed to make the first flights on all new Vultee aircraft over the previous three years . . .

'The Vengeance came out of preliminary design in March of 1940 and entered the urgent prototype development phase. Due to the urgency of scheduling in those days drawings were sent to Northrop for production planning purposes at about the same time they went to our own experimental shop. This led to the necessity for many changes later on as testing progressed, and this was very upsetting to Northrop's management. Lamont Cohu was heading Northrop at the time and Warren Kaneriem was his Project Engineer. Co-ordination of the two efforts was very challenging.

'As with most aircraft designs the center of gravity did tend to creep to the rear. This was corrected by lengthening the nose section. This lowered the pilot's visibility to the point where a wing incidence change was considered, but not implemented.

'The wing structure was interesting in that it had a very heavy skin reinforced with longitudinal U-shaped stringers to minimize the number of ribs required and thus provide space for larger bullet-proof fuel bags, each with its own motor-driven fuel pump. The wing structure and fuel bags proved to be quite satisfactory, but the plumbing complexity and frequent fuel pump failures led to a fuel system that left much to be desired.

'The dive brakes were also rather unique. They consisted of a heavy aluminum alloy channel approximately six feet long and eight to ten inches wide with a flange approximately one inch deep. They were

An early production Vultee Vengeance is given last-minute touches alongside two of same company's Stinson AT-19 Reliant light communications aircraft at Nashville. *(AVCO)*

mounted on arms that retracted into the upper and lower surface of each wing when not in use. The channels were perforated with slots making them resemble a picket-fence. They fitted into the wing surface with a minimum of interference when retracted. The slot configuration was easy to modify during testing to minimise vibration in the dive. Radio telemetering in aircraft flight testing was used to study these vibrations and to work out corrections. I believe this was the first use of telemetering in aircraft flight testing in this country.

'The landing gear was a particularly troublesome system. As the gear retracted to the rear the wheel was rotated through 90 degrees so that it would fit flat into the wing structure when retracted. To accomplish this the wheel was offset to the side of the shock strut and the strut was rotated 90 degrees by bevel gears at the junction of the strut and the wing. This resulted in a very flexible gear which produced uneven tyre wear and dynamic problems for the pilot in uneven landings.

Meantime, undisturbed by such traumatic events, over at Northrop's they were forging ahead and conducting their own test flying, as Ted Coleman recalled. 'The test flying of the Vengeance at Northrop was done by Moye Stephens and Dick Rinaldi. Moye was in charge of all company test flying during World War II. He was also Secretary of Northrop Aircraft Inc. I cannot recall any accidents at the plant. We set a remarkable record of test flying 400 Vengeance airplanes without an accident.'

Unlike the silver Vultees Gerald H. Balzer notes that uncamouflaged aircraft from Northrop's production generally were painted in the yellowish primer finish prior to the application of colours.

Let Moye Stephens himself take up the story in his own words. From his logbook it can be seen that his first test flight in the V-72 took place on 30 November 1941, and was a 45-minute hop from Mines Field (the mile-square nucleus of what has since expanded into LAX, Los Angeles International Airport).

'Vultee had produced an experimental ship, but we beat them into production, and my flight on our No. 1 constituted my first experience with the model. As soon as our production was established, I hired Dick Rinaldi to help with the test flying so that I would have time to spend on the N-1M.

'My initial impression was there was something inherently wrong with the ship. Included in its peculiarities was the British requirement of zero angle of incidence to facilitate dive-bombing. It *was* possible to dive straight down with a minimum degree of tuck-under; but, as a consequence, the ship's nose-high attitude in level flight effectively blocked out vision straight ahead. Among other novel first-flight impressions was an erroneous notion that the indicated airspeed had to be unbelievably modest.

'My first flight in the Vengeance took place just over a month after flying a Spitfire with a Hurricane the only other ship flown in the interim. A dray horse can't logically be compared to a thoroughbred; each has its place in the scheme of things, but the contrast

Autographed picture of Northrop's Chief Test Pilot, Moye Stephens, who flew the first production Vengeance. *(Moye Stephens)*

was impressive. Insofar as handling characteristics were concerned it was an honest airplane; though it had features not among the most desirable.

'Among the first of these to be noted was the ship's nose-high attitude in level flight. Its unusually long nose interfered with forward visibility. We were given to understand that this was due to a design requirement of little or no angle of incidence to aid dive-bombing. Another item which was questioned, was the incorporation of a small, intermediary, fuel trap tank in the fore part of the cockpit. It served as the focal point for fuel lines from the various wing tanks. Its outlet led directly to the carburettor.

'At the start of my take-offs, the outlet connection developed a leak which drenched a canvas-covered dynamotor directly beneath the tank. Cutting the combination ignition and electrical system master switch (another debatable feature) was the only means of shutting down the dynamotor. It was fortunate the failure hadn't chosen to delay its appearance for a few seconds further into the flight.

'Another item which caused me a moment of anxiety was a feature of the landing flap design. On each wing the flaps were in two sections: inner wing and outer wing. The flap actuating mechanisms were directly connected to the inner flaps only. On each wing, the outer flap was connected to the inner flap by a toggle near their trailing edges. The inner flap was lowered by the flap actuating mechanism; and the flap, in turn, pulled down the outer flap by means of the connecting toggle.

'Near the end of a final approach the toggle between my right hand flaps failed abruptly, allowing the outer flap to snap into the trail position. It took all the left aileron, much left rudder, and added power to right the ship with little altitude to spare.'

When asked by the author to elaborate his feelings about the novel electrical system master switch, Moye Stephens replied: 'I much prefer to have the ignition and electrical systems independent of one another. In the trap tank incident, if the substantial leak had started a few seconds later I would have been too far down the runway to abort. With the possibility of the dynamotor sparking the cockpit into an inferno, I would have had the choice of risking incineration or cutting the ignition-electrical switch and crash-landing in the abutting residential area of the city of Hawthorne. With independent switches, the electrical system could have been inactivated and a circle of the field completed with no sweat.'

Thus the tests continued and, one by one, the problems were found, and solved. Then, just when the British felt that, at last, they were going to get delivery of their long-awaited dive-bomber America was catapulted into the war by the bombing of Pearl Harbor on 7 December 1941. Almost at once this led to a totally new complication to the Vengeance's already complicated gestation story.

# Chapter 3
# Gestation

Comments by the RAF pilots flying the first of the Vengeance aircraft in the States were basically favourable. One Air Ministry secret report commented: 'The all-round view is good for all purposes. The diving speed is restricted to 290 mph with diving brakes extended. Pilots' reports from USA, while showing that certain improvements were desirable in flying characteristics, indicate only the usual "teething troubles" associated with early tests of a new type. Control is heavy but acceptable and bombs have been released in dives up to the vertical without trouble being experienced.'

On America's entry into the war she was forced to take stock of her own armaments and, like the French in 1939 and the British in 1940, she found herself in dire need of almost everything. Also like the two European nations, but with three years' less excuse, she found that her Army Air Corps had no dive-bombers designed for land-based operations at all. The A-20, for example, unless redesigned extensively to include dive flaps, could not be flown at the steep angle that the accurate attacks being achieved by the Japanese *Val* required. It is true that, on 8 June 1940, the Materiel Division, Washington D.C., had recommended procurement of modified versions of the Navy's Douglas *Dauntless* and Curtiss *Helldiver* types, given the designations A-24 and A-25 respectively. But only a few of the former were available for combat duties and

Production of the V-72 under way in the spacious new Vultee plant on the old Stinson Aircraft site at Nashville. Notice armour-backed padded head-rest at back of pilot's seat and height of undercarriage, size of wing fuel tank space with three men inside them. *(AVCO)*

the latter aircraft was subject to even worse delays and tribulations than the Vengeance. Also, the third alternative, the custom-built Brewster SBC *Bermuda*, was in even bigger trouble yet. Even when it got hold of dive-bombers, the US Army Air Corps found that, having little or no expertise, previous knowledge or training in the technique, the SBD in the hands of the Army pilots was but a pale shadow of the aircraft that Navy and Marine Corps pilots were to use so dramatically and effectively in the years ahead.

Not surprisingly, once the need was identified, envious eyes were turned to British dive-bombers being produced in American factories and thus ready to hand. On 16 January 1942, the Air Corps gave Vultee a Letter of Intent (AC-24664) for 400 A-31 dive-bombers, but since British contracts covered all the possible production models for the rest of 1942 the Americans could not

Another excellent view of Vultee's Nashville plant in full swing in 1942, showing working techniques and size of the plant at that time. *(AVCO)*

Body and engine line-up at Nashville. Note tails already have RAF insignia marked up, flush assembly awaiting bolting-on of inner wing section, double intakes with bottom one sealed for protection. *(AVCO)*

The main doors of the Nashville factory showing to good effect the size of the plant, with Vengeances wingtip to wingtip inside. Parked outside are AF934 in foreground (left) and one other completed aircraft. *(AVCO)*

hope to receive any Vengeance dive-bombers until 1943. This problem was solved by what became known as the 'Arnold-Portal' agreement under which a certain proportion of British production in American plants was turned over to the USAAC.

J. J. Llewellyn at the MAP was to write to Sinclair on 28 May 1942, scathingly, 'We were about to get deliveries when Pearl Harbor occurred. The U.S. Air Corps thereupon seized about 200 Vengeance and 192 Bermuda. The Arnold-Portal agreement increased the number of these which we surrendered, and sanctioned the seizure from our orders of 300 Vengeance dive-bombers, 158 of these were ex-contracts for which we had paid hard cash and 142 were Lease-Lend.'

The British Air Minister gently rebuked his angry colleague in a letter dated 1 June 1942. 'You should seek to place the blame for the delay in deliveries of dive-bombers on production, not on allocations. . . I do not understand how the U.S. Air Corps seized 200 Vengeance and 192 Bermudas after Pearl Harbor. None of either type were in existence at that time!

'What actually happened was that the proposals for the allocation of dive-bombers put forward by the Americans during the *Arcadia* discussions involved a cut of 492 Vengeances. In spite of our efforts we could not reduce this cut, but we were able to have the cut fall on Bermudas as well. The final allocations for Vengeances and Bermudas came out at 999 Vengeances and 556 Bermudas, involving cuts of 300 and 192 aircraft respectively. We retained 77 per cent of our original expectations of dive-bombers as compared with 66 per cent over the light bomber class as a whole.

'I think you are a little unreasonable in referring to the Arnold/Portal agreement as

39

"sanctioning the seizure" of these aircraft. It is, I suppose, possible to argue that the only satisfactory outcome to the discussions with General Arnold would have been for us to retain all our original allocations. In fact such a solution was never remotely practicable — or indeed desirable. Radical adjustments of allocations on the entry of America into the war was always a certainty.'

The noble Lord was far out of touch with reality, however. Even in the 1940s his old-world view of how diplomacy was conducted proved very obsolete! He of course was not privy to a telephone conversation between Lamont Cohu of Northrop to Colonel Orval R. Cook of the Army Air Corps Materiel Division at Wright Field, made on 26 January 1942. Had he been, he might have been disillusioned on the true American attitude to 'seizing' these planes.

Cohu requested clarification of a wire from Materiel Division which stated that the Air Corps planned to take January and February production of V-72s (A-31) for themselves.

He expressed some concern over the fact that British equipment would have to be removed and replaced with A.C. equipment and that authority would have to be obtained from the British for such action. Colonel O. R. Cook quickly set him right on this score: '. . . the British aren't running this country Mr. Cohu. If the Army decides to take them over, we take them over do you see!'

The initial agreement in fact provided for allocations of the V-72 to the USAAC of seven airplanes in January 1942, 16 in February and eventually a total of 300. But then the Air Corps had to decide whether or not the A-31, as it existed, was suitable to American needs. The two nations' specifications varied so much that it soon became obvious that important modifications would have to be made before the Americans could make tactical use of them. Accordingly a conference was held at the Nashville Plant on 29 January 1942, to see when these changes could be achieved.

On 4 February 1942, Colonel K. B. Wolfe,

AF841 rolls out from Vultee in the standard RAF paint scheme but with elaborate roundels and plain underwing paint scheme. Note twin-rear guns and wing guns. *(AVCO)*

Chief of the Production Engineering Section, reported on this meeting thus: 'It is apparent that we will not obtain a useful dive-bomber of any type before March or April, 1943. Therefore it is recommended that all contracts on A-31 airplanes be cancelled and concentration be given to obtaining a suitable dive-bomber, low-altitude attack fighter in its place.'

On 13 February 1943, Lieutenant-Colonel Thomas H. Chapman, Chief of the Inspection Section, requested that an acclerated inspection be conducted to render a final decision on the questionable items. When this had been completed at the end of the month a very long list of engineering changes required before the Americans could use it in combat was submitted.

Colonel Wolfe reported to the Assistant Chief Materiel Division in Washington that: '.50 caliber guns to be installed on 901st

Good close-up view of the Wright Double *Cyclone* at full belt at Hawthorne. Note production A-31s with early USAAF markings in background. *(Northrop)*

aircraft, and converting to a single-seat plane with armour plate, proper leak-proof tanks and redesigned fuel system on the 1301st airplane. Not enthusiastic due to large turning radius, long take-off, low rate of climb, limited manoeuvrability, which would be aggravated rather than alleviated by these changes. Recommended by Wolfe A-31 contract cancelled and A-25 or A-32 built instead.'

The following relative points were also noted around this time:

(1) Flight demonstrations, held at Wright and Patterson Fields on 14 February 1942, were not satisfactory.
(2) British pilots reported that the take-off distance was excessive and that the chin sank rapidly at speeds below 140 mph.
(3) Vultee and Northrop A-31s were not interchangeable despite the pious hopes still being expressed.
(4) Therefore Northrop-built planes, although completed earlier, were going to require extensive modifications before the British could use them in the front line. This was partly due to the need of Northrop to conform with their strict contract, partly to the fact that Vultee did not always get the modified drawings of design changes over to Vultee in time for them to implement them.

On 10 March 1942 another interesting telephone conversation took place between Lieutenant-Colonel C. E. Brandshaw, District Representative at Santa Monica, and the newly-promoted Brigadier-General K. B. Wolfe, about the fuel tanks in V-72s being unsatisfactory. After congratulating 'KB' on his promotion 'Charlie' got down to business.

'Well, here is the story, I have got to get it straightened out quick. Vultee is building the V-72, which is a Vultee job, engineered by Vultee and being built by Northrop on the Licence Agreement.'

'Yes, that is right, Charlie.'

'All right, the job is lousy. Got several things wrong with it, one of which is the gas tank.' He elaborated: 'Those gas tanks are no good — in the first place they are not bullet-proof and never will be bullet-proof. It is not the fault of the rubber company. Please bear that in mind in any consideration. They are built by Voit. Voit objected when they started to build them. Vultee thought they know all about rubber tanks and so they drew up their own specification, their own design, and made Voit build them that way. Result, they are not bullet-proof, and what is worse they are not leak-proof. I don't know if you knew that.'

'Yes, we suspected it.'

'Charlie' suggested that '. . . we have got to junk the tanks entirely and get some new ones, built to proper design specifications. . .' He also noted that the bomb-bay would not accommodate American bombs. He concluded it would be better to take larger batches instead of alternating with the British in small batches, and that the British take the first batch, giving the firm time to make corrections before the American batch was reached. With this there was some accord but events had already overtaken this.

One aircraft from the production line of each plant was made available to the US Army Air Corps but so many modifications were required, as we have seen, that, on 17 March 1942, General Wolfe recommened that:

(1) All A-31 airplanes be allocated to the British only — a reversal of the earlier decision.
(2) Production of the A-31 type be kept at a minimum consistent with the time required to re-tool for another, improved, model.
(3) If the above two could not be implemented, then the Air Corps take their Vengeances only from the Vultee line.

The thorny question of interchangeability was the subject of investigation by the Air Corps Production Engineering Section; its Chief, Colonel O. R. Cook, reported that a procedure for co-ordination between Vultee and Northrop of all engineering data had been formulated and was then in effect. We have seen the BAC memos on this subject, but this was all made academic by the adoption of one of General Wolfe's earlier recommendations: the allocation of the entire Northrop line to Britain and Vultee to the USA was implemented. This immediately reduced its importance.

Richard P. Patterson, Under-Secretary for War, Washington, contacted R. A. Lovett, Assistant Secretary for War (Air). General Knudsen had told him that little could be expected from the A-31 in the way of performance. He therefore recommended the ending of production and Nashville being used to build 'a plane of proven merit, such as the Douglas dive-bomber'.

Lovett replied on 30 March. Tests with A-31 at Wright Field confirmed unsatisfactory visibility and instability in the dive, location of gas tanks under the pilot and other equally objectionable installations, substantial changes and mods required. The British however were less perturbed about these unsatisfactory military characteristics.

In the interim, on 31 March 1942, the Experimental Engineering Section at Wright Field recommended that as few V-72 as possible be issued to American combat service organisations. At this time a crash programme of dive-bomber training was to be initiated, at the order of the same tough-talking Lieutenant-General H. H. 'Hap' Arnold, Chief of the Army Air Forces, and the setting up of suitable training schools was being discussed along with the allocation of suitable aircraft, initially with A-24s. The Engineering Section stated that the V-72 might be suitably employed thus as a training dive-bomber. In the same report however they recommended that the *whole* of the A-31 output be delivered to the British until a version more suitable to US needs could be put into production in its place. Nonetheless, the 300 A-31s taken over by the Americans were duly allocated for combat crew training and operations unit training schools. This brought a comment from the Director of Bombardment, Washington D.C., Colonel E. P. Sorensen: 'it appears that, even after reworking, this airplane will only barely be suitable for training and probably out of the question as a future combat model.' On 13 April came further criticism, General Meyers issuing an order in which he requested a complete report on changes required on the A-31 to satisfy operational training requirements. He further requested that action be taken to determine the possibility of closing down the production of the A-31 altogether.

Materiel Command gave careful attention to the possibility of adapting the V-72s allocated to the Army Air Force (as it had then become) to training purposes but the condition of the aircraft available and to be produced in the near future 'made such a program impractical'.

On 14 April 1942, Vultee's themselves insisted that the many changes wanted by the Americans over the British design could not be implemented until after the 500 V-72s of the outstanding British order had been produced, and that would not be until October. Materiel Command therefore recommended, two days later, that the start of the US Army's production run of 300 A–31s be delayed until September, by which time most of the desired changes could be incorporated. This would result in the re-allocation of the existing present and intermediate production of 360 airplanes back to the British again.

But Arnold was not to be fobbed off like this. He wanted dive-bombers and he wanted the latest, which meant the Vengeance, and the modified Vengeance at that! On 18 April 1942, he objected to the diversion of these A-31's 'for the convenience of the manufacturer'. He issued instructions that dive-bomber operational training units must be organised immediately. As only a meagre three A-24s were available for this duty he told Materiel Division to contact Vultee and tell them that they *must* get on and make the required changes forthwith.

Meanwhile, further attempts were being made in the USA to have the A-31 programme cancelled. General Wolfe had repeated his earlier attempt of February 1942

one month later. Also, on 29 March 1942, Mr. Patterson stated that, on the basis of information received from General Knudsen, little could be expected from the dive-bomber in production at Nashville; he indicated that it was time to put an end to the production of the A-31.

On 14 April 1942, Robert McCulloch, Works Manager at Nashville, reported to CHG Materiel Division on the modified A–31, the A-31-A. In addition to AAF requirements suggested on the basis of a 689 inspection, further changes would be made in guns, visibility, take-off, armour plating and fuel system, with the possible addition of a torpedo installation. Vultee advised of serious effect on morale of engineering and shop personnel and that subcontracting difficulties would result if an outside design were introduced. Confidence was expressed that the A-31-A would achieve results comparable to any other dive-bomber of later design.

After the radical changes in Vultee management the new controllers of the company came up with a proposal, on 14 April 1942, to produce a modified A-31, to be known as the A-31A, and they hoped that the big list of USAAF complaints against the earlier airplane would be rectified in this new model. Robert McCulloch put forward a schedule for the A-31A, which would act as the prototype for the new A-35, would be delivered in July 1942, and the last of the unsatisfactory V-72s would be delivered by October of the same year. There was a lot of confidence that this new model would suit the Materiel Command's needs.

Wolfe, now a Brigadier-General but still Chief, Production Division, concluded on 22 April 1942 that the A-35 'would be a suitable flying machine and military weapon comparable with the A-25 airplane.' He recommended that Vultee continue with production of the A-31 until such time that the A-35 could be introduced. General Echols and General Myers concurred in this recommendation on 25 April 1942, and it was to be taken up with Lieutenant-General W. S. Knudsen, Director of Production, War Department, Washington D.C., and Mr.

Robert P. Patterson, Under-Secretary of War, the following week.

General Wolfe advised the contractor to proceed with the redesign work, and to submit the necessary data for the initiation of a change order to the contract. This was the origin of the A-35.

General Wolfe himself had considerable faith in Vultee's new design team under McCulloch and the promise of improved operations at the Nashville plant. Nashville had set up its own engineering staff, separate from Downey, for on-the-spot solving of problems as they arose. B. R. Sherrell was appointed Works Manager of the Nashville Division by McCulloch. He had worked for Vultee Nashville before, having joined the company in California in 1940 as Assistant General Foreman of Experimental, and had worked on the BT-13 and the *Vanguard* projects. He later became Production Manager, Assistant Works Manager and

Works Co-ordinator at Nashville before leaving in June 1941 to join the Southern Aircraft Co of Garland, Texas. This company was one of Vultee's major subcontractors for the A-31.

On 7 March 1972 an inter-office memo from the Assistant Chief Materiel Division, Wright Field, Dayton, Ohio, to Engineering Production listed the following alterations required to make the A-31 usable for the USAAF:

A complete revision of the fuel system consisting of: (1) Removal of the seven submerged electrically driven fuel pumps, installation of an engine-driven fuel pump, installation of an auxiliary electrically driven fuel pump and emergency pump; (2) Relocation of metal trap tank located between the pilot's legs, which would flood the cockpit if pierced by a bullet and constituted a great fire hazard; (3) The fuel

AN869 parked on the concrete. Some indication of the long nose of the V-72 can be assessed from this view and how far back the pilot was seated. This made landing and take-off visibility poor but had a negligible affect in attack as the Vengeance was specially designed to dive vertically and not at the arbitrary 60-75 degrees as most previous dive-bomber types. *(Northrop)*

A V-72 pulls up very low during a practice dive-bombing trial against dummy guns and tanks before invited film and camera crews. *(AVCO)*

system to be resistant to aromatic fuels; (4) Installation of self-sealing tank material in lieu of that used.

Next, the revision of the hydraulic system and landing gear installations by: (1) Installation of an emergency hydraulic system; (2) Making the levers for the landing gear, bomb-bay door and dive brakes return automatically to the neutral position. This would obviate pressure on hydraulic lines which made them very vulnerable to one stray shot; (4) Installation of newly designed elevators and rudders to reduce stick and rudder forces. 'The Northrop A-31 airplane at present at Wright Field cannot be dived because of the excessive stick forces required to pull out of a dive.'; (5) Rework of the engine priming system; (6) Rework of the radio installation to provide for pilot control; (7) Relocation of pilot cockpit controls to Air Corps specification; (8) Installation of oxygen system; (9) Replacement of the .30 calibre guns with four .50 calibre guns in the wings. Thus was born the A-35.

Training and test flying continued apace. At Nashville, test pilot Howard Kincheloe conducted the very first dive-bombing tests of a production aircraft that July. At the old Sky Harbor airport he did a shallow 45-degree dive on a 200-ft circle target containing dummy tanks and anti-aircraft guns after only a few hours' flying the Vengeance. Despite this his bombs were on target and he expressed the view that the A-31 was 'one of

Dramatic shot as dummies are disintegrated by practice bombing during early media filming of the Vengeance in California. *(AVCO)*

the most stable airplanes he had ever flown'. A former Navy dive-bomber pilot, Kincheloe added that he considered the Vengeance to be 'far superior to any in use by the Navy at the time he was in the Service'. The tests were filmed by Scientific Films, *Life Magazine*, the Office of War Information and Associated Press and got the machine a much-needed publicity boost.

Over at Northrop, too, the test flying continued and the comments were hardly less scathing than in the Pentagon itself. Moye Stephens recalls the equivalent Northrop bombing test they conducted: 'It was to determine if bombs released in a vertical dive would safely clear the ship. The principal concern was the largest bomb (I can't

remember its weight). It was housed inside the fuselage and, on release, swung out on arms to be turned loose outside the arc of the propeller.

'With a full complement of dummy bombs, I landed at the Air Force field at Muroc Dry lake (now Edwards Air Force Base) and reported to the officer of the day for assignment to a bombing range. I explained that, inasmuch as I had never dive-bombed anything, I would appreciate a target in an area of the greatest possible isolation. He assured me there would be no one anywhere near my assignment.

'The target was a circular area cleared of desert brush with a straight, narrow lane of some length leading into it. I assumed the lane served as a sighting aid in horizontal bombing practice. I salvoed the bombs at a safe altitude and pulled out of the dive into a chandelee so that I could look back over my shoulder to be able to judge the extent of my "expertise". To my consternation, I discovered a car travelling up the lane toward the target. It reached the edge just as my bombs impacted the opposite edge.

'The unexplained intruder could have been a hunter who had unknowingly strayed into a restricted area. On the return flight to Northrop, I couldn't escape the reflection that if there were any way he could have known of my bombing experience, he might very well have considered the centre of the target the safest place to be!'

Moye remembers the diminutive Dick Rinaldi, who also flight tested the Vengeance at this time. 'Dick, the first of my pilots to be hired, was gifted with a whimsical sense of humour. He opined that a plan view of the ship suggested a number of things: (1) In its original form, the CG had proven too far forward. (2) The outer wings had then been swept forward to correct the error. (3) The change had overcompensated: the CG had moved too far aft. (4) The motor mount was then replaced with one moving the motor forward in order to move the CG forward. He pointed out that the space between the motor and the firewall provided "enough room to smuggle a couple of aliens into the country".

Moye's period of test flying lasted until 26 February 1942, and were mainly conducted from Mines Field. The longest 'hop' was one hour 30 minutes, many of the later ones 15 minutes only. On the whole, things went uneventfully but accidents could happen of course.

'I was obliged to make one landing in a Vengeance under circumstances which suggested the advisability of cutting both the ignition and electrical system. In view of difficulties with one leg of the landing gear, I elected to land at Mines Field. It was only two miles from the relatively narrow Northrop Field, and its greater area provided more room for whatever antics might ensue. On the final approach, with the landing in the bag, I

cut the combination switch. The landing was uneventful, though the airport's ground maintenance crew was of the opinion the trail of hydraulic fluid might just as well have been deposited on Northrop's runway.

'Under the circumstances, the combination switch was of no particular advantage. There would have been no need for haste in operating independent switches. It seems to me the combination switch would be of value only in the rare instance of a last-second perception of an imminent crash, and its disadvantages in more usual, less critical emergencies would outweigh that value.'

Since the beginning of the year the German General, Irwin Rommel, had defeated a numerically and materially superior British army in a succession of lightning thrusts, and even the proud fortress of Tobruk had fallen. All his sweeping successes had been led by the Stuka dive-bomber, which, despite constant belittling in the British press, continued to act as a totally successful instrument of close support. The fall of Tobruk was the last straw for some people and led to a motion of censure in the House of Commons on the Government's policy. One of the main criticisms was the continuing lack of any British dive-bombers, and the politicians had to pull every trick in the book to prove that it was not their fault there were none. Hasty memos flew to-and-fro up and down Whitehall between the various Ministries concerned.

In the debate itself, on 1 July 1942, Mr. Lyttelton, Minister of Production, was closely cross-examined on this question. His reply was to attack: 'Before leaving the subject of equipment, I think I must say something about the air situation. It has not been suggested that any justified criticism has been directed at our machines and the efficiency of our aircraft, except in one respect, and that is the lack of dive-bombers. The present Government have always attached importance to this weapon, and, in fact, a few weeks after the Government was formed orders were placed for dive-bombers in the United States.' He was interrupted by angry MPs crying 'How many?'. 'A large number.

My right Hon. Friend the Secretary of State for Air said in his speech on the Air Estimates on 4th March, that it was completely mistaken to suppose that the Air Staff have discarded dive-bombers.'

He went on to add to this remarkable statement the fact that 'we have gained the air superiority in more than one theatre of war, and this ascendancy, which is a prerequisite of the use of dive-bombers, means that we can now turn dive-bombers to good account. . .'. He added also that 'The House will know how

long it takes for a new type of aircraft to get into production, and, although there have been delays in production and modifications in design, we are today receiving deliveries under the contract which was then placed. Some dive-bombers are already delivered to one theatre of war, and others are on their way.'

As for deliveries, a memorandum issued in May 1942 gave the following position on the Vengeance: Number expected to be delivered from production and allocated to British

Patriotic slogans urge greater efforts to production-line workers at Hawthorne as A-31s share space with the P-61 'Black Widow' night fighter (foreground). The reference to Boeing was because Northrop was also subcontracting B-17E engine nacelles and cowlings. *(Northrop)*

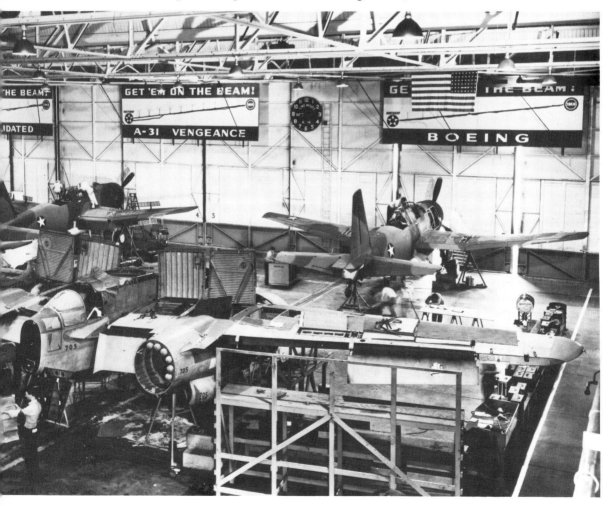

Group after the Arnold/Portal Agreement was supposed to be: March, 15; April, 33; May, 66; June, 91; July, 121; August, 148. Numbers actually delivered were one in March and 23 in April. It added: 'The last weekly statement of shipments issued by the Director of Movements, based on information received up to 21st May, shows that no Vengeance has yet been shipped to India but that five are *en route* to Australia.'

With this in mind, the statement later made by Major-General O.P. Echols, Assistant Chief of Air Staff, Materiel, Maintenance and Distribution, on 12 February 1943, can be perhaps better understood. He stated, looking back to this period, 'We tried to stop the A-31 and the British would not let us!'

Certainly the whole issue was a delicate one in terms of the new Anglo-American alliance. On learning of such talk by senior American officers being reported in the press, Air Marshal R. M. Hill of the RAF Delegation in Washington D.C. called an urgent informal meeting at the BAC on 19 May 1942. Also in attendance were Air Commodore A. C. Betts and Wing Commander R. C. Storrar, with Mr. A. C. Boddie of the BAC.

They quickly agreed that, 'In the original agreement there was no differentiation between the two production lines of Nashville and Hawthorne and, in fact, the allocations could only have been met by the Americans taking part of their allocation from Vultee and part from Northrop. It has, however, been subsequently agreed that the whole of the Northrop output, except for one aircraft retained for experimental work at Wright Field, shall be allocated to the British and the Americans shall take their balance of 299 from the Vultee line.

'Admittedly the production is lagging badly behind the initial contract schedules, but this is no uncommon experience with a new type of aircraft. So far as the Vultee factory is concerned it has been frankly admitted by the firm that this was fundamentally due to weak management, a defect which has since been remedied, largely at British insistence.'

Revised schedules of deliveries were given as:-

| | Cumulative deliveries | | Accepted to May 12 |
|---|---|---|---|
| | April 30 | May 31 | |
| Vultee | 15 | 48 | 19 |
| Northrop | 40 | 72 | 51 |

Thus, when the planes implacable opponent, Mr Patterson, decided, due to the unsatisfactory performance of the A-31, that production at Nashville should be held down to 40 per month (instead of rising to 105 per month by July, 1942,) and General Meyers informed Wright Field accordingly on 27 May, the fur flew. Air Marshal Roderic Hill, RAF, registered a strong objection to this decision. He wrote to Major General Echols that: 'I can only say that a heavy reduction in output of the A-31 (Vengeance) at this juncture, now that the development troubles have been substantially overcome, would be little short of disastrous to the arrangements in hand for reinforcing India, Australia, South Africa and Canada.'

This strong stand — and the recommendations of Vultee — Mr. Lovett reported to a meeting on 4 June 1942, at which Patterson reluctantly restored the A-31 schedule. But producing again at this rate led to another snag, for it meant that Vultee's contracts would run out early in 1943. The need to hold the workforce together as a viable entity, ready for production of the A-35 and other aircraft types the next year, meant that they had to be kept working. This in turn meant that a contract contemplated by the Letter of Intent of 16 January 1942 (for 400 airplanes at a unit price of $60,599) had to be approved, and this was done on 10 October 1942. Moreover, for mainly the same reasons, a supplement of this contract providing for 2330 airplanes, at a unit price of approximately $54,000, was also approved on 17 December 1942.

Further inter-Allied media difficulties continued to arise in the interim. For example, on 6 June 1942, a Personal Secret Telegram (No. 211) was sent from the British Air Attaché in Washington, Thornton, to Air

Marshal R. H. Peck, Assistant Chief of the Air Staff at the Air Ministry. It read: *'New York Times* of June 3rd carried quotation from speech by the Director of British Air Training Corps, at Erith, Kent, to the effect that we regard dive-bombers as obsolete. Such a statement incorrectly reported might prove embarrasing, especially if re-published in local press at Nashville, where Vultee is being produced.'

This led to a telegram reply from Peck on the 9th, which concluded: 'We want Vengeances and Bermudas in quantity and as quickly as possible.'

The deliveries were now set in hand from Northrop in good numbers. On 21 April 1942, Wing Commander McKenna, RAF, had conducted a simulated 'Blitz' of Northrop Field for publicity purposes and John Northrop had written in his column 'the V-72 is as fast or faster than any other American dive-bomber now in production and carries a much greater bomb load. The V-72 is fitted with many improved devices which enable it to perform its function more efficiently than ships of a similar type now in use.

'British pilots who have flown the Vengeance are well pleased with its flying qualities and feel that it will be exceedingly useful to them in their various campaigns, as the airplane is readily adaptable to service conditions in the tropics, in the desert, or anywhere in Continental Europe.'

But however much RAF pilots might, or might not, have expressed happiness with the A-31, no such sentiments were found in their USAAF equivalents. If they had to have the Vengeance then they wanted the A-35. General Myers issued a CTI on 4 May 1942, requesting that action be taken to modify A–31s to be allocated to the Army Air Forces so that they would be suitable for operational training. Lieutenant-Colonel L. G. Harman, Chief, Bombardment Branch, Wright Field, expressed concern lest the standardisation of the A-31s would divert engineering manhours from the projected A-35. Colonel T. A. Sims made the same point in a letter dated 11 May 1942 to the Joint Aircraft Committee, and he recommended that 'No further attempt be made to standardise the A-31 beyond the few simple changes now being directed on Army Air Force airplanes.'

And so, finally, the two lines were allowed to go their own way, while yet a third, the A–35, was got ready.

# Chapter 4
# Deliberation

No A-31 (for the original design 'A-31' was now the officially adopted USAAF designation, standing for Attack Aircraft, Type 31, and was being utilised generally in the States instead of the company designation V-72. However, both the British and Australians used their own designations of Vengeance I, Vengeance II etc, as we have seen, but far from uniformly) had joined any Allied fighting unit, nor was one destined to for some considerable time. The first Northrop-produced airplanes were beginning to be shipped out from both Atlantic and Pacific ports to England, India and Australia but their arrival by no means heralded their early usage on any front.

When the first Vengeance Is reached Britain and were given stringent tests at the RAE, the comments made were very mixed indeed. Serviceability was considered appalling and early aircraft totally unreliable. Fuel and oil consumption was reported as extremely heavy, economy low. Serviceability at the test units was one of the poorest recorded.

Once these many difficulties had been overcome trials were begun and some true facts and figures began to be assembled. The first trial showed up the unpalatable fact that, should the dive brakes jam out, it would be virtually impossible to land the aircraft. With dive brakes and flaps a 300 ft per minute descent could be obtained, but if the hydraulics were damaged through enemy action during a dive a pilot would not be able to lower the flaps.

The second trial was conducted to test the sensitivity of the controls in various positions and at various speeds. It revealed that at speeds between 50 and 60 mph elevator and rudder control became effective and that, without bombload, the Vengeance I was airborne at between 90-95 mph. The normal climbing speed was 135 mph; rate of climb at 2100 rpm, 700-800 ft per minute. The controls were effective down to 105 mph, which at full throttle and rpm was considered the lowest possible climbing speed for an emergency. The rate of climb was then 1000 to 1100 ft per minute, although the aircraft would still climb at 95 mph. Over a five-minute period the highest rate of climb was 1400 ft per minute with full rpm and boost. It was impossible to maintain formation in that instance as right rudder, as well as full right rudder bias, was needed to maintain a straight climb.

In level flight the elevator and rudder controls were heavy and the aileron control light. The aircraft was favourably reported as being very stable and would fly 'hands off' for periods. Stalling in clean condition with closed throttle was at 90 mph and the loss of height before recovery at 110 mph was 300 ft. In a climbing turn with 2100 revs stalling occurred at 95 mph, with recovery at 115 mph and height loss of 150 ft. With the undercarriage and flaps down, stall was at 80 mph, recovery 90 mph, height loss 200 ft. In a gliding turn, with undercarriage and flaps down, stall was at the same speed, but with recovery at 100 mph and height loss of 300 ft. With the dive brakes and bomb doors open, undercarriage and flaps up, the stall was at 85 mph. High-speed stall in turns started at 200 mph and occurred up to 170 mph, depending on the G exerted, while stalls in turns at cruising speed occurred between 90 and 125 mph.

The third trial concentrated on the aircraft's diving performance, the crucial point. Here the Vengeance I came out well and was reported as being 'very stable in a dive. Aileron control remains very light and all corrections must be made by aileron. Considerable pressure on the stick is necessary to pull out and at high speeds trim is helpful.'

It was found that, on entering the dive, the rudder bias had to be moved from the level flight position, which had considerable right bias, to almost neutral. It was considered by the RAE pilot concerned that 70 degrees was the best angle of dive, as once in a 90 degree dive the aircraft was hard to aim and correct.

Terminal velocity with the brakes out was 320 mph. During dives at 70 degrees from 10,000 down to 4000 ft at approximately one-third throttle, the speed reached between 270 and 300 mph and required between 1500 to 2500 ft for recovery and pressure exerted was 4 G. Following these trials in England the recommended diving procedure was given as follows:-

'On run up to diving position, increase revs from cruising to 2,300; engage low blower; rich mixture; and open bomb doors. At diving position, extend diving brakes and pull back throttle to approximately one-third open. Maintain throughout dive. At pull-out, if dive brakes are retracted at the start, more height is necessary for recovery but elevator control is lighter than if the dive brakes remain extended throughout the recovery. The extra speed gained by early retraction would be an additional asset in getting away quickly. Bomb doors are closed when level flight is regained and rpm should be reduced as soon as full throttle is no longer necessary.'

Other snags kept cropping up. Thus, on 12 June 1942, General Vanaman of the Materiel Centre, Wright Field, gave the Vultee representative information received from Eglin Field concerning deterioration of the fuel cells and defects on the leading and

Two A-31s built by Northrop. Note the single intake above the engine cowling on these units. *(Northrop)*

Vengeance airborne over UK and fitted with the standard RAF underwing bomb carriers for light (250 lb) bombs in addition to internal bomb load of two 500 lb weapons. *(National Archives, Washington)*

trailing edges on A-31 airplanes. A request was made that the contractor take immediate action to remedy these faults.

On 22 July 1942, Colonel D. C. Lingle, Recorder of the Working Sub-Committee on Standardisation in Washington, informed his opposite number at the JAC that a request from Britain that barrage-cutters be incorporated in A-31s on the Northrop contract was disapproved, due to the short time remaining before completion of contract and 'indeterminate status of continued production of this type of aircraft'.

Colonel Orval Cook was writing to Vultee again, on 21 September 1942. The 77 V-72 airplanes diverted to Australia from the 241 allocated to AAF on British contract A-557 were to be sent to Louisville for certain listed modifications. These airplanes were to be sent to Vultee in California where they would be crated for export.

While test flying was being conducted, other aircraft were on their way to the combat zones of India and Australia.

The process of dismantling the aircraft and preparing them for shipment in crates was later to be standard and was to demand a line of its own highly specialised experts. Vultee had pioneered a special form of crating in the late 1930s, when it had sold aircraft to Turkey, and this method was utilised. However, for the early shipments of the Vengeance, ordinary deck stowage on freighters with a tightly lashed tarpaulin to protect them on the long haul across the oceans to the other continents in slow convoys, meant that the weather often got in, with ghastly results for some of the more vulnerable parts of the engine.

On 28 January 1944, for example, M. M. Mason, Contracts Co-ordinator at Vultee Nashville, was informed that the AAFRR Contractors' Field Reps in Australia had reported that airplanes shipped as deck cargo were arriving with canopies in a badly corroded condition. In a response, dated 16 February 1944, Colonel F. R. Cook told Chief, Container and Packaging Control, Wright Field, that the poor condition of airplanes mentioned in contractors' letters should be called to the attention of the companies responsible for the packaging and crating of these planes.

Nor did all the aircraft despatched reach their destinations at all. Three (AN 869, 870 and 871) were lost *en route* to India on one early shipment when their vessel was sunk by a marauding U-boat. Another four (AN 873, 879, 971 and 973) were later to be lost at sea in the same manner.

The Australian Government had shown interest in dive-bombing and in July 1940 had sought to obtain 243 Brewster 340s (the Buccaneer, or in RAF parlance the Bermuda, as they were to become known) but the endless delays due to production problems prompted the British, in a telegram dated 28 September 1941, to offer to allocate the Vultee Vengeance in its place, provided the RAAF thought its specification suitable. At this time the two Downey prototypes had 90 hours' flying time behind them, their aerial performance was considered good and most of the faults seemed to have been ironed out. As no allocations had actually been made by 28 October strong representations were made for this to be done. The cost to the Australian Government, of outright purchase rather than Lend-Lease, was quoted as £90,000 (Australian), inclusive of the Bendix radio. Due to the changes incorporated after production model 255 it was made clear that, unless Australia would accept a mixture of models, she would have to wait until April 1942 for deliveries. By 8 May 1942 a total of 367 Vengeances had been ordered from the Northrop line for the RAAF.

The first Vengeances to reach Australia were serial numbers AN 853, 854, 855, 856 and 857, which arrived on 30 May 1942. These, and all subsequent Vengeances, were assigned the RAAF designation A27 and the first five planes therefore became A27-1, -2, –3, -4, and -5 respectively and were allocated to No. 12 Squadron, RAAF.

Before the arrival of the Vultees the RAAF had conducted makeshift dive-bomber missions using the Commonwealth Wirraway aircraft.

One of the first Australians to get his hands on the Vengeance was Flight Lieutenant Douglas Johnstone, one of three RAAF pilots acknowledged as the experts on this machine. Before the war he had taught himself to fly a little Moth biplane to patrol his sheep station in western New South Wales and he had joined the RAAF on day one of World War II. He was a senior flying instructor by 1942. He gave me this description of the work carried out on the first

arrivals when they finally reached Australian shores: 'They were assembled at Bankstown RAAF station on the outskirts of Sydney, NSW. American experts arrived with the aircraft and supervised the operations and were responsible for training the pilots that were selected to instruct on them. We remained at Bankstown for one month, getting to know the aircraft under the supervision of the Americans from the Vultee Corporation. They were obviously not Air Force personnel and each was an expert on the Vengeance in their own special fields, test pilot, hydraulic system engineer, electrical system engineer, and so on, and they remained with the aircraft for approximately six months.

'When sufficient aircraft finally arrived and were assembled, No. 4 Operational Training Unit (OTU) was formed. From Bankstown we were transferred on a temporary posting to Mildura RAAF fighter OTU, where we remained for approximately two months waiting for our permanent base to become vacant. We found the time spent at Mildura invaluable as it gave us time to become proficient on the aircraft and to work on a syllabus of training. As we had received *no* previous experience or advice from *any* source, this breathing space was welcome.

'The first course of trainees started their training on 5 January 1943. The original staff consisted of the CO, Wing Commander Fyfe, and six instructors, all familiar with Wirraway operations. We found the Vultee a very efficient dive-bomber and our instructors enjoyed training crews on them. They were very heavy on the controls for a single-engined aircraft and much use had to be made with the trim, particularly the elevator. The aircraft was remarkably stable in all phases of operations, even in the vertical dive. With dive brakes extended the maximum speed was 319 mph, but it was quite smooth and stable resulting in a very high degree of accuracy on the target.'

Air Commodore E. G. Fyfe, CBE, DSO, was Australia's first dive-bomber pilot and had commanded an RAAF squadron in Malaya. He confirmed the above and told me his part in the setting up of the unit: 'In September 1942, I was posted to command No. 4 OTU. My brief was to form the unit, to develop bombing techniques and tactics as well as to train a sufficient number of pilots to man three squadrons in order to form No. 77 Wing. The Wing eventually consisted of No. 21 (Squadron Leader B. Todd, DFC), No. 23 (Squadron Leader T. Philp, DFC) and No. 24 (Squadron Leader B. Honey, DFC).

'Late in September 1942, the first of the aircraft had been assembled at Bankstown, NSW, and test flown by Jack J. Kelley, a Vultee test pilot, before being handed over to my unit. The remainder were handed over later in the month and early in October. Subsequently the nucleus of the unit proceeded to Midura on the NSW/Victoria border, to develop tactics in conjunction with the fighter OTU based there.

'In November 1942 the unit moved to Williamstown, NSW, which was to be its home for the rest of its life. During this time aircraft strength was increased to meet the training needs and generally the aircraft performed well although casualties *were* suffered, which was to be expected considering the nature of the training and the inexperience of the trainees. In the main, casualties were caused by failure to recover from a dive, either because of poor technique or elevator failure during, or before, pull-out.'

Doug Johnstone explained how the training programme was run: 'As far as pilot conversion was concerned, this was very brief; as there was no dual control in the Vultee it consisted of a cockpit check and once thoroughly conversant with the layout of the cockpit you were on your own! The trainees were drawn from the service *Wirraway* training schools at Wagga and Dembirguin. On arrival at the OTU there were an equal number of pilots and wireless operator/air gunners, and they were given time to get to know each other and decide how they wished to crew up as it was important that they be compatible and got on well together. Once that was sorted out they then trained as a crew and were posted together to a squadron on completion of their training.

'The aircraft, after take-off, formed up in the standard "V" formation and climbed to the height of attack, usually between 7000 and 11,000 ft. They approached the target area and formed up in line astern position and followed the leader down. The leader positioned himself over the top of the target and eventually did a half-roll so that a very steep dive was needed; the steeper the dive, the less was the margin of error. In the case of the Vultee this technique was always used, the only difference being that when positioned over the target the dive brakes were extended and, with the bomb doors opened, the target could be seen through an aperture in the cockpit floor. The aircraft was then put into a half-roll on to its back and was then pulled down into a near-vertical dive, the angle depending on the position of the target. When it was in a stable position and lined up on the target, the bombs were then released, they being attached to a long arm arrangement in the bomb bay so that in the vertical position the bombs were swung clear of the propeller arc. Once the bomb was released the aircraft was eased out of the dive, the dive brakes retracted and the air speed was allowed to build up for the remainder of the descent for a quick get-away at low level. Practice bombs were of course used in most of the training until the pupils' final check-out, when 250 lb live bombs were used over the target area, which, at Williamstown, was in the middle of a big swamp area, well away from habitation. The course also included air-to-ground gunnery for the rear-gunner and low-level close formation flying.'

A similar story was unfolding at the same time in India. Here 168 Wing was to be set up with three dive-bomber squadrons and was to be followed in due course by a second. Ultimately both were to be joined by an Indian Air Force Wing. Wing Commander John M. McMichael of No. 82 Squadron, RAF, recalled that 'I was involved in the initial training of pilots in 82 Squadron at Karachi . . .' On 1 July 1942, he was issued with a hastily prepared but detailed memorandum to help initiate this, written by the Commanding Officer of 168 Wing, Group Captain Hunt. It was entitled *Rough Notes on Dive-Bombing Tactics* and contained extracts from the *Manual of Air Tactics.*

The Japanese carrier raids against the vital Ceylon (now Sri Lanka) ports of Colombo and Trincomalee were still fresh in everyone's memory at this time. Attacks by the Vengeance against a Japanese task force was therefore considered its prime possible, and imminent, role in this theatre initially, and much emphasis was at first placed on how to conduct such an operation in the face of the deadly *Zero* fighter and masses of anti-aircraft guns on the Japanese warships.

It was stated that any such fleet would have a limited number of fighters and that the ships would rely mainly upon their long-range and close-range guns for defence against all forms of air attack. This was based on faulty and obsolete reasoning, probably from Royal Navy experience. Certainly a British fleet would only have limited fighter defences, but not a Japanese one. The Nagumo Task Force that had attacked a few months earlier had six big carriers with a total of more than one hundred Mitsubishi *Zero* fighters embarked, each one of which was far superior to any Allied fighter aircraft operating in South-East Asia.

Long-range AA fire was not considered a suitable defence against dive-bombing because, in the words of the memo, 'Before the aircraft are committed to the attack they are free to manoeuvre, and are therefore unsuitable targets. After they are committed to the attack the speed of approach is so great that the fuze-prediction gear cannot function.' The main target to be studied by the Vengeance crews was either the capital ship or the aircraft carrier, and these would almost certainly be protected by a ring of lesser ships to form a screen of anti-aircraft fire.

As for the dive-bombing attack itself, it was estimated that a bomber attacking at a diving angle of 45 degrees and with a speed of 250 knots would be within effective range of automatic weapons for about 12 seconds before dropping its bombs. It was recommended that the approach to the diving position be made at as great a height as possible; that all aircraft should attack the

Experimental types. The Vultee V-85 was merely a modified V-72 which the Army used as a test-bed under the designation XA-31A, to try out in flight the new 3000 hp 28-cylinder Pratt & Whitney R-4360 engine. *(USAAF Official)*

ship from the same direction, the stern approach masking the majority of guns; that the initial part of the dive could be made from the *opposite* side of the ship to that which it is intended to attack and the crossing to the attacking position delayed as late as possible, thus restricting still further the time the guns that would fire at them would have sight of the aircraft; that individual aircraft should follow one another down in the quickest possible succession, making concentration of fire impossible; that in the final attack dive each aircraft should avoid attacking in exactly the same line as the one ahead, a five-degree variation was thought sufficient to stop more than one aircraft being brought into the same zone of fire; and, finally, that flexibility was essential.

Although it was stated (in marked contrast to earlier claims it will be noted) that 'it is a more accurate method of bombing than level bombing from 10,000 ft . . . ', it was also pointed out that although the time of flight of the bomb was considerably shorter in dive-bombing, avoiding action by the ship target remained a factor to be reckoned with, 'because of the difficulty in changing direction of a dive once started'. Here again the special qualities of the tab fitted to the Vengeance had obviously not been fully realised. Height of bomb release depended on penetration required; obviously, a heavily armoured battleship would be relatively immune, whereas the Japanese carriers (which like the American carriers of this period had wooden decks, not armoured like the British ones) would be highly vulnerable to even small bombs. Against small, narrow targets, such as bridges or destroyers, it was recommended that 'stick' bombing be used.

However, with no aircraft yet even assembled it was perhaps just as well that the Nagumo Task Force had been engaged by the American Fleet by this time, far away in the Pacific off Midway Island. Here the US Navy's SBDs had indeed caused the maximum damage with their dive-bombing attacks that had been hoped for from the Vengeance squadrons, sinking four of the big carriers and one of the large cruisers and

winning the battle almost on their own. There always remained the chance that further Japanese Naval task forces would return to the Indian Ocean however, seeking softer opposition, for the Royal Navy had been practically withdrawn from the area and was to remain but a token force throughout 1943 also. So initially, the watch on Ceylon was to remain one of the main functions of the Vengeance units.

The first nine aircraft for the RAF in India had arrived in Karachi on 4 August 1942, and six more had followed on 6 September. Three hundred were expected by the end of the year. They were collected from the docks by 301 MU, with the assistance and advice of two teams of experts from the Vultee factory. Between 16 August and 8 September 1942, Group Captain Hunt visited 226 Group at Karachi and spent considerable time with No. 301 Maintenance Unit (MU) at Drigh Road, where the off-loaded Vengeances were being assembled and flight tested. His object was to obtain as much information as possible about the Vengeance I, its probable rate of flow into India and of the supply of its maintenance equipment and spares. He subsequently submitted a detailed report on what he found there.

The first aircraft had been assembled by 17 August 1942, and the second followed about one week later. Unfortunately, the remaining seven from the first consignment were still being readied. Group Captain Hunt explained the reason for the delay in assembly. 'These aircraft have been built by Northrop under subcontract to Vultee, and are packed for shipment without first being assembled at the factory. Consequently, a number of small adjustments have been found necessary on assembly in this country. Two defects have been causing a good deal of trouble:

'(i) The neoprene gland washers in the electrical petrol pumps have been found to be distorted on arrival, probably due to heat during the journey. The result is that petrol gets into the electric motors. New washers have been ordered from CRO, Calcutta, and

Vultee's in America informed of the trouble.

'(ii) Some of the flexible pipes in the hydraulic system are designed for 850 lbs pressure only, whereas the system uses 1250 lbs. A number, usually those leading up to the undercarriage, have already started to leak. There is difficulty in telling which pipes are low pressure and which are high. *This defect is likely to lead to serious delay in the delivery of aircraft.* Latest type pipes have been despatched by air from America.'

There were a few spares with the first batch of aircraft but a number of cases arrived with the second batch and these were being sorted out at 301 MU. Two of Vultee's pilots were conducting flight tests before handing them over to Wing Commander McMichael, and Group Captain Hunt also flew the first assembled plane while he was there. He could therefore state from his own experience that the Vengeance I's flying characteristics were: 'Very stable. Light on ailerons, heavy on rudder and elevators. Gentle stall, with no tendency to spin. Fairly long take-off, and comparatively high landing approach speed (110-115 mph). No incidence on mainplanes and therefore flies with nose in the air. Very easy to make tail down landing. *In general the aircraft is easy to fly.*'

He found the cockpit layout 'Excellent. Flying position comfortable, with plenty of room for pilot and observer air gunner.' No exhaustive flying tests had yet been possible to evaluate performance.

'First impressions are that normal cruising speed will be about 200 mph Indicated Air Speed (IAS) although the most economical speed is considerably less. One full-speed test at ground level, without load, gave an IAS of 250 mph. The final figures will probably be slightly, but not very much, less than those given by the makers. No fuel consumption tests have been carried out, so it is not yet possible to say whether the maker's estimates of ranges are correct.'

Other features he commented on were that the general airframe and engine fittings were easily accessible, and inspection and maintenance would not be difficult. Air cleaners had not been fitted but 301 MU had designed one for the aircraft. The aircraft were fitted with American .300 guns but 301 MU had omitted these and had instead installed .303 English Brownings. 'Air Headquarters (AHQ) has now given instructions for all aircraft to be fitted with the latter. The necessary modifications are not very complicated or extensive.'

The Bendix general-purpose radio set was commented on most favourably: 'clear and strong and promises well'. No oxygen had been fitted to these aircraft and the Medical Officer (MO) of No. 220 Squadron, who had been engaged in Britain in high-flying experiments, pointed out in a report to Wing Commander McMichael the benefits of this in clearing the ears during high-speed diving. McMichael therefore had oxygen bottles fitted to the first of No. 82 Squadron's aircraft and asked AHQ to standardise this.

Group Captain Hunt reported that *full* night flying equipment was fitted, 'but the exhaust stubbs project from the sides of the nose, and no flame dampers or screens are fitted. Trials will have to be carried out to see whether night flying operations are possible with the existing arrangements, which I doubt.'

The ultimate fate of the XA-31A was a humiliating upside-down crash-landing in a tobacco field in Connecticut when the experimental engine failed completely during a test flight! Note modified National insignia on the wreck. *(USAAF Official)*

Back in the States, the earlier US Navy interest in a folding-wing Vengeance for use as a torpedo-bomber had now been terminated. This concept, the TBV-1, which was named the *Georgia*, envisaged the carrying of a 22-inch naval torpedo into action slung underneath the fuselage on special crutches. The studies and tests on torpedo conversion that had been held in the spring of 1942, during which Vultee had hoped to install necessary provisions for the carrying of a 2000 lb torpedo, continued. However, it was the rival Consolidated TBU-2 which was finally ordered, but only 180 were eventually built and the Navy concentrated their production on the well-tried Grumman TBF-1 (General Motors TBM) *Avenger.*

Despite this, further development took place which resulted in the Vultee XA-41-VU of 1943-44. One of these prototypes was built and flew successfully. It was a single-seater giant, with a weight of 23,359 lb, a wingspan of 54 ft and length of 48 ft 8 ins. To get this monster off carrier decks required a Pratt and Whitney XR-4360-9, 3000 hp engine, which gave it a speed of 353 mph. As a combined dive-and torpedo-bomber the Vultee 90 was a potent weapon. A glance at its picture and it betrays its origins in every line. But it was too big and it was too late! The plane was cancelled.

Other variants of the Vengeance appeared however. A solitary airframe was built by Vultee at Downey and was designated the V–85 and given the serial number 42-35824. It had no military equipment, nor engine, when delivered, for the Air Corps wanted it solely as a flying test-bed for the new type of Wright R–2600 engine. This was listed as the XA-1A–VU.

In fact it was not used for its original purpose but was instead equipped with the X–Wasp X(Major)-108 radial engine. But this was merely a cover name for the Pratt and Whitney XR-4360-1, which was a four-row, 28-cylinder engine, rated at 3000 hp (2237 kW). The aircraft was then re-designed as the XA-31B-VU. It was never intended to fit these to the A-31s or A-35s but it needed a large

single-engine mount for trials and the Vengeance fitted the bill. Obvious features were the forward-projecting air intake atop the nose just behind the engine cowling and the two large, rectangular-shaped scoops set in the underside of the inner wing section, above the undercarriage. Length was increased from the normal 39 ft 9 ins to 42 ft 3 ins, while weight went up from 13,650 lb to 15,000 lb with this power-plant installed.

Test flights were conducted from Wright Field during 1942 but the experimental aircraft had only a short lifespan, for, following engine failure on a flight on 15 September 1942, it crashed in a tobacco field in Connecticut and ended up on its back, a broken wreck. The R-4360 was tested further in other experimental models, not Vengeances, and was finally utilised on the Boeing B-50 in 1946.

In a similar manner was born the XZ–31C–VN. A normal RAF production V-72 was taken from the Hawthorne plant (AF 759) and was used by the USAAF as a flying test-bed aircraft for the Wright R-3350-13 'Double-Cyclone', a 2200 hp (1640 kW) engine, as had originally been intended for the XA-31A. This had been destined as the power-plant for the Boeing XB-29, prototype of the *Superfortress,* but it was causing problems and again the Vengeance was the biggest single-seater around to carry this power-plant, which weighed 2625 lb. Overall length came out at 40 ft 8 ins, weight was 14,270 lb. With it installed, tests were conducted to try to trace some of the faults more economically than by using the big bomber.

As a later continuation of the testing of the R-3350-17 and R-3350-37 engines the USAAF took out a further five Vengeance IIs from the Northrop line at Hawthorne and designated them as YA-31C-VNs. The aircraft selected were AF 756, 782, 845, 887 and 904 and they kept their RAF serials during USAAF use.

The give-away in appearance was the four-bladed Hamilton-Standard 16 ft 7 ins diameter, constant-speed, fully feathering propeller and a redesigned engine cowling.

The first Vengeances arrive and take over from the Wirraways in the first dive-bomber training units in the RAAF. This is No. 4 OTU, a newly completed Vengeance unit paraded with its crew and staff.
*(Doug Johnstone)*

With these five workhorses extensive tests were conducted at Wright Field and at Paterson, New Jersey, through the autumn of 1943.

The standard RAF A-31s plucked from Vultee's production line by the USAAF also failed to meet that service's basic design datum, as spelt out in great detail in the *Handbook of Instruction for Airplane Designers*. Vultee's had gone their own way with only the RAF's requirements to hinder them, and the result had been what today we would call 'user-friendly' layout which suited pilots who used it perfectly and was much praised. Initially the USAAF turned a blind eye, and, although this technically barred them from using the planes as 'standard

issue', carried on. The original designation of V-72 was retained, as were the original RAF serials and indeed the camouflage patterns. The RAF roundels were initially merely painted over with variations of the US white star with red centre, in a circle. On 15 May, 1942, the red centre was deleted as it was being confused with the Japanese red 'meatball' in the Pacific, and later still the white bars appeared either side the circle. At Wright Field large, white, blocked twin indicator letters appeared on the forward fuselage and also, slightly smaller, on the top of the tail fin. These were merely the last two digits of the original RAF serial. Individual squadrons, as usual, also adopted their own particular markings. Let us now examine these units.

Most historians have only credited one or two USAAF squadrons as being equipped with the Vengeance, but in fact it was supplied to at least a dozen, if only for very brief periods. It will be recalled that General Arnold had insisted that dive-bomber units be set up, and that the A-31 be sent to them, pending arrival of the A-35, to supplement the A-24s on hand. Added emphasis was given to his decision by the shortage of Navy SBDs in the combat zone at a time when their Army equivalents were to be turned out but not used!

Some of Arnold's new dive-bomber squadrons, officially termed Bombardment Squadron (Dive), had started life as Bombardment Squadron (Light) units, activated early in 1942 as the war expansion programme was initiated. The last five were formed as Bombardment Squadron (Dive) right from scratch. The first was of more mature origin. Typical of the units was the 57th, under Captain Ward P. Robinson, which had been designated a dive-bomber unit by US War Department letter AG 320.2, dated 2 September 1942. It had originally been constituted as the 57th Bombardment Squadron (Light) formed on 20 November 1940, becoming effective at Savannah, Georgia, on 15 January 1941 and equipped with the A-20. Later, on 10 August 1943, it was again re-designated as the 494th Fighter-Bomber Squadron and equipped with P-39s.

The complete list is given in Appendix One. There may have been others, for instance the 86th Bombardment Squadron (Dive) has been mentioned, but the USAAF could not produce documentation to confirm this fact. All these units were set up at the designated dive-bomber training school at Key Field, near Meridian City, Mississippi. A-31s equipped the 309th, 311th and 312th, A-35s the others. The 57th, the Replacement Training Unit and Operational Training Unit, used both before it moved out from William Northern Field, Tennessee, in August 1943.

Typical of these was the 311th, redesignated, as per General Order No.1, as a Bombardment Group (Dive) effective from 1 July 1942. The headquarters of the Group was no longer a separate squadron but was superimposed on one of the squadrons. Base was Will Rogers Field, Oklahoma, and the Group consisted of the 382nd, 383rd, 384th and 385th Bombardment Squadrons (Dive). The Group took departure from Oklahoma City on 2 July 1942, and arrived at Hunter Field, near Savannah, Georgia, on 4 July, before shifting base to Waycross in the same State. First Lieutenant R. B. James was acting as CO of the unit until 10 August, when Lieutenant-Colonel John R. Kelly was assigned to the Group as its first permanent commanding officer. Under Colonel Kelly the Group took shape, the majority of the personnel were assigned and began to function as a unit. After completing the first phase of OTU training the Group left Hunter Field to re-establish itself at Army Airport, Waycross, Georgia, on 22 October where it commenced the second stage of training.

Two complete units of combat crew pilots were trained by the Group. The initial unit was assigned to the North African theatre of war and the second went to the Indo-Sino-Burmese border territory. The first group cut its dive-bombing teeth on the V-72 and training continued with the Vengeance until December 1942 when it was discontinued. Thereafter it continued training and equipping with the P-51A and A-36 types, and it was these it used in actual combat. What the 311th thought of their V-72s is wryly summed up in the Group Official History: 'In December, 1942, much to the pleasure and satisfaction of both pilots and ground personnel, the V-72 planes were all transferred to Service Unit. (The gunners were the only individuals who regretted this change, since they were transferred out of the Group).'

Continued problems were found by the USAAF in setting up engineering production in readiness for the A-35 line. A CTI had been issued by General Meyers on 4 May 1942, requesting that action be taken to modify A-31s already allocated to the USAAF so that they would then be suitable for operational training. But the Chief of the Bombardment Branch at Wright Field, Dayton, Ohio, Lieutenant-Colonel L. F.

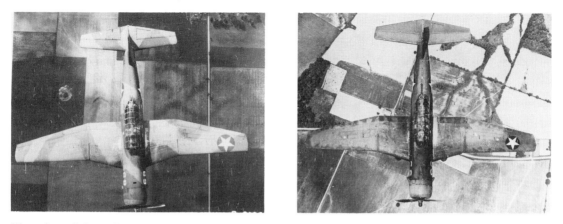

Plan view of the A-31 and A-35 respectively showing the small differences. These views were taken at different times near Patterson Field, the Proving Ground near to Wright Field, Dayton, Ohio, the main testing centre of the US Air Corps. *(Smithsonian)*

Harman, feared that such a standardisation programme, if thus introduced and implemented, would divert vital engineering manhours away from the A–35, and be self-defeating in the long-run. On 11 May 1942, Lieutenant-Colonel T. A Sims, Assistant Technical Executive at Wright Field, expressed the same sentiments to the Joint Aircraft Committee and recommended that — 'No further attempt be made to standardize the A-31 beyond the few simple changes now being directed on Army Air Force airplanes.'

When the prototype A-35B was ordered to Eglin Field, Florida, on 12 September 1942, for intensive testing, it was already two months behind schedule. Major-General M. S. Fairchild, Director of Military Requirements, pointed out that tests of this prototype would not be *conclusive* as to the first production A-35. One is left with the feeling that the Army top brass was doing everything it could to avoid getting dive-bombers. If this was the case they were initially disappointed, because the prototype came through its tests well and a favourable report was given on it on 26 October 1942. The Army, however, dug its heels in and insisted that one of the first production models be sent to Eglin for the completion of the test before making any decisions.

Although the engineering troubles which had delayed the A-35 in the summer and autumn had been successfully overcome, they were immediately replaced by production difficulties with the self-same effect. Adel valves and Weatherhead cylinders were in huge demand and the A-35 project (only rated Group 6) took a back seat to other types in provision of supply of these essential items. Without them the production line became virtually static for long periods. General Wolfe tried very hard to have the allocations changed for a short period to get the A-35 line moving again, to little avail.

Direct intervention by the military led to a heated argument. Major Williams, from General Meyers' office, visited the Nashville plant in November 1942 to examine the production difficulties at first hand. He and Robert McCulloch did *not* hit it off and the Vultee manager was so incensed by the visit that he stormed into General Wolfe's office to deliver his complaint in person, adding that he was ready to quit!

What followed was duly recorded for posterity. On 11 November 1942, Brigadier-General K. B. Wolfe at Wright Field telephoned Colonel J. W. Sessums in Washington to complain about how McCulloch had been treated.

'Have you got a boy by the name of Major

Williams working for you?', he asked and, when assured he had and that he ' . . . had been checking on that A-35 down at Vultee', Wolfe blew his top.

'Well, what for?'

Sessums replied: 'Well, everybody is growling about the airplanes not coming out . . .', but he was not allowed to finish.

'Well, now. Let me tell you what happened, he goes down there on an assignment from you people and goes into this Vultee show having never been there before or co-ordinating with us and he takes these people for a real joy-ride down there and McCulloch is up here now, the General Manager down there, is up here with his crowd just raising the dickens with us. We have been following that job down there, we are thoroughly familiar with it. We have had people down there on an average of once a week. I, myself, am following this thing very closely. We have given these people certain specific things to do, we have checked on them, given them what help we could, and now this chap unbeknownst to anyone comes in there and he really goes over this thing and raises the dickens with everybody.'

A veil is better drawn at this point, the General stating he was telling Williams to report back to Washington, 'because I don't want him down there and I am having a time here this afternoon with this fellow McCulloch. He wanted to throw up the sponge on that job before and Dutch was after him to come back and go back to work for him. I personally talked the fellow into staying on the job. I told Woodhead and I told Girdler that they had a good man there and if they would support him we could get this factory going. He has done an excellent job. Now if you know the backgound on this thing you feel like giving this fellow, McCulloch, a medal. He comes up here now, he says he thought he was doing the job the way we wanted it. But someone comes down from Washington and raises the dickens with them and reports to their Washington representative, and the Washington representative writes a letter out to Girdler and Girdler is just raising the dickens with

them. Now here he is, he wants to quit his job.'

After he had cooled down somewhat, further discussion took place in which Wolfe stated that the upgrading of the A-35 in Group 2 for priority materials would expedite production of the block of the Vultee dive-bombers.

Wolfe then wrote to General Meyers direct on 13 November 1942, suggesting that close co-operation between Nashville and Wright Field should be continued and that investigations, such as that which had been conducted recently, should be avoided in future by co-ordination of all visits to Vultee with 'particular Project Officers concerned in the Production Division'.

On 9 January 1943 Wolfe told Colonel J. S. Sessums in Washington that discussions had revealed that production of A-35s was suffering from serious shortages of materials. He listed Weatherhead actuating cylinders, Stewart-Warner heaters, Chromoly tubing, cable terminals, elastic stop nuts, Bendix valves, Parker fittings, ball and roller bearings and oxygen manifolds. But especially damaging was the shortage of hydraulic cylinders. He made graphic references to how at Vultee they 'had only one set of hydraulics. He puts it in an airplane, it is pushed out the door, flies it, gets it accepted and then he take the hydraulics off and goes back and puts them on the next shift!' The General also tried to get A-35s upgraded to take the A-24's place in priority if possible. Sessums listed numerous reasons why this would be very hard but finally agreed to go to work on trying to get 200 A35s further up the priority list. None of this helped the A-35 one little bit and the parts shortage continued throughout the winter of 1942-43, delaying and limiting production.

Reports from the plants continued to concentrate on the rate of output, and none of this in-fighting between the management and the Air Force was made known to the production line workers, of course. Some things, however, could not be hidden. An example was recalled for me by Walter E. Holt, at that time a lead electrical man on the Vengeance line at Hawthorne. In 1942 a

British inspector was watching him work at soldering electrical plugs on the V-72. The inspector seized the paste and took it elsewhere for analysis. It seems that ten to fifteen Vengeances from the line that had been shipped to Australia had arrived there with the plugs inoperative; sabotage was suspected. But it was later discovered that it had been the sea air on the long voyage that had really produced wire corrosion and failure!

On 29 October 1942, Brigadier-General Hume Peabody, Director of Organisation and Movement, Washington, wrote to the Director of Military Requirements. Peabody summarised a report on A-35 tests at the Proving Ground as follows: (1) A-35-B is superior to V-72 in respect to greater ease of handling and turning, increased manoeuvrabilty, lighter controls and improved visibilty. (2) It is also superior to A-24 as a combat weapon. (3) Mechanical help obtained from elevator forces which are too light should be limited. (4) It was recommended that A-35 be adopted as standard equipment. (5) One of the first production models was requested in order that tests might be completed.

Edward Peden describes his part in this process as a typical production worker on the line: 'Most of my time spent working on the V-72 was concentrated on the aft fuselage section. I was a group leader of several craftsmen, and our main function was the assembly of the armour plate, pulley brackets for control cables, electrical wiring for identification and navigation lights, installing the vertical stabiliser attachments, completion of any missing fasteners, painting the interior of the aircraft and camouflage painting of the exterior.'

A visit to the Vultee line was made by Major-General A. E. Pott, Commander of the Canadian Army 6th Division. At that time Canada was still expecting to equip her Army Co-operation units with the Vengeance in the near future, despite the priority being given to Australia and India. Another visitor later in the year was Navy hero Lieutenant W. D. Carter, who had flown SBDs at Midway and at Guadalcanal. A Nashville boy, he was shown round the plant and praised the A-31 as better than anything the Navy had! Certainly the A-31 could carry more, at higher speeds. Trouble was that the SBD was *doing* it; the A-31 still awaiting its chance and the war was moving on.

Examination of the pilot's handbooks and other official volumes prepared for the A-35B

131250 on the concrete awaiting tests with the 'Star and Bars' national insignia painted up on an otherwise plain bottle-green body. *(Smithsonian)*

give clear insight into the chief difference insisted upon by the US Army over the A-31. In order to reduce the nose-up flying attitude they demanded the reduction of the dive-bombing capabilities of the plane. Thus the feature insisted upon by the RAF, a nil angle of incidence to facilitate the main role of the aircraft, was sacrificed by the US Army to give a clear take-off and landing view to the pilot and the wings were set with a four-degree angle of incidence instead. This was a relatively easy modification to achieve.

The engine unit remained the same Wright *Cyclone* R-2600-19, which was more-or-less identical to the civilian R-2600-A5B fitted to the first models to start with. The gun armament, which had been modified by the British in India right away, as we have seen, was also much criticised in the States. The fixed, wing-mounted guns became .50 calibre (12.7mm) Browning weapons with 425 rounds of ammunition per gun. Likewise the twin rear-gun was replaced by a single .50 in weapon with 400 rounds. The bomb load was doubled up to 2000 lb (908 kg) and comprised one 1000 lb and two 500 pounders. Communications equipment was updated also, and the fuel control system simplified and enlarged. Control surface balance tabs were fitted to reduce control forces.

The initial run was 200 A-35A-1-VN from the Nashville plant. The prototype, as we have seen, first flew in September 1942, and was used for testing. A further 98 followed it before the specification changed again. Two more fixed .50 calibre wing guns were added to each side centre section, making a new total of six such weapons and, at long last, engine power was upgraded to a more realistic 1700 hp with the installation of the Wright R-2600–13 (and later -8) radial, which had a gear ratio of .5625. The Hamilton Standard Type 6359A-24 of 12 ft diameter was fitted. These were the A-35Bs, which the British termed the Vengeance IV. The larger engine put up unit costings to $91,640, although Vultee's new automated line had reduced airframe costings by $2000 in the interim. Two hundred A-35B–1-VNs followed on from Vultee and subsequent orders as A-35B-10-VN saw

further price reductions, to $60,965, as the line finally got into full swing. Another 430 A-35-B-15-VNs, in two blocks, came out at a cost of $52,123 per machine.

The arrival of the first Vengeance Is in India coincided with a crying need for a precision aircraft in that theatre of war. The army's attempt to drive the Japanese back along the coastal plain that autumn had not met with success and the men on the spot had little doubt of the reason—obsolete aircraft flying inaccurate missions. On 11 September 1942, AHQ Bengal sent a signal to AHQ India which spelt this out in no uncertain terms:

'I cannot exaggerate the importance I attach to the early arrival of Vengeance dive-bombers in the Command. Present equipment of Blenheims and Hudsons, though satisfactory for medium altitude bombing, are quite unsatisfactory for attacks on ships at sea or in harbour . . . Had dive-bombers been available I consider that our object at Akyab on 9th September could have been achieved at less than half the effort. Therefore submit that 82 Squadron should be moved into 221 Group. Form there and undertake their first operational training there. Would gladly release a Blenheim squadron in exchange if this is considered necessary.'

As the aircraft came slowly from the MUs, plans were afoot to equip 168 Wing and other units. The RAF planned to equip four squadrons initially, Nos 45, 82, 84 and 110, all equipped with the Blenheim. The formation of an Indian Air Force Wing was also originated and two Vengeance squadrons were to be set up for this to start with.

Numbers of Vengeance Is were delivered to No. 152 Operational Training Unit at Peshawar late in 1942. The Coast Defence Flights of the Indian Air Force had been disbanded and general reconnaissance duties over the shipping lanes taken over by the RAF personnel of No. 3 (Calcutta) and No. 6 (Vizakapatnam) Coast Defence Flights, together with IAF personnel withdrawn from Nos. 104 and 353 Squadrons, RAF. All the navigators released from the disbanded flights were distributed among the two squadrons.

The first to form was No. 7 Squadron, IAF, commanded by Squadron Leader Hem Choudry. Conversion training commenced in mid-December 1942, and was not completed until mid-February 1943. Technical and ground personnel received training on the Vengeance at 320 MU at Drigh Road, Karachi, and on 8 March 1943 the squadron assembled at Phaphamau, a recently built airfield near Allahabad. Here they collected their aircraft and then moved over to Bairaganh, near Bhopal, to do live bombing and gunnery training. In the interim No. 8 Squadron IAF had been formed at Trichinopoly on 1 December 1942, taking in the remaining personnel of 6 CDF and the Cochin Flight. Shortage of both aircrew and ground crew was a grave problem for this second unit and it did not finally obtain operational status until 25 June 1943.

# Chapter 5
# Consideration

Although No. 84 Squadron was the first RAF unit to be *officially* informed that it was to re-equip with the new dive-bomber, it was No. 82 Squadron, which was officially notified in July, that actually became the first RAF Squadron to *receive and operate* the Vultee Vengeance. In turn, No. 84 Squadron was the first actually to *bomb* Japanese targets with the Vengeance. In fact of course the squadron commander and most others knew well before these dates that they were to become dive-bomber squadrons, along with No. 45 and No. 110 Squadron. It is therefore appropriate for the then Commanding Officer of No. 82 Squadron, Wing Commander Dennis Gibbs, to relate how his unit made the initial conversion.

'No. 82 Squadron —the non-flying part—arrived in Bombay in May 1942. There were no aeroplanes ready for us so we were sent to Quetta where we wasted time waiting for some aircraft. My logbook reads that my first flight was on 29 August 1942. From then on we were into the engine problems due to the aircraft being shipped out with uninhibited engines. We moved down to an airfield near Madras (Cholavaram) and, in spite of one hundred per cent change of all the piston rings on all the aircraft, the oil consumption soon was competing with fuel again and all the engines were condemned!

'Other technical problems were the large number of electric fuel pumps. I think I am right in saying that these early Vengeances had two per tank and there were four tanks per wing and a booster for take-off. In all, seventeen pumps that were continually shorting out in the rainy and humid conditions. Luckily the Vengeance had a hand-driven wobble-pump and many aircraft returned from flights with the air-gunner supplying the fuel.

'The first operation was on 17 October 1942, looking for a Jap submarine. I have a feeling we had no bombs so what we were to do if it was spotted I forget! We all eventually returned to base, some trailing smoke and back-firing. Another problem with the early model was the twin .300 machine-guns for the air-gunner and I believe these mountings were altered and I think .303s were substituted. Certainly the four forward-firing .300s gave trouble as, unlike the .303, there was no rear gear on the gun to hold the breech-block in the rear position when the firing stopped. This allowed the air to travel through the gun and cool it. The .300 cooked the round up the spout so there was spontaneous firing until a cartridge broke and another round jammed in the barrel. So we would come back with all four guns out of action and damaged. The only cure was to limit firing to very, very short bursts. It was not until April 1943 that we obtained serviceable aircraft that could be flown every day.'

Although thus plagued with technical problems 82 Squadron continued to operate regular anti-submarine patrols over the Bay of Bengal. Identical problems were shared to a similar degree by every other Vengeance unit during 1942. The same month that Gibbs' squadron took delivery so did 110 Squadron, under Squadron Leader Freddie F. Lambert, based at Ondal.

His first flight in a Vengeance took place in AP100 on 31 October and consisted of 15 minutes' local flying. Further flights followed on 1, 3 and 5 November, with VV847 as his mount and a variety of passengers, and included the first dive-bombing test on the 3rd.

While his CO was detached with a small piece of 110 Squadron, his senior flying officer, Flight Lieutenant Don Ritchie, and

Australian officer serving with the RAF, was busy working out the details of how to use and operate the Vengeance back at Pandaveswar. His first flight in the Vengeance was as passenger to Group Captain Hunt in AN863 on 19 November. This was followed by a further back-seat stint of instruction from Flying Officer Hedley and then, all in the same day, Don Ritchie went up on his own for his first solo and local flying.

'One day, in came a Vengeance aircraft. This was the first one I'd ever seen, though I knew it was on its way to us. I didn't know a damned thing about it, not a damned thing! The Wing Commander put me in the back seat and up we went. Electric everything and plenty of room. The plane had several fuel tanks in the wings, interconnected. In the early days the pumps that kept the fuel flowing had a nasty habit of packing up. We had to "wobble" our way home. A bit tiring, hand-pumping, but it did get us back several times. Eventually they got this problem fixed'.

Between 21 and 29 November 1942 Ritchie flew AN919, 850, and 917 in local and formation flying, dive-bombing and low-level, making a total of seven dives in all.

'On the fifth day after the aircraft arrived I was pronounced fit to fly and teach the Vengeance! There was, I was told, some sort of alarm, some talk of enemy warships, submarines or raids. One of our young crews had been sent out from Karachi to have a look and had not come back. We had quite a lot of engine failures to start with. It was a big plane for a single-engine job. Quite heavy and very underpowered. These were Vengeance Is. As further planes were flown in from Karachi I tested them out and I flew about eight in the first week. In effect I was trying out the squadron's aircraft in sequence.

'At the time I was breaking in the first planes we were thinking hard all the time on how to use them. Knowing nothing about it we needed to! The basic flying unit we first adopted was in fours. Flying at first wasn't as intensive as one would have expected it to be. Because, firstly, they were only arriving in dribs-and-drabs, and secondly, at that stage there was a certain amount of uncertainty

about their use at all. Thirdly, I think it would be fair to say that the ground crew were as totally unused to them as we were. Our ground crews were pretty experienced; I knew one or two people back at Karachi, engineers, Flight Sergeants and the like, who had been with us in England.

'It was an aircraft, I have to say, that in its first few months was plagued with uncertainties with the engines. Fuel pumps packed up regularly. The two American Vultee reps used to say "Well, its those neoprene washers that are fouled up". Ultimately we had the rear guns replaced as they too were unreliable. In other words it was just a case of getting the whole act together from scratch. I don't think anyone in the entire sub-continent had any belief in the role of this aircraft. It was well known that the RAF had no dive-bombers and had always been dead against introducing them on principle. They believed in low-level bombing, despite the fact that it had not worked in France in 1940. They maintained that had the Germans not had air superiority the *Stuka* would not have been the great success it was either. The Blenheims had suffered far greater losses than had the *Stukas* in truth, as we could verify, but there was no bias against them.'

On 18 November 1942 the first three aircraft officially allocated to 110 Squadron arrived from Karachi; these were AN863 piloted by Flying Officer Hedley, AN919 (Warrant Officer McIlroy) and AN998 (Pilot Officer Rule). Circuits and landings were conducted on the 19th and local flying in the Asansol-Panda area next day, which gave the local AA some shooting practice. On 22 November bombing practice against a ship target was conducted and three more aircraft joined from Allahabad: AN850 (Fg Off Topley), AN927 (Sgt Allen) and AN862 (Sgt Davis). Formation and cross-country flying with three aircraft was conducted and Lambert rejoined his unit in AN917 from Karachi. Next day a signal was received from 221 Group suggesting that Vengeances be grounded pending completion of a crash enquiry. Lambert flew VV917 from Drigh

Road to Jodhpur, then on to Delhi next day and from there to Allahabad, arriving at Pandaveswar, the squadron's new temporary base. On November 27 1942, a demonstration for the AOC-in-C, before returning to Drigh Road. From here they conducted anti-submarine patrols.

A further three aircraft arrived from Karachi for the squadron on 5 December and next day the Wing moved to Madhaiganji and the first Vengeance, piloted by Group Captain Hunt, followed them there on the 8th. Three more arrived from Pandaveswar the same day, six more next day, a further three from Karachi on the 10th and three more, led by Lambert, on the 11th. They were joined there on the 16th by Vultee test pilot Leech, and two more aircraft. The last of the squadron's allocation of 20 units arrived on 17 December.

On 13 December 1942, Lambert led 110 Squadron on an advanced training operation which turned out to be a sortie over enemy-held territory. He recalled: 'The 260 miles from east of Calcutta to the targets at Cox's Bazaar/Chittagong—Jap held—sticks in my mind. It was most hair-raising—no one as far as I remember ever lived in this Sundarbans area—and to come down would be final. I only recall losing one of my squadron in this fashion.'

Formation flying with four aircraft, army co-operation, high and low-level bombing practices followed over Chittagong and the Arakan coast before commencing a move via Alipore to Madhaiganji, to join 82 Squadron again in coastal patrols. Aircraft flown by Lambert during December were AP128, 116, 129, 181, 121, 120 and AN863, 850, 920F, 918 and 127. These duties continued until the end of the year, 110 Squadron being joined by No. 45 Squadron with their first Vengeances.

Freddie Lambert told me: 'I remember taking my squadron in flight from the depot in Karachi to the Calcutta area but first doing an op from Drigh Road for some kind of elusive anti-submarine trip—dropping bombs on an object which (at that time) I suppose I *thought* was enemy!'

This attack took place on 2 December 1942,

some 575 miles south-west of Karachi, two 500 lb bombs being dropped and both forward and rear machine-guns being fired with vigour. After that, routine testing and trials continued.

'The engines had a habit of seizing up, which added to all our problems—not, I'm afraid, a very operationally fit aircraft.'

Freddie Lambert left the squadron on 2 January and was relieved by Wing Commander J. D. Gill, who had arrived in November. In the meantime No. 84 Squadron had received its first six dive-bombers on 22 December 1942, after moving to Vizagapatam in November.

Let E. L. Pidduck, at that time a young erk working as part of the squadron's ground-crew, take up the story from that viewpoint: 'By mid-December 1942, the Squadron received the first Vultee Vengeance for crew training from the MU at Karachi. Thus began the first of the teething troubles. The whole of the fuselage was just covered in engine oil, and the oil level in the tank dangerously low. This eventually became a major set-back and the order was received from GHQ to change all the piston rings on the Wright *Cyclone* (18 cylinders) as and when new supplies were available; this took a few weeks, but local flying and training carried on.

'The changing and fitting of new piston rings was no joke in those temperatures and had to be done of course on makeshift stands, no hangars, no shade, just press on to get them in the air again was the constant target.

'The next set-back was the electrically driven fuel pumps, which were going u/s day after day. It usually happened after the aircraft had been refuelled and, not having the best equipment to de-fuel the tanks, we would change the pumps *in situ*, i.e. tanks full. This meant a bath in octane petrol if you were not lucky enough to get the pump in the tank aperture first time and tighten up. These were not located in the easiest of positions for this to be done either, especially those in the bomb bay and the undercarriage bay.

'After several weeks of extensive flying training things began to run more smoothly, and in February 1943 the squadron moved to

Asansol, Bengal, almost ready for operations. Modified pumps were now arriving and giving less trouble.'

The first three aircraft from 45 Squadron joined those of 82 and 110 at Asansol at 1720 on 20 February and all three units continued training and evaluations, including long-distance flights conducted on 25 February by eight aircraft from 110, eight from 82 and four from 45 Squadron, two of which landed at Ondal, continuing to Madhaiganji and Asansol respectively next day. This type of combined training continued throughout the weeks that followed. On 15 March 1943 the three squadrons were visited there by the Air Officer Commanding Bengal, Air Vice-Marshal Williams, OBE, MC, DFC.

What of 84 Squadron? It had only been kept together as a unit after being wellnigh annihilated in the disasters of Sumatra and Java early in the year. Only a scattered handful had got back to India but Squadron Leader Arthur Murland Gill was determined his proud unit should not be disbanded and he succeeded in holding the nucleus together.

The first aircraft delivered to 84 Squadron was a Vengeance I, AP917, which Gill flew on 22 November 1942. The Harvard was FE415. A batch of six Vengeances soon followed, Gill himself flight testing AN900 on 24 December, but that was all until the end of March when AN117 and AN996 joined the squadron. Thereafter there was a regular influx of Mark IIs.

In the interim, on 27 January 1943, the squadron had moved to Cholavaram and the programme continued until 19 April. As with the other units above, this initial period was one of trial and tribulation. Arthur Gill described to me in an interview just what this all involved:

'The first concern, I think, was that there were no dual-control aircraft. Very few of us had ever flown aircraft like these, and like Spitfires, Javelins etc, there never was a dual-control model to train on. You just climbed in, looked at the pilot's notes and you were away. So the same thing applied to the Vultee. I had a lot of pilots there who were, firstly, comparatively fresh from training and had no

A pair of Vengeance dive-bombers from 110 (H) Squadron as the unit assembles over India.
*(Donald Ritchie)*

operational experience to start with, probably had flown Tiger Moths and Harvards and the like and that's all. So the first thing I asked for was to have a Harvard, and one was allocated to us. My first task was to take up all the pilots in the front seat and check out what I'd got. Once in the air I'd say, "It's all yours" and put my hands in the air and see what happened!

'It was virtually the same with the Vultee. At any rate, as soon as the the first airplane came in we uncrated it and flew it. I had Ken Dicks as my navigator and we flew from Karachi en route. Having taken off from Jodphur we got three-quarters of an hour flying time into our journey when the engine stopped! Fortunately we had a manual pump, so we pumped like mad and the engine picked up again and burst into life. And every time you stopped pumping the engine faded out on us. So I said, "Right Ken, back to Jodhpur", and we flew back there and we found we had constant problems with the same thing on every aircraft we got.

'We had an airman called Childs, a Londoner, who was always in trouble, always on charges. And I said to him finally I'm going to make you a corporal. Your responsibility is for these bloody pumps! He worked hard and did marvellously, stripped all the pumps down. He found out they had a washer shaped like a saucer, dozens of them, and they had all been assembled in America back to front, so that instead of pumping the fuel through they were trying to suck it backwards. So he stripped them all down, because they were petrol submergence pumps; there was a pump in each tank so that as you switched on each tank these pumps would start working. As you changed over tanks these pumps would start to pump the fuel through from the reserve and emergency tanks. He stripped them all down and from thereafter we had no more fuel tank problems.

'Another problem we had was with overheating of the engines. We eventually made our own modification and cut a hole in the side of the aircraft and inserted an air-scoop to cool it down more. I think basically the Wright was a good engine but I think that under the extreme conditions of heat and dust and humidity and heavy rain in India and the jungle, this really tries out an aircraft and the Americans had only tested them in the ideal climate of California. Having once been a desert squadron we knew what to expect from heat and dust. Due to the air filters, all the dust which you suck into your engine through your air intakes caused wear and tear on your pistons. As a result you use an enormous amount of oil, almost as much oil as you do petrol. The Vultee lacked suitable air filters and I think they just didn't realise I suppose. They built them for Europe and got caught out when they arrived in the Far East.

The squadron's chief engineer at this time was Flight Lieutenant John ('Engoff') Ramsden, a 'no-nonsense' northerner from Leeds. In an interview he recounted the engineer's viewpoint to me thus: 'The biggest problem that I can recall was with the fuel system. They were immersed electric pumps. They were of the old type, although radical and novel at that time, immersion pumps with a double impeller at the bottom. And the problems we had with those were that the seals round the impeller shaft failed, and the pump was flooded with fuel and failed. The pumps were in short supply and we overcame this by having a brilliant young bloke called Childs who was an electrician. What he'd been in Civvy Street I don't know but he was an electrician in the RAF. He helped form his own Pump Bay and from somewhere or other, I don't know where we got them, we obtained these stacks of neoprene washers which fitted round the impeller shaft. Whether we got them officially or otherwise I thought it best not to enquire, but we got them. As far as I can recall there was no repair scheme for these pumps but young Childs devised a repair procedure from scratch. We got stacks of these neoprene washers and he ran this bay with another man who built up the bay with tanks and immersion pumps and they kept these pumps, and therefore the aircraft, going.

'Another problem I recall with the Vengeance was the harnesses on the engines. They were susceptible to water were these, and I can remember we had a lot of problems changing them. They were hardly the thing for jungle warfare. But as far as I can remember we did not have a lot of problems with spares. Being an independent squadron, that is, self-sufficient, the NCOs and myself sat down and decided just what spares we would want with the American reps—we had four American Technical Officers (TOs) from the company — and the spare parts list. We used to sit down with them and order from the list and they were very good to us and used to get us anything we indented for. So much so that we got very ambitious and we found all sorts of bits of kit in these lists which we didn't know whether we were entitled to or not, and just asked for them and got 'em!

'So we had inflatable crash-bags, and I think that 84 Squadron was the first up on the Burma front to have them because the NCOs and myself had sat down and said, "Those things look good, let's try those!". It was just a matter of picking out what we wanted and so we had these crash bags on the Vengeance. Once again, whether they were British ones or

American ones I couldn't say, but we certainly had them, and they worked very well.

'The interconnecting fuel system worked well as long as you had these immersed electric pumps working correctly. It all depended on these damned pumps and they were the originals.

The Indian squadrons also faced similar difficulties. No. 8 Squadron Indian Air Force was led by a former army officer, Squadron Leader Niranjan Prasad, who had transferred to the Indian Air Force and had served with No. 1 Squadron, flying Lysanders in Burma. He thus had both Army and operational experience, the exact qualities needed for the dive-bomber squadron's future role. The pilots were ordered to report to 152 OTU at Peshawar, on 1 March 1943, to commence their conversion course to the Vengeance, while the location of the squadron adjutant and ground staff remained Trichinopoly.

The first ceremony the new squadron participated in was the tenth anniversary of the foundation of the Indian Air Force on 1 April 1943. At the end of a parade at Peshawar in front of the Governor, Sir George Cunningham, one of the new Vengeance dive-bombers made a fly-past to mark the arrival of modern aircraft and the coming-of-age of the young force. Conversion to the Vultee started on 8 April with the CO making the first solo flight that day. On the 16th Prasad had to make a crash-landing owing to a petrol pipe coming off its connection; his aircraft was slightly damaged after a belly landing. This was but the first of a series of such crashes which got the squadron off on a bad footing. On the 24th Pilot Officer Kamal and Flying Officer Khan crashed after take-off, half a mile from the field; both survived but were injured. On the 29th it was worse; the squadron took its first casualty when Pilot Officer M. K. Chand was killed in an accident. A month later and Pilot Officer K. S. Sandhu's plane crashed while conducting air to ground firing on 29 May. Both he and Sgt Rushtomji were killed when the plane caught fire. By July 1943 the squadron had eight Mark I and four Mark IA

Vengeances on equipment strength, but it was noted that 'Considerable difficulties are experienced with regard to the serviceability of the aircraft for shortage of parts. The maintenance crews worked under adverse conditions for want of proper equipment and tools.'

In No. 7 Squadron (IAF) the tale was a similar one. As the official statement recorded: 'Nobody was very happy . . . for the Vengeance possessed more than its share of teething troubles and defects and had to be withdrawn for a while.'

But they did manage to mount some kind of live combat operations from Quetta against dissident tribesmen in two North Waziristan villages as early as the end of January 1943. In general, however, training continued as did the normal struggles to keep the aircraft operational. Both RAF and Indian squadrons were restricted to eight machines per squadron during this early period, as deliveries continued to be spasmodic.

Don Ritchie, with 110 Squadron at that time, recalled: 'We also had communications problems to work out. The standard RAF wireless wasn't much good. We had been used to using the TR9s, standard RAF R/T that had a range of anything from five to seven, eight or nine miles. We had never seen VHF. Then we had the TR5D. The Bendix fitted in the Vengeance was undoubtedly better.

'My impression of the dive brakes of the Vengeance was very efficient. Mind you, I had never used dive brakes on anything else to compare them with. As they were fitted both above and below the wings they made little difference to your handling of the aircraft when they were extended. On 16 February 1943, I felt sufficiently at home in a Vengeance to do three slow rolls! (The pilot's handbook said this aircraft must not be rolled.)

'We had acquired a couple of American reps from Vultee, not servicemen but representatives of the company, Spencer J. Leech and a chap called Anderson. Both were bloody good chaps and "on the ball", as they say. They knew the aircraft backwards, any fault and they would jump in the plane and

EZ804 of 110 (H) Squadron. The tail-wheel retracted assembly is seen to good advantage in this photograph. Note painting of roundels at this early period of use, before actual combat period. *(Donald Ritchie)*

find out exactly what was going wrong. They were on our side, although representing the company, but tireless in their efforts to sort things out and they knew their job.

'We had problems with the piston rings in many planes not long after first getting the aircraft. Thus we had many instances of going off with a perfectly serviceable engine and coming back having to nurse it along with the windscreen covered in oil. We had one or two planes that had horrendous fuel consumption. I can only remember losing one plane to this problem but it was a major headache. I think 82 lost one crew due to the

engine seizing up, not on operations but on a cross-country flight. Nobody could figure out why. Everybody had got perfect engines, perfectly tuned. The problem was ultimately solved when we sent our Engineering Officer, ex Flight Sgt Debond, to Karachi where they had arrived in crates and he dismantled an engine to see what it was like before anybody used it.

'There were marks from an emery wheel, which led us to think of sabotage. About the same time the United States Navy had taken over Curtiss Wrights. Now there was no real reason given why they should had done so. We put two-and-two together and I suppose made five and put it down to the same trouble. Once that was discovered and put right everything was fine.'

Group Captain Hunt, CO of 168 Wing, prepared a secret memo on his unit's progress on 25 February 1943. In this the Wing's future training instructions and tactics were spelt out as far as they could be, and details of progress to date were recorded. As he pointed out: 'The tactics have been decided upon after considerable experiment by 110 Squadron, although it must be confessed that no trials were carried out with 9 and 12 aircraft, owing to unserviceability. The pilots have, however, had considerable success with the Vic of three, which is the basic formation'.

A summary of results over different weeks showed that, at this period, the six most experienced pilots were getting an average error of about 40 yards (sometimes from single dives, and sometimes from Vic) after an average flying time of approximately 50 hours in Vengeance aircraft. Both A and B Flights of 110 Squadron provided figures thus:

| | Average error: | | Number of | Bombs dropped: | |
| | *1st week* | *last week* | *of pilots* | *1st week* | *last week* |
|---|---|---|---|---|---|
| A Flight trained pilots | — | 42 yds | 3 | 105 | — |
| Untrained pilots | 166 yds | 118 yds | 7 | — | — |
| | — | 55 yds | | | |
| B Flight trained pilots | — | 37 yds | 3 | 108 | — |
| Untrained pilots | 158 yds | 96 yds | 6 | — | 102 |

At the conference a flight commander from each of 45 and 82 Squadrons attended and expressed general agreement with the tactics laid down. However, Hunt added the obvious rider that although, ' . . . it is essential to have some standardization of method, I am, however, well aware of the dangers of over-orthodoxy and over-standardisation, and I am encouraging the squadrons to experiment as much as possible, providing that all pilots receive adequate training in the standard method laid down. It is intended to improve these tactics, and also to develop entirely different alternative methods of attack'.

The ideal length of dive was estimated to be from 10,000 ft to approximately 4000 ft, which allowed a sufficiently steep dive and time to stay in it long enough to get an accurate sight, release the bombs and pull out with a reasonable margin of safety, although they could press down to 2000 ft to get a good

sighting if necessary. At such a low pull-out a high 'g' force was experienced. The terminal velocity (TV) with dive brakes out and one-third throttle was recorded at 320 mph at 90 degrees or 290 mph at 75 degrees.

As these early aircraft had no angle of incidence the angle between the datum line of the aircraft and the actual line of flight was nil at 90 degrees and negligible at 75 degrees. However, pilots were warned they must learn to judge the trail angle of the bomb, which varied with the angle of the dive. They considered a scheme of painting lines on the cockpit cover itself, like the German *Stukas* were known to have, but this was rejected without practice. 'The pilot must concentrate on looking at the target and the nose of the aircraft, and when his head is in a correct position for this, lines of 60 degrees and 75 degrees on the cockpit cover are outside his vision. To raise his head to look at them

A good underview of two 110 (H) Squadron Vengeances nicely 'tucked-up' tight illustrates how complex wheel fairings closed up flush to wings and the angle of the tail assembly contrasted with the rear of the inner wing sections. *(Donald Ritchie)*

*Diane* caught in flight. A good study of this No. 12 Squadron RAAF Vengeance over Northern Queensland in 1943. *(Cyril McPherson)*

during the dive would interfere with the sighting and would also be difficult physically. The angle of 45 degrees is not sufficiently steep and would merely confuse the pilot.'

The heights of bomb release were from altimeter readings, with negligible lag compared with the speed of the aircraft's descent. In other words, pilots would not worry about 100 feet or so when approaching the ground at more than 400 ft per second! The Vengeance, the men on the spot emphasised, 'should be confined as far as possible to the role for which it was designed and in which it is effective, i.e. dive-bombing, *and not frittered away on odd jobs for which it is unsuitable.'*

Nonetheless, with dedication, results were achieved in this new concept. No. 7 Squadron were recorded as achieving impressive results after a few months of this training: 'they could place their 500 lb (227 kg) bombs within 15 yards (13.7m) of the target.'

Another summary on the operational use of the Vengeance made much the same point when discussing low-level attacks. 'The aircraft is manoeuvrable near the ground and good results have been obtained in low-level attacks against a ship target (80 per cent hits). The view of the pilot directly ahead is obscured by the large nose. Moreover the aircraft, although manoeuvrable, has only a moderate speed and with its one engine will probably be very vulnerable to light automatic fire from the ground. Therefore, although it is possible to use the aircraft for low-level attacks, it is not by any means the most suitable aircraft for such an operation.' In contrast, of course, 'The Vengeance is a good dive-bomber and by reason of its accuracy could be used with effect against comparatively small targets. In steep dives the aircraft is steady and easily controllable laterally and good bombing results have been obtained by pilots after some practice. The experienced pilots of 110 Squadron are now getting an average bombing error of only 40 yards.'

On range, it was noted that extensive tests had not then been possible but results obtained at Cholavaram gave a radius of action, with full warload, of slightly over 200 miles and the rough figures obtained by 110 Squadron substantiated this.

Don Ritchie of 110 Squadron recalls this early training: 'When I started with 110 Squadron we had two young Flying Officers sent out to join us straight from the US Navy Dive-Bomber training school at Pensacola, Florida. They had loads of theory and diagrams and manuals when we acquired them around the end of 1942. They were sent to us in good faith because the RAF knew nothing about dive-bombing, Meanwhile we, in our ignorance, had evolved our own ways of doing the job. Now in my own personal view, the most outlandish aeronautical manoeuvre that exists is the bunt, an outside loop with the "g" exerted in reverse. You feel as if you are being flung out of the cockpit, and this was the method they basically tried to teach us. But, I suppose because I personally hated this manoeuvre, I evolved what was, to me, a much more comfortable way to fly dive-bombing attacks, the "Wing Over". They tried to have this stopped. Well, fair enough, they had been sent to the States on this course especially to learn how to do it and then come and spread the word to us. They were Flying Officers, but had never been on ops. Although they joined 110 Squadron I imagine they were there to instruct the whole Wing eventually.

'Our own immediate thoughts on the actual dive early on concerned the bomb release itself. The two main bombs were held inside the bay on forks which swung out and, when you released the bombs in a vertical dive, flung them clear of the prop. But there was a lot of lack of confidence about whether this would in fact happen! I'm glad to say that in practice it always did! Whomever was senior had to try everything out first, and that was me at that period.

'Anyway we had got our act together ourselves *before* the Pensacola boys arrived and tried to change it. The squadrons had all

done it individually, of course, although we were the first. Group Captain Hunt was appointed to take over the Vengeance Wing, 82 Squadron joined us and then, I think, 45. We were in Bengal to start with and 82 was somewhere down on the east coast of the peninsula, somewhere down at Madras; the others had at that time not yet re-equipped. I cannot recall how 82 decided to do it.

'But in the end my way of doing it won the day. It was very, very accurate on the target. Group Captain Hunt, with no experience at all, had to come down and make a decision. What I did was very simple. I just slid the nose of the aircraft along, keeping the target in sight. Let it disappear under the wing-root. In my experience we found it was something like seven or eight seconds and you just counted it off. As soon as you rolled over, past the vertical, you could see the target. Now, instead of a bomb-sight, which was an ordinary plain ring-sight, I had a black line painted straight down the nose of the aircraft. Later it was to become a yellow line but it started off as a black line. Having flown Blenheims, in which we had "jinked" on the way out, we decided to do likewise in dive-bombing after the pull-out. The German *Stuka* boys' method, as we understood it, was to follow a predetermined path, which of course was predetermined for the AA guns as well. We, fortunately, didn't adopt that!

'The next problem was, what height shall we bomb at and should we go for altitude or should we go for the deck afterwards. It was literally up to your own judgement. Again we decided on the latter; the aim was to bomb as low as possible and get our fast. We bombed from something like 800 ft. The operational scientists from the theoretical side had their own ideas. They watched us and took photographs. They reckoned we were not diving at 90 degrees but at maybe 75 degrees. We said, well, it felt like 90 degrees to us and our instruments thought so as well. *And* it works! So we got on with it. But anyway we were immediately sent off on a detachment to Doiswah on 17 March. Seven planes were sent down and next day we bombed the Japanese HQ with a box of six. That was the first

Refuelling operations with No. 110 Squadron.
The wing fuel tanks were another special Vultee
feature; they were fine but the pumps which
operated them presented constant problems for
air and ground crews alike in the early days.
*(Donald Ritchie)*

combat mission that I know against a land
target with the Vengeance, and we recorded
100 per cent hits!'

The date of this attack was 19 March 1943,
and Ritchie flew in Vengeance 'G' (927N)
with Pilot Officer Vincent in the back seat.
The other aircraft of 'Dog Group', as they
were codenamed, were 'N' — Pilot Officer
Rule, 'A' — Flying Officer Topley, 'P' —
Flying Officer Brooks, 'Y' — Flight Sgt
Davies and 'L' — Flight Sgt Duncan. Each
Vengeance carried two 500 lb general-
purpose (GP) bombs. The dive was made
from 11,000 ft down to 1000 ft against a
Japanese HQ in Htizwe village. All twelve
bombs burst dead-centre of the target and the
formating, both before and after the flight as
well as the actual dive-bombing, 'was
executed as on a practice flight'. All the
aircraft returned safely.

This exercise was repeated next day when
the target was the village of Thaungdara, and
all the bombs save one were direct hits on the
target. On 21 March 1943 the Vengeance unit
sortied out once more, this time against a

Japanese strongpoint in Donabik village and
again the box of six had 100 per cent success.
Flight times for all these missions were one
hour 55 minutes. Next day they struck at
another Japanese HQ located in the Pagoda
of Lawngchaung. Dives were made from
10,000 ft down to only 600 ft and target was
totally destroyed. One final attack brought
this diversion to a most satisfactory
conclusion, six Vengeances attacking a
Japanese pill-box at Donbaik which had been
holding up the Allied advance.

Don Ritchie recalls: 'I had asked that we be
given *fluff* (smoke) on the target for this
mission. The Army argued that if they put
smoke on the enemy the enemy would put
smoke on them. I replied that they could
always change the colour of the smoke from
day-to-day or mission-to-mission. Have a
colour of the day. Eventually they agreed to
lay on the smoke. But on this occasion they
didn't use mortars, they used 25-pounder
guns and these had a virtually flat trajectory,
which was not very accurate for our purposes.
It didn't take us long to get down from 10,000
ft to 600 ft going downhill and the Army were
just not ready for us. The fluff was just too
late, it fell some 200 yards north of the target
according to later signals. Our last plane
down saw one extra white flash after the
bombs exploded and two green Very lights
were fired. It didn't matter because we hit the
target anyway.'

A box of four had been used and direct hits
were scored by three of the aircraft. 'All this
proved our tactics, our way of aiming, the
crude bloody black line down the nose, all of
it worked'.

Soon congratulatory signals began pouring
in. From the AOC Bengal: 'Very glad indeed
to see that Vengeances of 110 Squadron have
joined in offensive against enemy on this
front. Congratulations on highly successful
bombing during first attack. Good hunting.'

From 221 Group: 'Results proved the
Vengeance can be a great asset assisting
Army.'

The Vengeance had arrived!

# Chapter 6
# Hesitation

While the Commonwealth air arms were receiving their first batches of Vengeance dive-bombers, overcoming the many mechanical problems, working out their tactics and, finally, first taking them so successfully into battle, the picture elsewhere was somewhat confused. The USAAF continued to treat the A-31 as totally unusable and its successor as little better, Other air arms either had their desire to obtain the Vengeance frustrated, or found that its inherent problems were too much for them to overcome in the same manner as the British, Australians and Indians were doing. In contrast, on the production front all the irritating delays and hold-ups were resolved one by one and the airplanes finally began to roll out in substantial numbers. Let us examine each of these facets before returning to the Vengeance's combat career as it really began to get under way.

In addition to the consideration of the use of its A-31s for training purposes it had been suggested that the USAAF might employ them as glider-towing aircraft. However, this idea was rejected by the Experimental Engineering Section in a report dated 5 August 1942.

Nothing daunted, Production Engineering Section had also been exploring the possibility of using them as target-towers. It had been found that there existed a requirement for 500 such aircraft and so trials were requested. The first tests in this respect were conducted on 15 January 1943, but the failure of the electrical priming system

A27-17 of the Royal Australian Air Force, a Vengeance II in British parlance, ex-US 41-30930, ex-British EZ881, delivered to the RAAF on 23 February 1943. Classed by them as a Vengeance I she force-landed at Williamstown eight months later and was scrapped without seeing combat.
*(RAAF Public Relations via Wayne Brown)*

interrupted them and also, two days previously, the Engineering Division at Wright Field said that the new A-35 would be a better aircraft for the job anyway! On 26 July the Production Division at Wright Field, reported that target-towing equipment was also being considered for aircraft which were to be delivered to the British and this was accomplished on 25 November 1943.

As for the A-35s, the parts shortages had continued over the winter of 1942-43 and, by February, only 11 had been accepted at Nashville, although the original schedule had called for the delivery of over 300 by that time. General Meyers requested that ten of these aircraft be subjected to special tests. As a result of this the Commanding Officer of Key Field in Mississippi, Colonel Norman R. Burnett, made a detailed report on 12 March 1943. His comments were generally unfavourable. He stated that the A-35Bs could definitely not be used for combat and that it was not as suitable as other aircraft for training purposes.

As if this were not bad enough, a serious rust problem was discovered in certain of the Wright R-2600 engines in March 1943, and this of course held up, still further, production of the A-53. Typical of the way the Vengeance was being viewed in the States at this time are the comments of Edward Peden. He had left Northrops and enlisted in the Air Force and he found himself transferred to a Ferry Command base at Memphis, Tennessee.

'The first thing I noticed was a large quantity of V-72s stored, parked row-after-row, out in the open in one area of Memphis Municipal Airport. I began to ask questions: "Why are all of these aircraft here instead of in England being used to fight the enemy?" One ferry pilot that I talked to remarked that the English did not want the V-72 and the entire weapon concept was ill-conceived, by a committee perhaps. The range of the V-72 was short, and looking at a map of Europe, one would ask the question, where to find a suitable target flying from England to warrant the expense of the aircraft and perhaps the life of the pilot to achieve a questionable object?

Such a misconception of the Vultee shows a basic misunderstanding of its role of course, and if such views were commonplace then it was probably due to the one-sided reflection of strategic bombing in the media. It also begged the question of the fact that hundreds of heavy bombers were being sent out nightly from England and were being slaughtered with the loss of many more crew members per aircraft and at far greater cost than a Vengeance. Nor were more than a tiny fraction of the thousands of tons of bombs they carried each night destined to cause the enemy any *military* damage. In fact Germany's production of war material actually *increased* ten-fold under the strategic bombing offensive.

Being an engineer himself, however, Peden could identify the basic problems that had held the Vengeance back from playing a more active role up to that date. 'The V-72 had mechanical problems that may have been remedied. One of these that I knew of was the hydraulic system, especially the landing gear. I witnessed two belly-landings where the main landing gear had stuck mid-way between gear retraction and extension. Luckily both pilots were not injured. In my negative opinion this aircraft should have been cancelled, diverting labor and material to aircraft that were desperately needed. I question the Government's wisdom in continuing to manufacture this aircraft, then to put it into storage while urging their citizens to turn in their pots and pans for the war effort'.

Peden was far from alone in the opinion, however, for about this time a special board of officers of the USAAF met to consider the disposition of all dive-bombers, including the A-25 as well as the A-35. On 27 March 1943 Mr Lovett wrote to General Arnold recommending the termination of the contract and the substituting of the A-20G or A-26 instead.

Tentative arrangements were made with Vultee to bring in A-20 production as rapidly as possible. On 6 April 1943 General Wolfe wrote to Vultee commending the workforce and assuring them that the transition would be accomplished with the minimum of break

Very nice aerial view of three Vultees of No. 12 Squadron RAAF, with A27-216 closest to camera, then 209 and 261. Although formed early, the squadron only saw limited work on coastal patrol duties until they made a memorable first Vengeance strike against the Japanese island base of Selaru in June 1943. *(Australian War Memorial)*

in their continuity of employment. On 20 May 1943 the contractor was officially advised of the cancellation of 2035 A-35s.

At Nashville the production plan to be adopted with reference to A-35 operations was outlined in a teletype from the Materiel Division, Washington D.C., on 16 August 1943. In order to maintain the Vultee labour force for the A-20H work, it was directed that an additional 250 A-35s be procured from Vultee. This quantity, following the 881 covered by existing orders, was thought sufficient to occupy the facility until August 1944. Production of A-20s was scheduled to commence in June 1944.

On 14 September 1943 General Arnold ordered that the A-20 project at Consolidated-Vultee, (or Convair as the company had officially become on 31 March 1943), be abandoned. The problem of maintaining the labour force until it could be used on P-38 production came up in this situation, just as it had in the case of the A-20.

If the work force was to be held together by continuing the production of A-35 airplanes, additional orders would have to be given to the contractor. Back at the plant, production was now getting fully into its stride.

At Northrop both contracts had been completed on time. The first for the RAF was completed on 22 August 1942, and Mr Cohu in New York City received a telegram from C. R. Fairey, Director General of the BAC in Washington, which read: 'On behalf of the Minister of Aircraft Production, England, I should be grateful if you would convey to all workers of your corporation, our appreciation and gratitude for the magnificent effort they have made in completing the Vengeance contract six weeks before due time. The standard they have set is an inspiration to us all.'

Less than a year later, on 18 May 1943, the second contract was also completed. The last A-31 was flight-tested by Dick Rinaldi and the AAF Resident Representative, Major C. R. Douglass, from Northrop Field. Then it was disassembled, carefully crated, loaded on its Union Transfer and Storage truck and trailer with motorcycle escort and, after being signed out by Lewis Gravante of the Army Office and E. W. Stevens of the Traffic Department, started on its long journey.

Over at Nashville, work on the original RAF contract was completed in March 1943, and that of the first batch of the A-35s on 25 May 1943, when Ferry Command pilot Second-Lieutenant James D. Crowley, a former Vultee paint shop employee, flew it out to Memphis.

Meanwhile the fully automated production

Of the three No. 12 Squadron RAAF aircraft featured here A27-209 (ex-AN540) crashed into the sea off Merauke, New Guinea; 216 (ex-AF934) and 261 (ex-AN538) both survived the war and were not finally scrapped until 1949.

*(Australian War Memorial)*

line was now working flat out. Its originator was by now the new Vice President of Manufacturing at Vultee. The then forty-year-old Charles W. Perelle had been a graduate of the University of Washington. After working at Boeing's Canadian plant he joined Vultee's Field Division as superintendent, installing the first mechanised assembly line as already related. Named 'The Merry-Go-Round' by the workers of Department 62, because of its oval overhead conveyor system, the official line was now working double shifts and round the clock. By mid-1943 it had been extended and was assembling more than two-thirds of each Vengeance. The system, under overall control of Elmer Prieskorn, General Foreman, comprised 23 work stations plus three inspection stations and was manned by a total of 24 lead men, four supervisors and two foremen, J. B. McWhirter and John Matthews, as day and night foreman respectively, with two supervisors per shift.

Each embryo Vengeance moved from Dept 90 into Dept 62 at Station 'O' where the installations began. All the parts from the fabrication departments were brought in by Dept 49, Production Control, and other parts flowed in from Dept 15, Stockroom. At the initial station some of the main assemblies were installed, department-made jigs being used and holes drilled from templates for hydraulic lines and electrical equipment. At Stations 1-2 hydraulic and bracket assemblies were installed. Moving to Stations 3 and 4 the main hydraulic assemblies and shear web overturn structures were installed. At Stations 6, 7 and 11 electrical equipment went in.

The airplane then moved to Stations 8, 9 and 10, where engine controls, flight controls, hydraulic assemblies, pulleys, cables and brackets were put into place. Self-sealing rubber fuel tanks were installed at Stations 13-14 and they were closed at Stations 15, 16 and 17, where the windscreens and canopies were put in and a continuity check and an air check were made. With the main central section of the aircraft complete, the inner wings were 'hung' at Stations 18-19 where an all-girl force had replaced the former all-male force. Additional hydraulic lines were also connected at this point and control cables were installed. At Stations 18-19 the wing main fuel tanks were closed, a complete air check was run, a hydraulic flush was made and the landing gear was rigged. Finally, at Stations 22 and 23, both mechanical and electrical inspections were carried out. Department 3, 'Inspections', also conducted 'shake-downs' at Stations 5, 12 and 17. Any differences between production and inspection were worked out at this point.

Testing of the .50 calibre machine-guns was also done at Nashville. Each aircraft was wheeled into place in front of the log-built, prefabricated target and loaded. Twenty-five rounds had to be fired from each gun to meet Air Force specifications and Major K. O. Thorpe, Resident USAAF Representative, examined the results to see if all the forward-firing guns converged at the specified range. The aircraft were then handed over to the Flight and Field Operations Department.

These were the mechanics, flight inspectors, tractor drivers and Company and Army test pilots, radio experts, armament technicians, Dept. 21. After the aircraft left the final assembly its records were turned over to the flight inspector's office and copies were sent to the office of the Flight and Field Superintendent, 'Cy' Younglove.

The plane was then prepared for an engine run. Routine checks were made on carburettors, spark plugs, etc prior to this and the aircraft was 'pre-oiled'. Once the initial engine run was completed this oil was drained off and checks were made for possible leaks. Then a second engine run was conducted and all necessary adjustments were made. On a satisfactory completion the aircraft was handed over to the company inspector and the plane then had its compass 'swung' and checked out.

Once in the flight area a safety inspection was carried out on the plane and then it was turned over to the company test pilot for a shake-down flight. Test pilots at this period were the two veterans, Younglove and Joe Dyer, along with Ed Rosenberg, Rex Cudney

and James Warren. This was followed, again if no faults were found, by an inspection by the Army who in turn handed it over to an Army test pilot for a second run. The AAF inspectors then went over each plane again, checking for loose equipment or other shortages. Finally, the ferry pilot took it out to its destination. By the fall of 1943 this routine had become a well-tested and smooth-running operation at Nashville. But just *what* the destinations were to be for the flood of A–35s coming out of this system, was to become more and more of a problem towards the end of 1943.

One nation that no longer had any interest in the Vengeance was Canada. The earlier postponement of the establishment of its first dive-bomber squadron was followed by continuing changes of schedule until. ultimately, outright cancellation resulted. This took place on 30 April 1942, in a telegram sent to the Dominions Office and it was subsequently endorsed by the Joint Chiefs of Staff on 12 May, despite Canadian protests.

Shortly after this another Allied nation was more fortunate, although it had to wait a long while for its dive-bombers. Brazil had declared war on the Axis powers on 22 August 1942, due primarily to U-boats sinking Brazilian merchant ships off the port of Bahia. Following this, the need for modern aircraft was felt to patrol her coastal waters and take suitably aggressive action should any German surface ships venture into those same waters on raiding missions. Accordingly, the embryo *Federale Aeronautica* (Brazilian Air Force) sent two of its officers, Colonel Julio Americo Dos Reis and Major Renato Rodrigues, on a tour of American aircraft factories. In October they visited the Nashville plant, arriving at Berry Field in a War Department plane with USAAF Colonel H. N. Burnside, and toured the facility. This visit was because of an order for 50 A–35s, which were to come out of RAF production capacity under the terms of Lease-Lend. The background to this was as follows.

On 29 July 1942, the Technical Executive at

Wright Field had received a letter from Major Newhall of the Office of the Chief of Staff in Washington. It stated that the planned allocation of 28 V-72 airplanes on contract A-557 had been made to Brazil on the basis of 10 in August, five in September, five in October, five in November and three in December. Because major changes were being made to some items it was suggested that a homogeneous block allocation would be more advisable, in that correctly interchangeable spares would be delivered concurrently. The first batch so assigned were 28 standard Vengeance IIs, AN581-AN592 (as V-72s) and AN593-AN608 (as R (Restricted) V-72s), but they were listed in the paperwork as A-31s and given American markings. These initial allocations were complete by early 1943, and their actual delivery was accomplished by 4 February 1943, although not without incident.

Flown down to South America direct by US pilots, one (AN607) crashed in Guatemala and was destroyed completely. A second (AN594) crashed *en route* but was later repaired and eventually reached Brazil. All 27 were handed over to the 1st Dive-Bombing Squadron FAB, which was based at the Santa Cruz Air Station near Rio de Janeiro. But these aircraft were subjected to exactly the same mechanical problems as the rest of the order from which they had been taken, and soon all bar one were non-operational. On 26 January 1943 Colonel Sessums told the Technical Executive at Wright Field that information had been transmitted, via ATC, to the effect that all but one of the A-31s delivered to Brazil had been grounded because of engine trouble of one sort or another.

Even as late as August 1943, 11 of the 25 machines on hand were listed as unserviceable. On 2 June 1944 Brigadier General Orval R. Cook directed the AAFRR at Vultee Nashville to take necessary action to deliver 50 A-35-B airplanes in the shortest possible time to ATC for delivery to Deer (Brazil). Airplanes were similar to British A-35s except that AAF bomb racks were to be used and the SCR-695 radio was to be deleted. The entire delivery was to be expedited with contractor working seven days a week if necessary.

The FAB took delivery of this second batch in September 1944, five A-35B-15-VNs, with US serial numbers 41-101412, 101421, 101422, 101426 and 101435, but with Brazilian national insignia painted up. They joined the 2nd Dive-Bombing Squadron, FAB, based at Sao Paulo. In May 1945 the FAB assigned all its aircraft new blocks of serial numbers, the first batch becoming 6000/6025 and the second 6056/6060 respectively. In the interim several had been written off through crashes. With the ending of hostilities many of the grounded Vengeances were put into reserve and rotted away. By June 1946 a mere six were still operational and these survived until 17 May 1948, when they were struck off the list completely. Other then limited anti-submarine patrols they had seen no action.

Yet another ally was to become the recipient of the Vengeance at this time, and also to suffer the endless engine problems that went with it. This ally was the newly reconstructed Air Arm of France, born again with the final liberation of its North African territories and the overthrow of the Vichy government. It was appropriate that the originators of the Vengeance should finally get the chance to take delivery of their (much-changed) protégé for use at long-last against their oppressors. Indeed, it was the self-same Lieutenant-Colonel Chemidlin from the original pre-war mission who was to be directly in charge of the A-35s which served in the French Air Force during 1943-4.

On 3 March, 1943 the US Army Command announced an initial allocation of 67 A35s to the reconstructed French Air Force. They were to be delivered at the rate of approximately 15 per month and arriving mainly at Casablanca, Morocco. One of this original batch was lost in American hands (131200) Immediately the French Air Force HQ anticipated the formation of three dive-bomber squadrons equipped with these aircraft. Initially two *Groupes de Bombardement*, GB I/32, based in North

83

Into the dive! No. 12 Squadron peels off. After their initial attack on Selaru the squadron moved into Merauke, in the late summer of 1943. *(Australian War Memorial)*

Africa and at that time flying DB-7 twin-engined bombers, and GB II/62, based in West Africa and at that time flying Martin 167F (*Maryland*) twin-engined bombers, were to re-equip with the Vengeance.

On 8 April 1943, Brigadier General C. E. Branshaw, Materiel Command at Wright Field, asked the AAFRR at Nashville to supply the serial numbers and expected delivery dates of the block of 15 A-35-As to be delivered to AAF for the North African French. On 17 April 1943 a memo from Lieutenant-Colonel Barber revealed the planned allocations of the A-35 from January to December as follows: Army Air Force 1149; North African French 67 (15 A35-As in April, 15 A35-As in May, 15 A-35Bs in June,

15 A35-Bs in July, 7 A35-Bs in August); Australia 190 (all A35-Bs); Brazil 41 (all A–35Bs, 5 in July, 5 in August, 5 in September, 5 in October, 10 in November, 11 in December); and Britain 651; giving a grand total of 2098. These were broken down as follows: A-35A: DA AC 119-99; A-35B: DA AC 119-201; A–35B: AC 24 664-2730, for a total order of 3030 machines.

A memo dated 11 June 1943 was sent from Lieutenant-Colonel P. Chemidlin, Chief Air Secretary, to Colonel J. Milles, Materiel Division, Washington. Colonel Chemidlin forwarded information to the effect that the French were anxious to get their 67 Vultee airplanes as soon as possible and that the 27 modifications, as requested by the BAC and RAAF for their versions, were *not* desired on these French Vengeances. Four days later Colonel S. R. Brentnall confirmed to Vultee that the 37 A-35 airplanes allocated to the French could be delivered without modifications to British requirements and that an effort was being made to reach a similar arangement concerning 41 aircraft allotted to Brazil. The third group, GB I/17, was never ultimately to be equipped because the Vultee dive-bomber very quickly proved a disappointment in service. The engines were very frequently out of use and oil consumption was extraordinarily high (up to six gallons per hour). The troubles began even before delivery to the FAF, for they occurred during the reception flights conducted by US personnel to the French North African bases.

GB II/62 had begun its A-35 conversion during August 1943, initially using a I/32 aircraft. But this unit was ordered to merge with I/32 only a few days later, on 31 August 1943. Its CO, *Commandant* De Maricourt, became I/32's commander on 18 September 1943. II/62 was definitely disbanded on that date.

But it was GB I/32 *Bourgogne* that initally received the A-35s. The aircraft delivered were listed as A-35s and A-35As but they apparently comprised both A-35As and A–35Bs, as noted serials proved. This French unit began to fly with the Vengeance type during June 1943, under the command of

Vengeance A27-209 NH-L, 12 Squadron, under camouflage netting at Cookstown, North Queensland, August 1943, just before the unit moved to Merauke. Cyril J. McPherson, the RAAF's most experienced Vengeance skipper (standing on the wing), named this aircraft *Diane* after his daughter.
*(Cyril McPherson)*

*Commandant* Besnard. He was later to be relieved by *Commandant* De Maricourt on 18 September 1943. The initial delivery batch consisted of serial numbers 131193, 131201, 131203, 131204, 131207, 131211 to 131214, 131216, 131217, 131219, 13122, 131224, 131226 and 131231, which arrived during July 1943. During December 1943 a second allocation arrived, comprising serials 131266, 131269, 131275 to 131277, 131283, 131289, 131292, 131294, 131296 to 131298. But the unit actually used far more aircraft than this. Despite having an establishment of 24 aircraft, it was said 'to have consumed ninety aircraft from October 1st, 1943, to 20th April, 1944, mainly in the gunnery training role at the Agadir, Morocco, air-gunners' school'.

Meanwhile Lieutenant-Colonel Chemidlin, who was directly in charge of the French A-35 programme, held discussions with the US

authorities and received all the subsequent reports concerning the many difficulties. In one such report, made by Vultee Field Representative Engineer Brent towards the end of September 1943, an explanation of these troubles was given as being due to: '(a) Lack of spare parts. In fact the FAF had at that time still not received the necessary hydraulic control pieces and lines which Brent judged absolutely necessary. (b) Poor quality maintenance work by the French mechanics.'

However, much of the trouble originated *prior* to French acceptance, while the aircraft were still in American hands, and were probably compounded by the problems of sea transport from the States to North Africa. Brent's visit took place at the same time that the French Command began to abandon the idea of using the A-35s operationally. Brent listed many aircraft, 131193, 131298, 131207,

131209, 131211, 131214, 131216, 131217, 131219, 131221, 131222, 131224, 131226 and 131228, all of which were serving with I/32 and all suffering various mechanical defects. Among the problems listed were high oil consumption (up to 30 litres per hour) and sensitivity of the undercarriage to the rough secondary North African landing strips. Other documents mention 131220, 131225 and 131275 as having defects.

During October there was an undercarriage crisis and all the A-35As had to be withdrawn from service and handed over to the Vultee technicians. The A-35Bs were not affected by such failures. Among the cripples was 131198, under repair at Agadir, The next month, for economic reasons apparently, about half the A-35s had their .50 calibre guns replaced by 7.5 cm moveable guns in the rear cockpit.

A CO's report, dated 16 November 1943, read as follows: 'GB I/32 possesses twenty-four planes, of which only 25 per cent are available. Unit flew 341 hours 10 minutes total during the past month but failures of the A-35s did not permit execution of all the planned missions. There were four accidents caused by material instability. This aircraft is unsuitable for gunners' and radio-operators' training. About 50 per cent of flights were for gunnery training . . . .'

On 30 November 1943 an official protest was made concerning the continued American use of A-35s which were announced as being delivered to the FAF. The USAAF was still using 131213, 131220, 131225 and 131227 at its Training Centre at Telegma, and 131200 had been destroyed in a crash with an American pilot there before effective delivery to France. The French Commander wanted to know if in such a case the plane was still included in Lease-Lend regulations?

Deliveries recorded in early December were 131275, 131294 and 131297, which had just been assembled at Oran, while 131285 and 131290 were being delivered to I/32. In January 1944, dispositions were recorded as four with GT2/15 as target towers; two at Oran; 21 serving with GB I/32; five in service at Meknes; nine more being repaired at

Meknes and 18 being repaired at Casablanca, giving a total of 59 machines. On 22 January 1944, an allocation of spares indicated that this number had increased by one, with 26 Vengeances with GB I/32, 14 under repair at Casablanca and 20 under repair at Meknes.

A letter was written on 31 January 1944 to the French Air Attaché in Washington asking him to convey to the USAAF HQ the position on the A-35s, which was serious. It listed the cripples thus:

| | |
|---|---|
| Casablanca | 8 A-35s waiting for engines |
| | 9 A-35s waiting for landing-gear accessories |
| Meknes | 8 A-35s waiting for engines |
| | 8 A-35s waiting for landing-gear accessories |
| | 3 A-35s had just been repaired following landing accidents |
| Agadir | 2 A-35s waiting for engines |

On 2 February 1944, FAF HQ was requesting from Allied Command the replacement of the 18 new A-35s, due to be delivered in the first quarter of the year, by A-24s, as these were far more useful. They mentioned the fact that oil consumption on the Vengeance quickly reached 20 litres per hour, rising to 35 litres per hour after 50 hours' flying time, and that numerous engine changes were necessary. When the US authorities announced on 10 February, 1944 a supplementary allocation of a further 36 A-35s the French refused outright to have them. Despite this, because the French had originally requested 100 more A-24s, the Americans offered 100 more A-35s which initiated the following strong protest to the Chief of the French Air Mission in Washington:

'We ask you to strongly intervene to obtain a second batch of A-24s. US are proposing delivery of A-35s and refuse to supply A-24s. A-35s were ordered to be used as dive-bombers. Allied Command having decided that such planes will not be used above European battlefields, we have used this aircraft as gunnery trainers. But A-35s proved unsatisfactory because of extravagant oil consumption. Further — it cannot be used for pilot training since it is too heavy and not able to be fitted with dual controls. And it cannot be used by "Policing" units because of engine unreliability'.

That would seem clear enough and, as if to emphasise their point, on 7 March 1944, it was proposed to stop all A-35 flights with both A and B types. Meanwhile, in an attempt to overcome this reliability factor, an enquiry was made direct to Vultee, dated 18 March 1944, which asked if the R-2600 A5-B5 engine could be adapted independently to the A–35As and Bs. The answer they received was: 'These can be directly mounted on As and with only minor modifications on Bs. Since A5B5 or R26000-19 are less powerful (by about 100 hp) only extra precaution needed is for slightly longer take-off distances to be maintained.'

The first French A-35s to receive the A5B5 engine were 131202, 131203 and 131204. Neither of the supplementary batches of 18 and 36 A-35s respectively was delivered but the one hundred A-24s asked for *were* (and

were used over European battlefields with great success and minimum losses). Of the original order for 67, 66 were delivered as we have seen (see Appendix 3 for full listing) and replacement orders continued throughout the winter of 1943-44 to keep up with write-offs. Among the latest were those used by the Americans (131220 and 131225) mentioned earlier. By 27 March 1944 a total of 56 A-35s were in use including 14 with GB I/32 and three with GT II/15. The same number of effective planes was recorded on 17 April 1944, 19 with I/32 and two with II/15, plus a further 11 listed as being out of use since deliveries commenced.

From May 1944, I/32 began to convert to a Martin B-26 *Marauder* unit, having previously merged with GB II/62.

GB I/17 *Picardie,* led by *Commandant* André Noel was ordered to re-equip its second *Escadrille* with ten A-35s which were to be ferried partially by its own pilots, after training in Algeria, and partially by I/32 aircrew. During January 1944 the decision was taken to replace their A-35s with A-24

Line-up of newly completed A-35s at Nashville. Despite the many improvements, which made it an excellent dive-bomber, the USAAF resolutely set its face against the type for ideological reasons and the failure of its own A-24 units to come anywhere near matching the Navy's SBD's achievements in the Pacific. *(AVCO)*

AF877, an early A-35, completed with the large-type 'White Star' insignia by Vultee. *(AVCO)*

(*Dauntless*) dive-bombers. Thus, although a few of their pilots had been trained on the type, I/17 never actually *used* the A-35.

One *Escadrille* of *Picardie* was ordered to leave French North Africa for the Middle East with ten A-35s during January 1944, but the unit reported that its serviceability rate quickly diminished from 22 to 13.5 per cent and commented,'soon all planes will require more than 30 litres of oil per hour'.

It had been re-equipped with A-24s and was flying these during February, and in that same month came the decision ultimately to re-equip it with *Marauders*. The A-24s had been

used by this unit pending the arrival of sufficient A-35s and they had been despatched to Syria with them for desert practice purposes. Then they had to return to North Africa after only a few months. One pilot of this unit, who had flown both types, later commented that: 'During these long flights over sea and western desert during our travels from Damascus to Mekines and, later, from Morocco to the South of France, we were glad not to be flying anything as unreliable as the Vengeance!'

Although the A-35s could carry much higher bomb loads this advantage was negated, in this French pilot's view, by a lack of manoeuvrability compared with the old SBD: 'the A-24 was much more manoeuvrable, so we were able to dive closer and to "pin-point" more accurately . . .'.

Jean Cuny summed up the reasons for the short life of the A-35 in French service thus: 'There were troubles with the engines, but these were never as bad as on some other American aircraft that were used. I believe the French would have made the same serious efforts as did the British and Australians to overcome these and use the aircraft. It was the fact that by the time the first French squadrons began to equip with them the Tunisian fighting, in which they could have

AF907 showing the single .5 calibre rear machine-gun and other improvements. The nil angle of incidence was abandoned and extra wing guns worked in by the USAAF, who had no taste for true vertical dive-bombing. *(AVCO)*

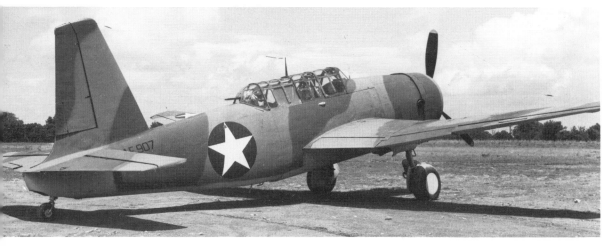

EZ856 being flight-tested over the oil-storage tanks of California; note depth of fuselage. The Vengeance was a deceptively big machine for a dive-bomber with an all-up weight of over 11,000 lb. *(Northrop)*

played a part, had ended before many French crews had become operational. Then for about a year the FAF prepared to fight a war on mainland Europe and to most of the HQ people the classical dive-bomber seemed an obsolete weapon in the face of expected German flak and fighter opposition. This consideration condemned the Vengeance as the FAF, lacking both industrial plant and sufficient experienced aeronautical mechanics, could not afford to waste its limited resources to do so much on what was by then considered a secondary plane'.

From September 1943, therefore, the A-35s were mainly used for gunnery training and from the beginning of 1944 they served mainly as target-tugs. Thus it came about that a third unit of the FAF did continue to operate the Vengeance. This was GB II/15 *Anjou*, commanded by *Commandant* Boizet. It was

originally a transport unit but among its duties was target-towing for the training of AA artillery. From January 1944 it received a few A-35s, modified for this job. Generally it possessed two Vultees but this complement was increased to four or five from August 1944. Among the French serials received were 131213, 131220 and 131225. In February 1945 the unit was re-equipped and target-tug duties were abandoned. Final use of the Vengeance (131225) by this squadron was a series of engine troubles and subsequent test flights during January-February 1945.

Back in North Africa, although most of the A-35s had been handed back to the American authorities, two were reported as still flying with the FAF at the Agadir mechanics school. These were 131203 and 131216 which were listed as being used for ground crew instruction.

In Australia, the problems were getting hold of enough machines both to train aircrew and to equip squadrons. Being closer to the oncoming enemy then any of the other Allies gave them a somewhat sharper focus on what was necessary and the urgency of supply. Those in Whitehall could afford a more academic approach, as was made obvious by a memo dated 25 March 1942 from the Chiefs Of Staff to the Joint Staff Mission in Washington. In response to Australian requests that more Vengeances be made available they stated blandly that: 'We agree we cannot press U.S. to release Vengeances or additional Kittyhawks for Australia from American quotas. U.S. Chiefs of Staff should, however, be made aware of Australian requests'. They also added that 'we should revise the allocations of British aircraft which we have made to Australia'. After adding that Canada should be asked to forgo allotments, they concluded: 'On receipt of a reply from the U.S. C.O.S. it will be necessary to explain to the Australian Government the reasons for the decisions we have beem compelled to make.'

Thus it was that it was not until October 1942 that the first RAAF unit, No. 12 Squadron, began receiving its aircraft at Batchelor Field, near Darwin. By Christmas it still had only an operational strength of 18 machines. With such limited numbers the squadron was perforce restricted to conducting anti-submarine patrols, convoy escort missions, searches for missing aircraft and Army co-operation exercises throughout the first half of 1943.

In May the squadron was ordered to prepare for a move to the forward airstrip of Merauke, partly completed by US 'Seebees', to operate as part of 72 Wing. Before this could be carried out there came a much-welcomed change of situation. On 18 June 1943, 12 Squadron finally got into action with a long-range strike by 12 Vengeances against the two Japanese fortified villages of Lingat

Aussie pilot George Limbrick was one of those lucky enough to walk away from his Vengeance crash. It was not his first mishap, nor was it to be his last, but this one he was lucky to survive with only hospitalisation after the first ever belly landing by a RAAF Vengeance. *(George Limbrick)*

George's unfortunate mount, A27-38, after he put her down on the deck *sans* undercarriage. His CO took off and flew in company while those on the ground tried everything they knew to release the stubborn undercarriage but eventually he had to take the final option! Sticking wheel legs was a common problem early on, due to the complexity of the design. *(George Limbrick)*

and Werain on Selaru Island, north across the Arafura Sea from Darwin. This was the most southerly of the Tanimbar group located between Timor and New Guinea and barred the way to the Banda Sea. It was only some 300 miles from Darwin and the Japanese feared the Allies might choose that route to outflank their main forces. Construction of an airfield was first noticed from photo reconnaissance pictures taken on 13 June 1943, which showed a 5500 ft clearing in the centre of the island. A pre-emptive strike was decided upon against the construction workers thought to be housed in the two villages.

Air Vice-Marshal F. M. Bladin called up 12 Squadron to mount a precision attack, and allocated six Beaufighters as escorts in case of interception. The island was just outside the range of the fully-laden Vengeance, but with each aircraft carrying a single 1000 lb (454 kg) bomb only, and with a fuelling stop laid on at Bathurst Island, they managed it without difficulty.

Cyril McPherson has supplied me with this detailed account of the first Australian Vengeance mission:

'We were to take two flights of six Vengeances each and there was naturally much wheeling and dealing among the crews to ensure a place in the team, but it fell to me and my fellow flight commander, Flight Lieutenant J. B. 'Berry' Keys, to make the selection. In the forlorn hope of saving any argument, I decided that I should take those crews who had been longest in the squadron and naturally had the greatest experience with Vengeances, irrespective of rank or seniority; but if I thought that my decision was going to make everybody happy, I was badly mistaken. Such was the morale of the Squadron that every crew wanted to be in on it.'

He recalls the composition of the force as being:

**B Flight**
Flt Lt Berry Keys/Fg Off Denis Holmes
Fg Off Berry Newman/Flt Sgt Ron Davies
Plt Off Alistair Bond/?

91

Line-up of A35B-1s of the French Air Force at Marrakech, Morocco. These units have just been unshipped after crossing the Atlantic aboard merchant ships in convoy and being assembled ready for use. They are protected against infiltration by the desert sands. Notice the tricolour tail-markings and the variety of other indicators. Nearest camera is 13128 (the French merely dropped the US initial character 4 and the hyphen from the original designation, i.e. 41-31282, but the last digit has also been inadvertently covered). Not so the rest, which are from the second batch of deliveries. Note also that the one nearest camera has USAAF bars still showing, while the next aircraft, 131280, had the French Army *cockade* overpainted. *(ECPA, Fort D'Ivry)*

Flt Sgt Andrew Fisher/Sgt 'Doc' Davis
Flt Sgt Bob Logan/Flt Sgt Rod Kefford
Flt Sgt Jim Purdon/?

### C Flight
Flt Lt Cyril McPherson/Flt Sgt Ken Smith
Flt Off Jim See/Plt Off 'Pop' Hodgens
Wg Off Don McKerracher/Plt Off Noel Aldous
Plt Off Bob Laughlin/Flt Sgt Neil Hargreaves
Flt Sgt Roy Pedder/Flt Sgt Joe McKenna
Flt Sgt Bill Lockley/Flt Sgt Ralph Davies

'The plan was for B Flight, under Berry Keys, to attack the Werain target at the western end of the airstrip, while my flight would attack Lingat at the eastern end. Because Selaru Island was approximately 370 miles from Batchelor airfield and the two-way trip would have stretched the Vengeance to the limit of its range and beyond, it was decided that we should land at the emergency airstrip on Bathurst Island, about 100 miles north of Batchelor, where our fuel tanks would be topped up. Each aircraft carried four 250-lb bombs and take-off from Batchelor was at first light on 18 June.

'B Flight took off from Batchelor a few minutes ahead of my flight and when we neared Bathurst Island I was surprised to see all six B Flight Vengeances circling in what appeared to be a holding pattern. The reason became apparent as we drew closer and were able to see that a shallow but thick fog completely covered the airstrip. The morning was bright but very still and there was no way of telling how long it might take the fog to lift. As all twelve aircraft circled the strip, the same thought was going through everyone's mind — would the fog delay us to the extent that we would not be able to make our rendevous with our Beaufighter escort. Such was our eagerness to get into action that we would happily have gone on without them as we did not expect much, if any, fighter opposition, but we were under orders to abort the mission if we failed to keep the rendezvous.

'We made our rendezvous with the Beaufighters at 0935 and set course for Selaru some 270 miles across the Arafua Sea, flying in two flights of two Vees of three each, or more correctly in my case, a three and a two. In perfect weather, the flight was uneventful and on sighting the island, the two flights separated and headed for their respective targets, flying at about 10,000 feet. As visibility was good, I had no difficulty picking up our target and, with no opposition, my flight formed echelon right as we approached and carried out a copybook attack, diving vertically and releasing the bombs at about 2000 feet. Although the target area would not have been more that 50 yards by 100 yards, all twenty bombs scored direct hits, a result which we learned later had astonished some of our escorting Beaufighter crews.

'As we climbed away and regained formation, I looked to the west and saw the bombs from B Flight exploding on their target, and I mentally registered the fact that mine had been the first bombs to find their target. My flight encountered no opposition, but some B Flight crews spotted a Japanese fighter which, however, made no attempt to intercept them.

'One or two aspects of this operation may be of interest. As you may be aware, there was a rectangular opening in the floor of the pilot's cockpit between the seat and the control column. This opening was approximately 10 inches by 5 inches and when the bomb-bay doors were open, it was possible for the pilot to see the ground directly

Fine aerial study of French Vengeance A35B-1 (131219) over the North African coastline. The French encountered the same initial problems with the Wright *Cyclone* engine as had the British, Australians and Indians but had not the time or the resources to spend rectifying them, subsequent to an Allied decision which prevented their use in Europe. They merely used them as gunnery trainers and later target-tugs and hacks after initial training work. *(SHAA via Jean Cuny)*

below him. Quite a lot has been spoken and written about the difficulty experienced by pilots of these aircraft in judging the exact point at which to commence a dive in order to ensure that the dive was as near as possible to the vertical. This supposed problem was caused by the fact that the leading edge of the wing was several feet forward of the pilot's position and at, say, 10,000 feet in level flight, the target would disappear from the pilot's view quite some time before the aircraft would be directly over it.

'In the absence of any other explanation, I accepted that the hole in the floor was designed to give the pilot a vertical view of his target. I could think of no other reason for it being there. In practising dive-bombing attacks, pilots in 12 Squadron had made use of this hole to line up targets, with considerable success, but of course it must be admitted that this technique could only be used against readily identifiable targets. Because of the restricted view it would not, for example, be of much use in trying to locate a relatively small target in jungle country. In the case of our attack on Lingat, the circumstances were ideal for employing this technique. The target was right on the coast and easily identifiable in relation to features of the coastline, of which I had a very good map. I was therefore able to fly north up the island's east coast and, when two or three miles from the target, open my bomb-bay doors and follow the coastline through the hole in the floor until the target was directly below me. I then rolled left onto my back and into a vertical dive, followed closely by the rest of my flight.

'I stress, however, that conditions had to be right to do this. If there was fighter activity about, for instance, a flight commander could not afford to have his head down in the cockpit, peering through a hole in the floor. It is significant that this technique was never taught nor used at the Vengeance OTU. The procedure there was to count several seconds after the target had disappeared under the port wing root, then wing over to port. With practice it was reasonably easy to achieve dives between 80 and 90 degrees by this method. In all dive-bombing attacks, the dive brakes were extended a few seconds before entering the dive.

This remained No. 12 Squadron's solitary war mission, unfortunately. An advance party of 270 ground personnel from the unit arrived at the Merauke strip on 8 July 1943, but no accommodation existed, nor had even been commenced by the 15th. This resulted in the Vengeances and their aircrews remaining in Australia, being transferred to Cooktown, on the west coast of Queensland, instead, and the routine sea patrols and convoy escort missions continued as before until September 1943. The Vengeances then finally moved into Merauke on the southern coast of Dutch New Guinea, hoping to see more action.

However, it was not to be. Their only brush with the Japanese occurred on 9 October, when one Vengeance chased an enemy float-plane and engaged it with machine-gun fire at long range until lost in the clouds. Normal duties consisted of a regular patrol beat to Cape Valsch, up the coast to Cook's Bay and back to Merauke.

Doug Johnstone described this period to me: 'Our squadron at Merauke was mainly engaged in patrol work and supply dropping. Our daily patrol of two aircraft entailed covering approximately 500 miles over the Arafura Sea in the search for any Japanese movements and north-east back along the Eilanden river north of Cook's Bay, where Japanese supply barges were reported to be hidden, and back to base. The nearest Japanese base was at Timuka west of the Lorentz river which was just out of our operational range for bombing.'

This standard routine continued until 9 June 1944, when the squadron ceased operations, returning to Strathpine, Queensland, later that same month. The aircraft were subsequently ferried to Laverton, near Melbourne.

The same month of June 1943 that had seen 12 Squadron move into New Guinea also saw the arrival of fresh batches of Vengeances to equip No. 24 Squadron at Bankstown, NSW, which initially received ten and which it operated alongside five obsolete Brewster

No. 12 Squadron RAAF spent much of its earlier career on boring anti-submarine patrols from its base at Cooktown, North Queensland. Here is an excellent view of Vengeance A27-204 taxying to the dispersal area armed with depth-charges instead of bombs. *(Cyril McPherson)*

Buffalo fighter planes. Next, No. 23 *(City of Brisbane)* Squadron received a quota at Lowoods, Queensland, to start the replacement of its *Wirraways.* Conversion training, Army co-operation and sea patrolling followed the established practice of 12 Squadron.

George A. Limbrick gave me an account of his early days with 23 Squadron. 'I eventually flew my first Vengeance (A27-233) solo, on 22 July 1943.'

With Sgt Griffin and other passengers embarked, Limbrick flew daily on high dive-bombing practices (with 88 yd error on his first attempt), Army co-operation flights, formation bombing and DR plotting tests. Among the aircraft he flew during this first week were A27-234, -253, -45, -54, -57, -28, -55 and -38. It was while flying the last, on 13

September, that he had his second crash-landing.

'The belly-landing was at the end of a DR plot which was around the Queensland interior. On returning to base I found that I had lost my hydraulics and the emergency pumping system was only 20 per cent effective. I was on R/T with the control tower and the Engineering Officer and my Flight Commander gave several orders which I carried out, to no avail. Flight Lieutenant R. Marshall took off and flew alongside me in the circuit (to encourage me I guess). As far as we knew at that time nobody had ever put a Vultee Vengeance down on its belly.

'At approximately 1630 I was given landing instructions. Bring her in at 115 mph (it was normally 110-105 mph). Having tested the rate of sink when the motor was cut at height

The dispersal area at Cooktown, North Queensland, with No. 12 Squadron RAAF Vengeances under netting. The Thunderbolt was one of two damaged in a landing accident at the base and awaiting repair at the time. Known as the 'Big fighter' an interesting comparison in size with the Vengeance can readily be made! When comparing performance figures 'experts' prefer to forget that the Vengeance was a bomber, not a fighter, but, if therefore slower for this basic reason, it had an enviable manoeuvring capability. *(Cyril McPherson)*

this worried me a little. I had acres of grass to spare so I brought her over the perimeter at approximately 100 ft and at 135 mph. As I cut switches the aircraft slowed and sank slowly. I did balloon her a bit at one stage but then sat her on her tail and she eased down on her nose and stopped quickly.

'Our CO, Wing-Commander Tom Philp, in an interview next day, told me that everyone thought I had buggered it up when I ballooned up to 30 ft but it finished up well and, had we been on ops, a new cowling and propeller would have seen her flying again.'

He resumed the normal daily flying exercises the next day. On 19 September 1943 they had a little taste of the real war. 'The squadron had its first scramble. B Flight was

ordered to load our guns and proceed to a point on the North Coast of NSW where a Japanese submarine had been sighted. Because A Flight were on leave and speed was of the essence I was fortunate enough fo fly as WAG with Flight Lieutenant Marshall. We strafed what appeared to be a submarine just below the surface and stationary. We were told next day that it had been sunk by Beauforts from Evans Head.'

No Axis submarine was in fact sunk that day, however. Throughout the rest of September and October training continued in A27-57 but then came another tragedy and also a disappointment.

'On 11 October 1943, I ferried A27-57 to Richmond RAAF base near Sydney and flew back to Lowood on 13th with a new Vengeance (A27-44), one with a new 2000 hp Wright *Cylcone*. Our early models had the 1650 motor I think. Flight Sgts Peter Cosh and Salty Jenkins had been working on their new aircraft for two days and at about 1000 they took her up on a test flight. I had gone up to the control tower to see my close friend Eric Nicholls who was Duty Pilot and Peter Cosh came over the R/T that he was going into a dive from (I think) 12,000 ft. Very shortly we heard this terrific and terrible noise of a motor so over-revved it was beyond imagination. We saw the aircraft explode about fifty yards off the perimeter road in a cow paddock. Flying Officer Bluey Wearne, seated outside A Flight office, watched the whole incident and saw something leave the aircraft and flutter away. It was later found and was the fabric from the elevators. The hole the plane made on impact was at least 30 ft deep and 50 ft wide.

'All our Vengeances were immediately grounded and on examination it was found that the fabric on a lot of elevators was torn and marked by pebbles etc when revving and testing motors. Moreover, the fabric was finished off into wind. A modification (official) was immediately implemented. All the fabric had to be criss-crossed, finished off to the rear and Egyptian tape used on metal frames and joints. No doubt there was more to it than that but I only remember these points. The only other point to come out of this was that a lot of the Vultee Vengeances had come to Australia as deck cargo and the salt-water had helped the fabric and framework to rust and deteriorate.'

# Chapter 7
# Fruition

It was not only the Australian and Indian squadrons that suffered occasionally from horrendous accidents as the initial 'teething' period of mid-1943 gradually changed into the more confident operational period later in the year. Nobody was immune. Even Don Ritchie, for all his pioneering work with the Vengeance, fell victim to chance fate. He recalls how this took place, with some irony, in the immediate aftermath of the first highly successful combat missions. 'We went up to a place called Ranchi and did our gunnery exercises there. It was here that I had one of my lucky escapes when I walked away from a mid-air collision and a three-part crash.

'We had taken off in formation. As normal, I was leading and I immediately checked my number two. He was OK. I looked over at number three and then, suddenly, there was a shadow over my aircraft, then an almighty crash! What had happened was that my number two had slid across me from above and his prop cut through just in front of my windscreen. He went straight in and there was practically nothing left of him and his crew.

'We were in trouble and there was no time to do anything other than concentrate on trying to get her down. I looked ahead. We had been climbing and there was nothing ahead of me but paddy-fields on a gradual upward slope, in steps. This helped me as it slowed us down when we struck. Even so, we broke into three major pieces on impact with the ground. We hit it hard with our belly. We had three people aboard; some of the other aircraft had four people up. I had Reg Wilson as gunner and a passenger whose name was Lawrenson. The immediate eye witness was number three, and, although it all happened very quickly, he thought that apparently, just prior the collision, number two had slumped

forward over his seat. Who knows what happened? All we do know is that he just slid across me and bang, that was it!

'I cannot recall any accident noises after the initial bang as his prop bit into us, no screech of metal or very much else about the crash. You very quickly lose 600 feet in an aircraft which was climbing steadily when it suddenly runs out of power. First thing was to drop the nose to try and get some airspeed to control the plane and see where you are going. Otherwise, up to impact all you would see would have been sky. And usually the windscreens were fairly dirty. I thank the Lord the Vengeance was a very tough aircraft. They were built like tanks; you had to really knock them about hard to hurt one as I did that day. I had a very high opinion of them in this respect, but they lacked engine power to go with it.

'I did not lose consciousness and when we stopped thought, "Let's get out of here." No pain. It was quite extraordinary. I had a bloody nose, my scalp was split and bleeding, so it looked worse than it was. Reg Wilson was out cold. That was his second time, as well as mine, of being involved in a major accident. Lawrenson was thrown out and later died of his injuries. Reg was badly broken up, his arms and legs smashed and I've not seen him from that day to this. In those days he lived at Cardington, Bedford. I walked away from it.

'After you've hit there was the thought of fire and getting out quick. I just slid the top half of the canopy back and climbed out.'

The date was 21 April 1943, the aircraft was a Vengeance II, Number 623N. Ritchie was out of action for an incredibly short time and was back flying Vengeances by 2 May. Others had less spectacular prangs, of course,

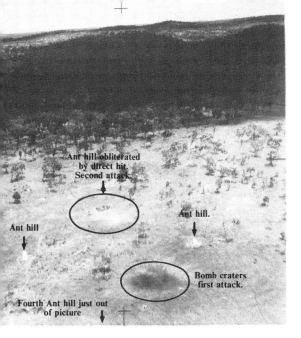

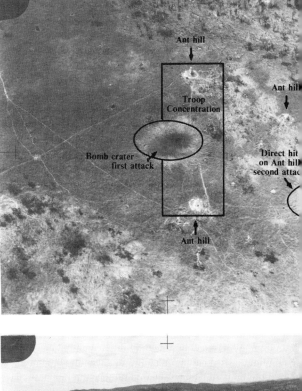

Army co-operation practice by No. 12 Squadron in Australia. Cyril McPherson took part in this demonstration of the accuracy of the Vengeance to Australian Army officers who had hitherto been highly sceptical that the Allies could do what the *Stukas* were continually doing! Four termite mounds painted white were allocated as targets by the Army. He had to hit in the middle of two of them, and try to hit one of the others in two separate attacks. These photos show the results of his two attacks.

In the first attack the bomb crater is in the centre of the target indicated but slightly off to one side. In the second a direct hit was scored on one of the remaining two termite mounds completely obliterating it. The Army were convinced! The USAAF CO in New Guinea, however, remained resolutely opposed to the RAAF Vengeance units, despite equal accuracy in real-life combat missions. *(Cyril McPherson)*

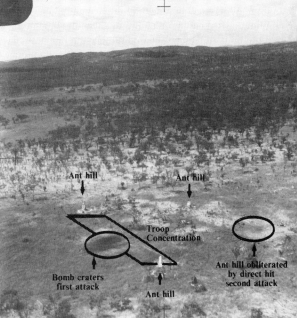

including Flight Lieutenant Henry S. P. Brooke, who was a pilot seconded from The Honourable Artillery Company. A well-educated, intelligent and well-meaning officer was how he was described to me, but on one occasion he made a very heavy landing and not even the Vengeance's undercarriage could cope!

The Squadron Medical Officer was Doctor Peter Latcham and he gave me this picture of the black-out effects and other medical problems. 'There were two medical problems which had not arisen with Blenheims. One was not complained of, but I used to worry that the aircraft were not equipped with oxygen. Targets were approached at, say, 14–15,000 ft and at this altitude human skill is impaired. Letters to Group HQ about this were soaked up with a feather pillow. The second difficulty was that some of the aircrew began to black-out when pulling out of the dive. I don't think this was ever a very serious problem. Healthy people's resting blood pressure varies a good deal from one person to another and I took all the aircrews' blood pressures to see if there was a correlation between low resting B.P. and a tendency to black-out. But there wasn't. Fatigue and low spirits seemed to be more important factors, but this is a personal impression which cannot be quantified'.

'I don't think the aircrews on the whole were conscious of the effects of diminished partial pressure of oxygen at 12,000 ft, although their skills would almost certainly be impaired to a slight extent. At 16,000 ft I think many of them would have experienced the tendency to gloom, and malaise if they were at that height for more than a few minutes. On 29 September 1943, for example, I took a trip in a Vengeance in order to experience what aircrew had to put up with and to lend some impetus to correspondence I was having with 221 Group to try to get oxygen equipment.

'As for black-outs, well, the vertical dive is tremendously exciting. On operations the gunner would be facing backwards but as a passenger I think I usually faced forwards — which was possible with the swivel seat — and sometimes we were three-up which is pretty crowded in an Vengeance. I never actually blacked out nor had the "red vision" often described. The most striking feeling for me was that of great heaviness of course. It would be very difficult to raise one's boot from the floor — a feeling of great pressure on the feet and of a dragging down of the corners of the mouth and eyes, especially the outer halves of the eyebrows.One's shoulders are bowed forward and down. I often had grey vision. I think peripheral vision closed down. But all these feelings lasted for a very short time and occurred when the crews knew they were pulling away at very great speed from the danger zone.

'I believe that a good deal of work has been done on the prevention of the effects of "G" on the circulation in the head.' As for training against it, Dr Latcham remarked that this was 'probably the practice of pulling in one's

abdominal muscles and tensing the muscles of all four limbs in an effort to squeeze blood out of those areas so as to be available in the head. It helps a little.'

As for the more prosaic problems of bombing-up the Vengeance during training, provision was made for the fitting, on adaptor brackets, of either two No. 1, Mk I or II, or two No. 2, MK I or II, Universal Bomb Carriers in the fuselage bomb bay and one on each wing outboard of the undercarriage. The bomb carrier assembly, i.e. bomb carrier and adaptor bracket, could quickly be fitted and removed as required for missions. Located in the fuselage bomb bay were the sockets for the fire-pin plugs. These were readily accessible from the underside of the bay. It was not possible to plug in the fire-pin plugs from inside the fuselage, however, nor was it necessary. The sockets for the wing carriers, however were rather awkwardly situated. One major snag the armourers encountered on the Vengeance was that all the electrical wiring ran through on conduit, making fault-tracing on any individual wire complicated and difficult to repair.

The carrier-and-adaptor bracket was secured and crutched to the bomb whilst the bomb was on the bomb trolley. A winch was mounted on the mainplane, whose cable passed through it and was connected to the adaptor bracket. The bomb was hoisted in the usual manner by winding the winch handle, but at least one armourer had to steady and guide the whole assembly fully home. However, this did not require great exertion. A linched lever locking device was operated by four locking pins. These were described as being 'not very robust' and were easily distorted or broken. Likewise, the lead springing catch, being in an exposed position, was easily damaged. None of the Vengeances was fitted for practice bombing on arrival from the States, but Mark II adaptors were found to fit on the brackets, one per wing, and Light Series carriers fitted with auto-selector switches meant that eight practice bombs could be carried and released independently during training flights.

The winch itself was the Standard Type C3

US Army Winch mounted on a winch bracket, positioned on top of the mainplanes. It had a lifting weight of 2200 lb but, surprisingly, they were hand rather than power-operated, and as a result were rather slow in action, a 500 lb bomb taking three minutes to hoist into position. Both 'B' and 'C' type bomb trolleys could be used under the fuselage.

As for bomb release, the switchboard contained the master switch, indicator lights, selector and fusing switches, and two jettison switches, and was situated on the port side of the pilot's cockpit, mounted on a beam raised about three inches above the floor. This position and layout was described by RAF personnel as 'excellent in every way'. The bomb firing switch was an orthodox press-button mounted on top of the throttle control handle, again in an ideal position, and the switches were clearly marked.

A young Canadian pilot, Bud 'Red' McInnes, joined 110 Squadron early in 1943.

'It was to be a few days though before we were to get a chance to take an aircraft up, because the squadron was plagued by engine troubles. The first Vengeance aircraft with the Wright *Cyclone* engine were just not standing up. Some of the engines indeed were just packing up after seven or eight hours of flying time. It got so that the mechanic said that the rings in the pistons were made out of swiss cheese. However, it came time to get airborne and of the six in our draft who joined the squadron I was the first one to take off an aircraft by myself. Naturally there was no way to get the feel of the aircraft beforehand, but that didn't concern me too much as I had gone through the solo first time with the Hurricane being a one-seater and so I took off on my first trip in a Vengeance.

'I did know that I was going to fly nose-up, more so than any aircraft I was acquainted with, because of the lack of incidence in the wings. The Vengeance, as you know, only had a few seconds of incidence in the wings so that in a vertical dive there would be no creeping forward. It made for an excellent bombing platform, a very accurate one indeed, but took some getting used to in the air. The other point was that no one had thought to mention to us the extremely high wing-loading. The boys who had been flying Blenheims of course couldn't do very much to help us as they were not familiar with the Hurricane's characteristics. Anyway, I took off on my first solo and had no trouble in the circuit. I cut back the throttle in the circuit as I would in a Hurricane to check the undercarriage and made what I thought was a beautiful approach, practically dead-stick, again as I was accustomed to doing in the Hurricane! However, when I went to pull up to level off previous to touch-down, I got practically no response and I was too close to the ground to recover, and I really believe that had I been in any other aircraft I would have driven the undercarriage right through the wings. As it was I'm sure I bounced at least 25 or 30 ft high. I immediately recovered from that, however, gunned the engine, then took off and made another circuit. Having been burned on my first approach I naturally brought it in with a fair bit of power and succeeded in making a very fine landing.

'I mentioned that the Wright *Cyclone* engines were giving trouble at this time by packing up after a few hours. I would not want you to believe that any of them, let us down entirely at any one item. Once they started to go we had plenty of indication in the high oil consumption and gradual loss of power so that generally speaking once they started to go you had two or three hours' flying time left in the engine so that you could avoid any unnecessary landing or getting trapped away from home unless you were really a great distance away. Another point that was strange to us was the tremendous amount of room in the cockpit compared to Harvards and Hurricanes. It just seemed as though we were inside a massive greenhouse. The greenhouse effect of the cockpit top was noticeable in flying in the bright sun in that it concentrated the heat on the back of our necks. Consequently, many of us had a khaki flap made for the back of our flying helmet to ward off the heat of the sun while flying.

'The "mushing" effect of the aircraft, although it took a bit of getting used to, was

29 May 1943. A Vengeance of No. 84 Squadron RAF banks away from the camera over Ceylon.
*(Arthur Gill)*

One. As far as formation work was concerned, several formations were tried but eventually we wound up with the box of six being one flight and flying in the double-vic formation. This formation was used right throughout final training and on operations.

'Once we were familiar with the handling of the aircraft in formation and normal flying, the next thing was to check it out and learn how to dive-bomb. We knew of course that the aircraft had been constructed for a truly vertical dive. To my knowledge, it's the only aircraft that was, because, having no incidence, the aircraft did not creep, so, theoretically, a perfect dive should be possible. There was nothing by way of a bomb sight, indeed even the gunner's sight was an American reflector type which no one knew how to use or operate. That was of secondary importance because we only expected to ever use our forward guns for strafing purposes and dead accuracy was not required. The dive however was a different thing. We wound up with a one-inch stripe painted down the length of the hood in front of the pilot. This was the only bomb sight we ever utilised.

'As to procedure, going into the dive, it varied a bit with different individuals. My own practice was to fly over the target, bringing the target up into the area of the wing where the break took place, where the wing changed its shape. I would count to three or four and then wing-over almost completely on my back, to the left if I could because I was getting better results that way. And on operations the whole squadron tended to operate the same way. On my first couple of dives on practice I just concentrated on trying to get a truly vertical dive. After a few dives one tended to become comfortable in this posture and just concentrated on the target. I think I dove maybe half a dozen times when I took up practice bombs. I went to the bomb area which consisted of concentric rings and we had observers at the site all the time and I found that I very soon became quite accurate. In June 1943 they were transferred to a field with paved runways at Digri, about 100 miles from Calcutta.

'By this time, too, it seems as though the

not too great a factor. The only other time that it was a factor, with me was when I was doing low-level bombing against what we called a ship target. This was the silhouette of a ship constructed on the ground out of bamboo and filled in with burlap sacking. On one occasion I came back with some of the burlap sacking in the bomb rack that held the small practice bombs I was using. Thus it was obvious that I was pulling up a fraction too late and the aircraft was "mushing" into the target!

'Now at this time, so far as I know, three squadrons had been issued with these aircraft and no-one, but no-one, knew anything about them or dive-bombing or how to go about it. Consequently it was trial and error from Day engines we were getting were of a much superior quality and we were having not a fraction of the ring problems that we had with the early issued aircraft. During the summer of 1943 we proceeded with practising all situations — formations, dive formation, dive-bombing, low-level, army affiliation, hunting for tanks — and on occasion would even take Army observers to see what our difficulties were and, in turn, we would go and spend time with the British Army in tanks.'

The summary of 110's initial detachment over enemy lines is impressive. On 13 May 1943, at 1500, they had dive-bombed supply dumps at Maungdaw left by retreating British forces; the attack was very successful and fires were still burning that same evening. On 19 May five aircraft attacked Kyautaw and bombs were seen to burst on and near the larger buildings of the town. At 1410 next day five Vengeances hit the rice mill and warehouses near the mouth of Satyogya Creek, Akyab, and direct hits were obtained on the targets and an AA position in the vicinity was silenced. On 21 May at 0715 four Vengeances attacked the Narigna Road bridge and direct hits were again obtained, which caused the collapse of the north-eastern section of the bridge. At 1010 six aircraft attacked a small lock on Royal Lake, Akyab, but the attack had been spoilt by cloud over the target. Two of the Vengeances therefore attacked Zawmadet village instead. At 1800 on 15 May 1943 six aircraft attacked the jail and courthouse at Akyab, and at 1500 next day the Narigna Road bridge was again attacked. Bume wireless station was the target for another six-plane attack at 0810 on the 17th. One aircraft was hit by AA fire over the island and the undercarriage was damaged. On return to base only one leg would lower and thus the crew baled out safely over the airfield. Just after midday on the 18th the same number attacked warehouses near the mouth of the Satyogya Creek but again low cloud made observation of results difficult. On 24 May at 0720 five Vengeances hit the village of Udaung, which was known to be a Japanese Army assembly area, and on the 27 May at 1810 five aircraft scored bomb hits on

the waterfront at Yegyanbyin. When 110's detachment had pulled out from its trial combat raids against Akyab Island a similar detachment from No. 82 Squadron took their place and carried on the good work.

Dennis Gibbs recalled how. 'We were now posted up to Asanol, a coal-mining town to the west of Calcutta, and were able at last to get on with bombing and operational training. On 23 May we moved to Salbani, an airfield that had been constructed near Ranchi. On 31 May we went up to Chittagong to see how the aircraft would perform on operations, and on 3 June we bombed Buthidaung jetty, the next day Akyab, and so on. On 17 June the monsoon really broke and on the 25th the detachment went back to Salbani after completing nine operations, or some 90 sorties.'

No casualties were taken at all in this period. On 3 June 1943 six of 82 Squadron's Vengeances attacked Buthidaung naval jetty and nine bombs were seen to burst among buildings in the target area. The following day saw attacks by a similar number of machines on warehouses in Akyab town and direct hits were observed. On the 5th, Buthidaung ferry and adjoining warehouses were the targets and eight bombs fell right on target. An abortive raid was launched by six aircraft on 6 June against fuel dumps at Akyab airfield, but nine-tenths cloud over the target caused all to return with their bombs.

On 10 June the new shallow dive attack was initiated by six Vengeances against the Rathedaung jetty area and buildings were demolished. Conventional dive-bombing on Akyab jail and courthouse followed at 0832 on the 11th, scoring direct hits on both buildings and occasioning the much-quoted comment by one pilot that 'as I was going down I passed the jailhouse on its way up . . . '. The same afternoon another six planes hit Padali village on the island, again scoring hits with four bombs. At 1145 next day the steamer station at Buthidaung was the target for another attack, and on the 14th the wireless station at Akyab received direct hits.

Concentrations of Japanese vehicles

concealed in the trees at Maungdaw were dive-bombed by 82 Squadron at 0805 on the 15th. A second strike was made at 1205 with a low-level attack on Japanese HQ at Letwedet, while at 1620 that evening the third mission saw eight direct hits on the National School at Akyab. This hot pace was maintained with a six-plane dive-bombing strike against enemy concentrations at Athet Narra and Sinch and shallow dive-bombing once more of Buthidaung jetty at 0930 on 17 June.

As 82 pulled out in its turn so its place was taken by No. 45 Squadron, to keep up the non-stop momentum by the Vengeance units. A detachment of seven aircraft left Digri for Chittagong on the 26 June 1943. This comprised Squadron Leader Traill ('V'), Pilot Officer Halley ('H'), Pilot Officer Curtis ('Q'), Warrant Officer Osborne ('E'), Warrant Officer Hocking ('Z'), Flight Sgt Jewell ('C') and Flight Sgt Matthews ('M'). They were later reinforced and continued operations from Chittagong until 14 July 1943, when the monsoon finally forced a termination.

Their first attack took place on 1 July 1943, against the north end of Akyab itself, with eight aircraft at 0845. Six planes mounted a second attack at 1225 on camp concentrations. The old favourite, Narigna bridge, was 'weathered out' with ten-tenths cloud on 2 July. On 9 July eight aircraft dive-bombed huts as Taugdara. Eleven bombs were seen to fall on the huts and a fire with blue-grey smoke was started. And so it continued throughout the month. One unusual mission was the mounting of a precision attack on a photo-reconnaissance Spitfire, which had crash-landed at Alethangyow inside enemy lines. To stop its top-secret equipment being seized by the enemy the Vengeances of 45 Squadron were sent in and destroyed it.

The 8th July 1943 was notable as the first-ever time that a reference to Vengeance aircraft operating in Burma was given by the BBC in London. Hitherto, Air Ministry policy had been to pour scorn and ridicule on dive-bombers and dive-bombing at every opportunity and the media had faithfully reflected this policy. The successful use of dive-bombers, with no losses and maximum efficiency, was in such stark contrast to the previous three years' proclamations as to leave the RAF hoist with its own petard. There was considerable embarrassment and it was only with reluctance that they finally admitted a few of the facts.

This grudging admission had been wrung from the Air Marshals by the actions of AHQ in India, which had signalled Whitehall on 3 June 1943: 'Propose releasing Vengeance as being operational here.' They added, 'We have not lost one Vengeance in operations and it has been able to do its job effectively and with impunity.'

The immediate reaction from the Air Marshals was predictable enough: 'Vengeance dive-bomber publicity presents many pitfalls from standpoints both of security and publicity.' They added that they considered any release of news on the Vengeance successes as 'somewhat premature'.

It took further pleading from AHQ, who stressed the amount of dedicated work the Wing had put in to achieve such results with a new aircraft and new tactic, only to be continually told via the BBC that both were considered 'obsolete' when the facts were daily showing precisely the opposite, before limited consent was finally given; even so, the dive-bomber aspect was played down and the Vengeance was termed a 'light bomber'.

As well as their own propaganda back-firing on them, the recent decision they had made not to use the Vengeance in future European land campaigns also probably influenced them at this time. This decision had been made in the light of tests conducted at RAF Feltwell during June 1943 by the Bombing Development Unit. It was revealed that the only BDU pilot with any experience of dive-bombing techniques had been posted and that these trials were conducted without him. They concluded that the Vengeance was 'rather worse, in almost every respect, than the Battle.'

As a result, the Air Ministry stated: 'It is considered that the employment of the dive-bomber of the Vengeance type would be most

A few mishaps! On 8 June 1943 in Ceylon (Sri Lanka) an attempt by a pilot of 82 Squadron to land his aircraft *through* a Cedar tree had this (almost) negligible affect on his Vengeance. *(Arthur Gill)*

uneconomical if used against targets in Europe. The use of specialised dive-bombers of the Vengeance variety against targets such as enemy transports or troop concentrations is not justified and would be of little operational value.'

From this view the Air Marshals never wavered. Back in Burma, where the exact opposite was being daily demonstrated to anyone who cared to notice, the weather began to close in, so proper dive-bombing had to give way to low-level attacks. While this inevitably resulted in a reduction in accuracy it gave the aircrew further experience in working out tactics for all situations. With the withdrawal of No. 45 Squadron there was a lull as they prepared for the next major offensive.

Meanwhile, 84 Squadron had been detached to Ceylon as a counter for the expected Japanese naval attacks. Arthur Gill recalls that this required close co-operation with the Royal Navy. 'On 19 April 1943, we moved to Ratmalana, Ceylon, for the defence of the island and to train with the Royal Navy. Several exercises were carried out at sea with warships and we bombed Gongala Rock, off the northern tip of the island, almost daily. In fact we did train with the Navy quite a bit, naval ships. And we had exercises with warships off Ceylon whenever possible. They didn't have any carriers on station at that time, but we carried out dummy attacks on other warships.'

From an examination of the ships' logs the following can be confirmed. On Thursday 29 July 1943, the light cruiser *Newcastle* was sailing from the Seychelles to Colombo. At 0740 she was attacked in turn by three Liberators with high level bombing, then by four Beauforts and finally a spectacular dive-bombing attack pressed home by six

105

Vengeances of 84 Squadron. *Newcastle* 'engaged' the aircraft with her AA personnel closed-up and took avoiding action. The second trial was against a small, high-speed target, the destroyer *Scout*, and this took place on 3 August. Finally, on Thursday 5 August 1943, the heavy cruiser *Suffolk* was *en route* from Colombo to Bombay and at 1100 she recorded that aircraft from Ceylon commenced combined air exercises on the ships at sea, which was completed at 1140.

One Australian pilot with 84, Ken Tonkin, remembers how: 'While in Ceylon we carried out a lot of cross-country flying, low-level on land and sea and practice dive-bombing with the Royal Navy. The latter was very exciting, seeing all those guns pointing at you when you were in your dive. We usually went into our dive at about 10,000 to 12,000 ft at an angle of 75 degrees plus, reaching a speed of about 350 mph with our dive brakes out and then retracting our brakes after dropping bombs and pulling out about 3000 ft. You had to be careful not to be too hard on the pull-out otherwise you could black out.'

John Ramsden also recalls this period of gearing up to attack a naval task force. 'The first time we dived I can recall vividly in Ceylon a rock we used as a target just off the coast. It was frightening and exhilarating. I can remember greying out. You went from 10,000 ft to 2000 ft; it seemed like a long time. Four or five seconds hanging on the brakes, but it seemed like a long time and the first time you wondered if you were going to come out of it. A good pilot would talk you through it. Arthur Gill was a remarkably good pilot and he talked me through the dive. Others wouldn't and you were never quite sure if you were coming out of it.'

Doug Morris gave the navigator/rear gunner's viewpoint of this period in an interview, as follows. 'In Ceylon the squadron were held ready to deal with the Japanese Fleet should there have been a re-run of the 1942 attack by the Nagumo Task Force. We practised bombing on this isolated rock in the sea and also practised target-towing for B24s from Ratmala near Colombo. The navigators could turn their swivel seats right round if we

so desired but in the operational zone we had to sit back-to-back to fire the rear guns and check astern in case we were jumped by Japanese fighters, but we never were.

'From the cockpit it was difficult to see where you were going because of the Vengeance's big nose. On one occasion, on a training flight over Ceylon, I was navigating as usual by dead reckoning. My pilot said to me, "Where are we?" and I replied, "In a few minutes we will be over Jaffna Lagoon" (on the north end of the island). My pilot didn't believe this so I said, "All right then, lower the nose and you will see it right ahead." I then crossed my fingers because we had been flying a long while and I was not one hundred per cent as sure as I tried to sound! To my relief when the nose came down there was the lagoon, as predicted, dead ahead!'

A classic remark by Flight Lieutenant Hawke during a 'beat-up' of Colombo harbour was recorded for posterity in the Squadron Line Book: 'I could smell the smoke from that chimney by the harbour. I thought it was the wireless set, till I noticed the chimney behind us!'

It was intended that 84 Squadron should also move to Chittagong, to take their turn after 45 Squadron, but the monsoon ruled this out and so they stayed in Ceylon until 18 August 1943, when the squadron moved back to India, to Ranchi in Bihar, where they continued to train, this time with the Army.

Arthur Gill was later to record how: 'By December 1943, 84 Squadron was ready to move forward to the Arakan, even going as far as to despatch an advance party to Chittagong (where they bought a large brood of hens for the squadron's Christmas dinner). Two days before we were due to move, however, the AOC No. 221 Group flew to Ranchi to say that we had been selected to support General Orde Wingate's Long Range Penetration Group (3rd Indian Division), the Chindits, and so, on 6 December 1943, we moved to Maharajpur, Gwazlior, to train and exercise with General Wingate's forces.

L. R. M. Tibble, then a RAF Sergeant, gave me this detailed and valuable description of a typical Vengeance training syllabus, as carried out at Peshawar in the November 1943-March 1944 period: 'The first part of the course at Peshawar was on Harvards, familiarisation of approximately ten hours total. There followed a conversion course to the Vengeance and teaming up with a gunner, followed by a total of some 25 hours' training.

'My first flight in a Vengeance was in the rear seat for fifteen minutes and then I was instructed to go solo, fly around and land. It was 0730 or thereabouts. The first time for early morning flying. I careered down the runway, head somewhere in the cockpit of this great machine compared with the Harvard. Airborne, selected wheels-up and looked ahead. Normally one would keep a look-out at all times and would instinctively glance at the instruments every few seconds. In view of the situation, I was a little more preoccupied then normal inside the cockpit. I was therefore astounded at, say 1000 ft, nose coming down (the nose of the Vengeance was such that direct forward vision was poor, and when climbing non-existent) as the aircraft levelled out and looking ahead, I saw the 180 degree view of the Afghanistan foothills some ten to fifteen miles from the drome, giving way to higher and higher ground and then on to snow-capped peaks in the distance.

'Then the next 50 hours in the Operational Training Squadron included a trip to release four bombs on the target, situated in open country, some fifteen miles from the drome which took approximately 1½ hours. After each dive the climb back to 10,000 ft took some 15 to 20 minutes.

'My flight, numbering thirteen men, was one of four flights passing through the OTU at the time, totalling some fifty pilots. You will know that casualties at OTU have always been a greater percentage than on operations. Two were killed in a Harvard, but Sergeant Brown was killed with his gunner in a Vengeance during bombing practice when he dived into the practice target from 10,000 ft. Numerous factors were put forward to explain the incident, one being that, whilst diving, the gunner, with his feet on the rudder bars, and with the weight released from one's seat, allowed his backside to lift, thus allowing his parachute to ease forward with the possibility of fouling the rear column socket (the rear stick was normally stowed) and it is thought that the gunner's parachute might have slid forward and fouled the socket for the rear control column. This could have impaired the pilot's pull-out. Such an (unproven) theory would have explained contact with the ground close to the target, as opposed to any initial pull-out, when the crash would have been some distance from the target.

There was nothing to be seen at ground level where the plane had impacted, just disturbance of the ground.

'Of the cockpit drill for diving I recall the following: We approached the target from a direction which allowed it to pass under the port wing (or indeed starboard, subject to conditions) and, as it appeared tight to the side of the fuselage, selected bomb doors open and allowed the target to continue towards the rear to a count of ten. We then selected dive brakes out, then made a tight downward turning and inverted turn to either port or starboard back towards the target having, of course, arranged in advance the return course to base to be adopted following final pull-out. It was essential to settle in the dive immediately to allow as long a period as possible to ensure that the entire craft was pointed directly towards the target without any slip or skid. The path of the aircraft had to align with the fore/aft axis of the craft.

'From 10,000 ft, approximately 1500 ft was used for entering and settling into the dive. The first check pull-out was commenced at 3000 ft from the 70 degree dive angle to 50 degrees. Approximately 5000 ft was therefore available for assessing that the dive line was correct, identification of target in detail and final aim and release of bombs. The time available was never sufficient to feel fully confident that everything had been properly gauged. It was really a matter of instinct. Hence the best dive-bomber pilots dived themselves at the target and reacted instinctively. Even as a fighter pilot felt that he was himself carrying out all the manoeuvres with the aid of the aircraft strapped to his back, so with dive-bombing; one felt that the aircraft was only a vehicle to help one to hit the target oneself. It will be realised that in the 70 degree plus dive angle the pilot himself was virtually standing in a crouched position on the rudder pedals.

'The gunner in the rear seat officially should have faced backwards to man the guns. Most gunners however did not like the manoeuvre of diving going down backwards and usually faced forwards, and of course yelled the thousands of feet to the pilot on the intercom. Most of us pilots always heard the three thousand foot warning from the rear seat. The rear cockpit had an altimeter, air speed indicator and of course the socket for the control column. Many pilots would pull out at lower heights, but apparently 2000 ft was quite a dangerous height to be changing from 70 degrees, or more, to 50 degrees. The constant speed of the dive brakes out was about 300 mph, so that the time of dive from satisfactory alignment to pull-out was only a matter of seconds. It seemed a long time, but was really no time at all. At 300 feet per second or more downwards the altimeter unwinds like a spring on a broken clock! Dive brakes selected on directly the attack angle

The same aircraft, AN956, showing damage to tail assembly by this accident. Note the trim tab and also the markings used by 84 Squadron at this time. *(Arthur Gill)*

was checked to 50 degrees and the drill would then be to hare for home on the deck. The stability and feel of flying the Vengeance at a steady 300 down to 250 mph near the ground was quite exhilarating and it was surprising how long the speed could be maintained with only a very slow movement down of the air speed indicator needle.'

Group Captain John Gerber, OBE, AFC, had provided a detailed account of the RAAF's training methods in this same period, which make a useful comparison with that described by Tibble as being conducted in India by the RAF and Indian Air Force, Having flown Wirraway and Boomerang aircraft during 1943 Gerber had completed a tour of duty with No. 4 (Army Co-operation) Squadron in Papua, New Guinea, and in November 1943 he was posted to command No. 4 OTU forming at Williamstown, NSW.

'Flying training was divided into two phases. The first month included refresher training in the Wirraway aircraft, formation flying and armament work. The second phase was devoted to Vengeance conversion and advanced training.

'The Vengeance was equipped with flight controls in the rear cockpit but, unfortunately for the pilots undergoing conversion, there were no trim devices. This made flying the aircraft from the back seat almost impossible except for men built like Samson! The size and weight of the aircraft required pilots in the front seat, during circuits and landings, to work continuously on the trims.

'The pilot undergoing conversion training was placed in the rear seat and given a short familiarisation flight. Then the rookie pilot was placed in the front cockpit and told to go to it. The first flights of pilots under instruction were monitored from a "pie cart" stationed at the touchdown end of the duty runway. This phase of training was usually completed without too much drama.

'The high dive-bombing phase from 12,000 ft was, however, not without incidents. The old hands usually approached the target, rolled over and down on the target and selected dive brakes out in a well co-ordinated operation. The difficult part was to

The only way to break a Vengeance! The Vengeance was an enormously tough and strongly constructed machine, able to take the greatest punishment. On the rare occasions they did break, it was into the three main component segments of the fuselage. Here are the remains of AN623 which was involved in a horrific aerial collision on 21 April 1943. *(Donald Ritchie)*

judge the release of the bomb and the pull-out from the dive. Here the old hands counted to themselves on the way down at 300 knots, released the bomb, broke the dive at about 2000 ft, and, at an angle of about 60 degrees to the ground, selected dive brakes in, and escaped at high speed at ground level. There was little margin for error. Unfortunately, new boys made mistakes, with disastrous results. Courts of Inquiry were not rare at RAAF Station, Williamstown. The usual finding was pilot's misjudgement. As a result all training was directed to develop procedures to release bombs safely and accurately.

'The culmination of OTU training was a squadron dive-bombing attack on Bird Island, a bombing target about 80 miles south of Williamstown. The squadron was usually led by the CFI or one of the senior pilots. A well-judged approach and attack could have eight aircraft in the dive pattern at one time!

'During its brief life the Vengeance OTU trained two-man crews for half a dozen Vengeance squadrons which were then on the RAAF Order of Battle. The destined operational role of those squadrons was, probably, air support, including close air

support, for the Army in its field operations. However, their full employment in this role was never achieved.'

Cyril McPherson has this to say on the Vengeance's trump card, the accuracy of delivery. 'It is a matter for regret that Vengeances never had the opportunity to demonstrate their destructive ability against shipping. With the degree of accuracy which they achieved in vertical dives, I believe that they could have been tremendously effective in attacks on shipping. Admittedly, as with torpedo-carrying aircraft and other dive-bombers, they would have had to run the gauntlet of anti-aircraft fire in attacks on naval targets, but the fact that they dived vertically and, if permitted by high authotrity, could have blazed away their six machine-guns at the target vessel during the dive, would have made the job of the AA gunners considerably more difficult and uncomfortable.

'We Vengeance pilots tended to take the high accuracy we regularly achieved for granted, and after a few practice bombing exercises, most reasonably good pilots came to expect bombing errors of no more than a few yards. To illustrate my point, take an

109

Army co-operation exercise we conducted south of Darwin early in 1943. At this time I had 35 hours' flying on Vengeances and my logbook shows that I had carried out only one practice dive-bombing exercise involving six attacks with $11\frac{1}{2}$ lb practice bombs. In addition I had made perhaps ten or a dozen dummy dives without dropping bombs.

'The Army co-operation exercise called for the dive-bombing of "enemy" positions represented by four termite mounds which, for easy identification, had been painted white. They formed the corners of a rough square, roughly 80 to 100 yards apart, and I was briefed to destroy these enemy positions. Although I was carrying four 250 lb bombs, my orders restricted me to two dive-bombing attacks. On pointing out to the army that I could not effectively destroy all four positions in two attacks, I was told to assume that two of the termite mounds were the extremities of one enemy position and to aim for the midpoint between them; then, in the second attack, to assume that one of the other termite mounds was a field gun which was to be destroyed. The exercise was carried out in ideal conditions and I commenced each dive from about 12,000 feet, releasing my bombs between 2000 and 3000 feet. In the first attack I aimed for the midpoint between the first two mounds with an error of about five yards. In the second attack I aimed at one of the remaining mounds representing a field gun and scored a direct hit, completely obliterating it. I recall that the army officers present at the demonstrations were quite impressed. In recounting this episode, I have no wish to shoot a line but merely to illustrate the high degree of accuracy which was obtainable with a Vengeance. I am sure that most of the other pilots in the squadron could have achieved the same results.'

He could not have known it, but in high circles moves were afoot to negate any such demonstrations. The hidden moves that saw the long-desired 'killing off' of the Vengeance by the RAF despite its unexpected success in combat were as follows:

On 23 March 1943, at the VCAS's office, a meeting was held on dive-bombers. A memo from DDO(A) to ACAS(P) pointed out that, as the Brewster Bermuda was not available, there were 1300 Vengeances on order and India would not require anything like that number. 'We could if necessary, divert to this country sufficient Vengeances to build and maintain four Army Support Squadrons for an indefinite period . . . .'

The War Office was advised in a communiction dated 27 April 1943 that 'The Air Council have no doubt that the decision to substitute the Vengeance for the Bermuda will not in any way decrease the value of the squadrons nor delay the date at which they became available for operations.' On the Vengeance it was stated that 'their performance is markedly superior to that of the Bermuda'.

On 30 April 1943 came the reply (D.Air to DMC) asking if they were dive-bombers and adding, 'It is desired to know whether these aircraft will be used in the role they were originally designed for, namely dive-bombing in the true sense of the word, or for low and medium level bombing as carried out by light bombers, or in both roles.' Although the DMC replied that the Vengeance squadrons would be used 'for dive-bombing, since this is the role for which these aircraft were primarily designed,' he unfortunately added, in face of all recommended advice to the contrary from the operational squadrons at the front, that 'This does not however, preclude their employment on level bombing if particular circumstances make this desirable.'

The Air Officer Commanding Tactical Air Group, Air Marshal J. H. D'Albiac (who had led the RAF in Greece in 1941 when the *Stuka*-led Panzers had cleared the peninsula in a week) and his two Group AOCs, soon killed off this plan. At a meeting held on 2 August 1943, to consider the organisation and equipment of the TAF, they 'expressed themselves most emphatically against being equipped with the Vengeance dive-bomber'.

This decision to block the use of the Vengeance was quickly followed up by the

A fine study of a Vengeance flown by Squadron Leader Arthur Murland Gill of No. 84 Squadron, with Flight Lieutenant D. J. Hawke as Navigator/Gunner, over the Mount Lavinia hotel and railway station on the coast of northern Ceylon, 29 May 1943. *(Arthur Gill)*

DCAS, who wrote to the Secretary of State for Air on 9 September 1943, confirming the decision *NOT* to employ this dive-bomber, or indeed, *any* dive-bomber, to support the Army. 'In amplification, I have placed a short enclosure on this file, setting out the tactical reasons which led us to abandon the dive-bomber type of aircraft, the gist of this note being that the fighter-bomber type of aircraft combines to a certain degree the characteristics of the dive-bomber with that of the fighter, and is far more preferable on grounds of economy and flexibility.'

This arbitrary ruling was thus made even *before* the Vengeances' greatest achievements and was adhered to in spite of them. As has been seen, the RAF and USAAF had always wished to do this and, having got their way, were instrumental in extending their will both towards the RAF and Indian units in Burma, the French North African units still forming, and the Australian units in New Guinea.

# Chapter 8
# Consolidation

The formation of SEAC (South-East Asia Command), and the setting up of the Tactical Air Force to direct the Army's planned offensive, saw the four RAF Vengeance squadrons come of age as dive-bomber units. For them the period of experimentation was largely over and now they began to apply their skills with considerable impact. In October the Allied land forces began to move down the Arakan yet again to the west of the Mayu mountains and very soon came up against fierce resistance from the well dug-in Japanese. The British were stopped and a Japanese counter-attack was launched and fighting continued until February 1944 on this front. Previous campaigns had foundered here and so the Vengeance squadrons were called upon to see if they could assist. No. 82

Squadron bore the brunt of the initial attacks commencing on 8 October 1943, mounting maximum efforts which saw, for the first time, twelve-plane boxes of Vengeances going out to the target, sometimes with fighter support.

It was here that the squadron suffered the first combat casualty of any Vengeance unit, when, on 17 October 1943, Flt Sgt R. G. Holding's aircraft was hit by flak over the target, and was observed to crash behind the enemy lines. The squadron continued to fly mission after mission into the island.

In the middle of October both 45 and 110 Squadrons moved up to Kumbhirgram in support of the Army's next probe, seven aircraft from the former arriving on the 12th of the month and 14 of the latter unit leaving Digri on the 15th. Further aircraft from both

84 Squadron over the Indian Ocean, Summer 1943. Persistent rumours of the return of the Japanese Carrier Strike Force from Singapore led to 84 being placed on readiness to repel such an attack but, in the event, nothing materialised. Much practice dive-bombing work was done against ship targets and in co-operation with Royal Navy warships at this period, however. *(Arthur Gill)*

units followed and, on the 16th, six Vengeances from 45 Squadron were in action at 1047 to attack Kalemyo. Squadron Leader Antony Traill arrived on 18 October and another attack was delivered against Mawlaik the same day. On the 19th six planes from 110 joined in against the same target. Operations during the next month can be summarised thus:

| Date | 45 Sqdn | 110 Sqdn | Target |
|---|---|---|---|
| 19 Oct 43 | — | 6 | Mawlaik |
| 20 Oct 43 | 6 | — | Myohla |
| 21 Oct 43 | — | 9 | Kalemyo |
| 22 Oct 43 | 6 | — | Kalewa |
| 23 Oct 43 | — | 6 | Indainggyi |
| 24 Oct 43 | 6 | — | Vowalumual Summit |
| ,, | — | 6 | No. 3 Stockade |
| 25 Oct 43 | 6 | — | No. 2 Stockade |
| ,, | 6 | — | Webula |
| ,, | — | 9 | No. 3 Stockade |
| 26 Oct 43 | 6 | — | Webula |
| ,, | — | 6 | Indainggyi |
| 28 Oct 43 | 6 | — | Theizang (aborted) |
| ,, | — | 6 | Tintha |
| 2 Nov 43 | 6 | — | No. 2 Stockade |
| ,, | 6 | — | Yesagyo |
| 3 Nov 43 | — | 6 | Pontoon bridge at Hpaungzeik |
| 4 Nov 43 | — | 12 | Paungbyin |
| 5 Nov 43 | 6 | — | No. 2 Stockade |
| 6 Nov 43 | 6 | — | Le-U |
| 7 Nov 43 | — | 12 | No. 3 Stockade |
| ,, | 6 | — | Basha East |
| 8 Nov 43 | 6 | — | Kawya |
| 9 Nov 43 | — | 6 | Basha East |
| ,, | — | 6 | No. 2 Stockade |
| 10 Nov 43 | 6 | — | Pontoon bridge at Hpaungzeik |
| ,, | 6 | — | Pinma |
| 11 Nov 43 | — | 6 | Basha East |

Maintaining this high sortie rate was the responsibility of the sweating ground crew and their contribution should not go unrecorded. Let E. L. Pidduck, who was with 45 Squadron at this time, record his memories of Kumbhirgram:

'I cannot recall any set-backs and the aircraft were mostly ready for immediate take-off and, whatever HQ asked for, those machines were on standby, ready to go. Without any more major teething troubles the VDB (Vengeance Dive-Bomber, the erks' colloquial term for the Vultee, sometimes used by historians in error) was no problem to keep serviceable.

'I can remember one particular instance when a ground engineer, a wireless operator, Sgt McClandish, went up on air-test to do some checks. After reaching altitude the pilot turned his head round to his passenger and put his thumb up as a gesture of something unknown to his rear crew member. Taking no chances, like a shot he was out and over the side, baling out. None the worse for his experience he was back on the squadron in a few days, treading his way through the jungle.

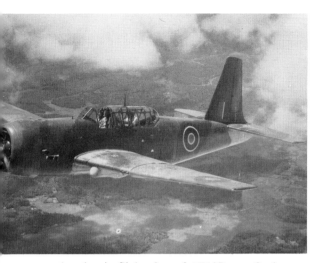

'Very few of the Vengeance aircraft were lost as I recall, perhaps about three from 45 Squadron up to Christmas, 1944. The conditions in general were not the ideal way of living, as one would find in this country. Food in camps was much the same, day in and day out, fat, greasy bacon from tins, and so were the sausages. The so-called potatoes were a yellowish colour and had the taste of a swede turnip.

'Normally the day's work would commence at 0800 but quite often it was earlier if operations planned from HQ for some reason required an early start, say at 0600. This usually meant a second sortie was planned for the same day when the aircraft returned from the first, so it was refuel and bomb-up and stand by for take-off. It was standard practice for the ground crew to ask the pilot if he had any snags as soon as he landed; if so, the airman concerned would get cracking to rectify any such troubles, sometimes it would

Another in-flight view of AP137 over Ceylon with Squadron Leader A. M. Gill at the helm. Note additional exhaust slot cut into the fuselage adjacent to engine cowling by the squadron's own ground mechanics to aid cooling under tropical conditions. *(Arthur Gill)*

Two 'Vics' of three over the Indian Ocean in June 1943. Various formations were tried out by the RAF squadrons during this early experimental period. Warship targets differed from merchant-ship targets; ground targets varied according to type. Everything was untried and the various squadron commanders were given a wide brief to form their own best attack ideas for dive-bombing with very little 'official' material to guide them other than their own experience and reports based on captured German aircrew and US Navy combat accounts. *(Arthur Gill)*

A Vengeance of No. 84 Squadron RAF undergoing maintenance under the camouflage net on the Indo-Burmese border. Maintaining a very high sortie rate under trying conditions marked the RAF ground personnel as among the best during this campaign. Earlier unreliability had been beaten largely through their own efforts and the Vengeance was able to keep up almost daily non-stop missions against the Japanese attacks. *(Arthur Gill)*

be a quick one, sometimes longer, but always getting assistance from someone on another aircraft which had no snags.

'At the end of the day's flying the final job was to carry out the DI (Daily Inspection). This procedure was every 24 hours, throughout the RAF in those days. What DI meant was that each aircraft was refuelled and checked by the engine fitter, then engine cowlings were removed and a thorough check made, plug leads secured, oil and fuel checked for leaks, all items tightened if necessary and as per book. Always a keen eye was kept open for cracks, breaks or anything that should not be. Having satisfied that all was completely OK the cowling was refitted and aircraft's Form 700 was signed up. This was a history of all the work carried out on any aircraft from the beginning of its life; sometimes an aircraft would have many of these. When all the tradesmen had completed their respective duties and signed up, then the senior NCO in charge would sign and clear the aircraft for flight. With 45 Squadron we were just a large team, everybody pulled their weight and morale was always high.'

Although no aerial opposition was encountered over the target the success of the dive-bombers finally stung the Japanese Air Arm into a retaliatory attack to try and curb the Vengeance operations. This took place on 11 November 1943 and took the form of a low-level surprise attack against Kumbhirgram airfield by 18 bombers escorted by six fighters. The enemy were sighted in the vicinity at 0824 at Silchar but the raid did not finally break over the airfield until 0912, by which time all possible aircraft were scrambled away to safety. Some did not make it, some only just, as 'Red' McInnes of 110 Squadron vividly recalls:

'Several days prior to this attack I had taken off with the full 1500 lb bomb load and was supposed to be in a formation of six which was going well into Burma. On take-off I noticed my aircraft was a bit sluggish but once I got straight and level it seemed to straighten out and it seemed OK until I went to form up in the formation and found I couldn't catch up with the rest of the aircraft with the normal amount of boost. I realised that I should have aborted while I was still in

115

Vengeance of No. 8 Squadron Indian Air Force being refuelled at a forward airstrip. *(Hugh Seton)*

flak during an attack on 13 November. His Vengeance crashed and he was killed, but his navigator/gunner survived and rejoined the squadron later. Bud McInnes describes some typical missions during this period when he rejoined the squadron after leave early in November. Both 45 and 110 were acting mainly over the Assam/Burmese border, east of Arakan, in direct support of the 17th Division.

'I did my first operation against the Japanese on 7 November, against enemy supply dumps at Basha East. You can imagine my embarrassment when I got back from my first trip to find that I had dropped my two 500 lb bombs in "safe" condition. I had neglected in my nervousness to arm the bombs. I wasn't the only one to pull such a *faux pas* but that wasn't much consolation.

'We did quite a few trips and at that time we were only dropping two 500 lb bombs. Later, we added some 250's under each wing. When our missions were successful we used to mark our logbook entries with a little strawberry. In case you are not familiar with this, a 'strawberry' was when we received word from the Army or the Navy that we had done a

the circuit, but no one liked to abort, it was always a reflection on you even if it were a mechanical problem and people were always suspicious. And where there was such a thing as lack of power it was always questionable and a bit nebulous. So I persevered but never did catch up with the squadron until we were over the mountains and right into Burma; and although I had the squadron in sight I never did succeed in catching them because every time I went to overboost, well, then my engine started to get hot.

'However, we were flying down the upper part of the Irrawaddy and I was losing more and more power so I was forced into abandoning the operation and throttling back into a comfortable setting for the engine and heading all the way home. And of course we were forbidden to drop our bombs except on the target or in extreme emergency so I brought the bombs all the way home. I was subjected to quite a bit of criticism from our CO at the time and he had someone else air-test the aircraft who couldn't see that it was so terribly out of condition, but naturally didn't try to use it in a catch-up situation. So the aircraft was marked as OK for another operation and again the pilot aborted.

However, a serious casualty was that of Flight Lieutenant J. H. Stevenson of 45 Squadron, whose aircraft was hit by enemy

A good close-up of a Vengeance of 84 Squadron in which the double-folding bomb-bay doors can clearly be made out. As described by some pilots, this special feature proved admirable in holding beer bottles in large quantities, whether in India or New Guinea! *(Douglas Morris)*

An excellent aerial close-up of a French Air Force A-35B of I-32 unit during its later days when employed as an air-gunner's training mount based at Agadir in Morocco. The old town seen below the Vultee's tail was to be totally destroyed in a post-war earthquake. *(SHAA via Jean Cuny)*

particularly good job (the opposite to a raspberry in fact). There were numerous strawberry signals received during our operations. Also, while we were doing combat ops, there was still quite a bit of practice flying. To a large degree this resulted from our having quite a turn-over in our aircrews and the newcomers would have to be broken in. By this time the OTU was operational in northern India and we were getting crews that had been through the OTU and just needed familiarisation with the squadron.

'Our main enemy at that time were the mountains. We had a good field and a good runway but we had to gain a fair bit of altitude before we could even strike out for Burma. Being the dry season though, we didn't have to worry too much about cloud cover at this point in time and almost invariably the targets were clear. After a month or so on ops we started carrying the large incendiary bombs under the wing and the squadron did have one accident in this regard — where one of these incendiaries was a 'hang-up' for some reason. Although the pilot knew he had a hang-up on return to base he landed anyway, and the bomb fell off and exploded right under his wing. Needless to say the aircraft went up in a ball of smoke and no one was saved.'

Glyn Hansford was an armourer with 110 Squadron. His mount was a three-ton Chevrolet truck rather than a dive-bomber, but he and his companions played their full part in this campaign. It was one continuing round to keep the planes flying, but some incidents stood out, as he related to me, and the one just mentioned was one of them.

'There were many acts of courage and devotion to duty. One of the most vivid was that of a Canadian pilot, Flying Officer Duncan, who returned from a sortie with a bomb hung-up, which he could not shake off at all. He attempted to land with it on, a very risky thing to do, and it blew up as he touched down. He and his aircraft were totally destroyed, along with his little pet dog, which he had taken with him on every mission.

'I well recall one instance when we had bombed-up a Vengeance with delayed-action bombs, the target being a road used by the Japanese to bring up their supplies which had to be bombed twenty-four hours a day to keep it non-operational. The pilot of the aircraft in question was Sgt Shay Waltham, a Londoner and a real character who, on this occasion, somehow contrived to drop his bomb load on the deck just before take-off! His words were, the printable ones at any rate, 'Put 'em up agin, lads'', and we did. He took off and made a successful sortie with very little time to spare.'

Back in the air, Bud McInnes had some other interesting recollections of this time: 'Another point we had to be on the look out for was, as you can imagine, targets in the jungle which were almost impossible to see and when we would be working with the Army we would depend on them to mark the target with smoke using their mortars. As you can imagine, it didn't take long for the

Another shot of an I/32 A-35B over Agadir's mountains with the historic old fort atop the hill clearly visible. *(SHAA via Jean Cuny)*

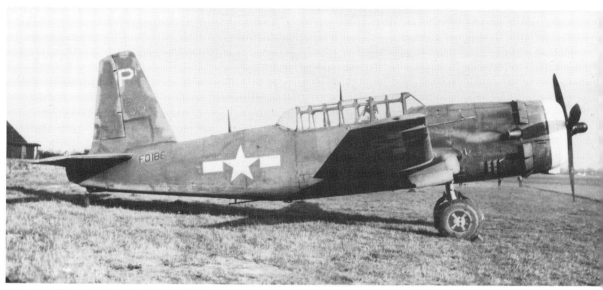

A test A-35 at the Proving Ground. Note drab olive paint scheme, with P for Patterson Test on tailplane, US national marking but RAF serial number, exhaust fumes marks on body and the white band on engine cowling to mark a test aircraft. The skull and crossbones on the wheel hubs give some indication of how the test and ferry pilots felt about the Vultee at this stage of proceedings! *(Smithsonian)*

Japanese to catch on to this, so that they would just fire smoke back at our boys so that from above we had to be extremely careful. We eventually got coloured smoke to the troops but communications being what they were it wasn't easy to get the required armaments up to our troops in the forward positions.

'On December 23 I had an interesting trip. I took off and just before I became airborne I noticed that my airspeed indicator was not working. It was too late to abort the trip on the ground at this point so I took off and had no difficulty as I was only carrying two 250 lb bombs. The aircraft was behaving perfectly otherwise and I was not leading, so I decided to go anyway, rather than abort the trip, as there was no back-up aircraft at that time. And I went on the trip and successfully bombed but, for some reason, on the way back the leader remained behind, I think he was taking photographs, so I had to lead on the way back. So I used throttle settings as the sole indicator of my speed and after landing I asked some of the other boys if they noticed anything — and not one of them was aware of

the fact that my instruments were out. I just mention this in passing to illustrate just how one can become accustomed to one's own aircraft.

The rest of the year these two squadrons continued their daily close-support operations unceasingly. During December some of 110 Squadron's Vengeances were utilised in the novel role of 'Pathfinders' for some Wellington bombers doing area bombing work.

Meanwhile 82 Squadron had moved into Dohazari airfield and continued to support attacks on Akyab, mounting up to three sorties a day against the same port and dock installations as before. A six-plane mission, on 15 December 1943, was mounted against Satyoga Creek and its shipping. This strike was led by Flight Lieutenant D. W. Metherill and, during the dive, his aircraft was hit by AA fire, burst into flames and crashed, exploding on impact with no survivors. This same day saw the arrival of reinforcements in the shape of No. 8 Squadron, Indian Air Force.

119

The Indian squadrons had continued their preparations. Lack of personnel for No. 8 Squadron, then at Charaa, was remedied by drafting in of RAF personnel. On 26 November 1943, for example, 20 aircrews were drafted in, two Australians and 18 RAF men. By 14 December 1943 the unit had moved to Double Moorings, near Chittagong, and were preparing for their first operations, planned for the following day, in a state of high excitement.

On 15 December 1943, at 1430, the first mission got under way with six aircraft each carrying a 1000 lb bomb load. The mission was to cut Japanese lines of communications at Apakuwa. Led by Squadron Leader N. Prasad, their target was a bend on the river and roadway. On approaching the target they could see damage in the enemy-held village but no enemy movements could be made out. The weather was generally good, with three-tenths cloud at 3000 ft in patches. At 1535 they tipped over into the steep attack dive from 9000 ft down to 2000 ft at 300 mph. Bombs were seen to burst in various parts of the village and close to the waterfront. All bombs fell in the target area save for two bombs which were brought back. No opposition and no flak were encountered.

Further raids soon followed this one. Next day another six-plane attack was mounted against buildings thought to be a Japanese HQ on the northern side at the foot of a hill at Point PN3030. Twelve 500 lb bombs were dropped in steep dives from 11,000 ft down to 2000 ft. One direct hit was scored on the main building and much smoke and dust resulted from the attack. Later on, huts and villages were strafed by four of the aircraft and there was again no opposition.

Attacks continued on a mounting scale in the same area, a supply dump at Thaungdara on the 17th, and at Laungcmang on the 19th which left big fires burning up to 2000 ft. Pauktaw and Kyauckaung were attacked on the 21st and three big fires started at Kwazon. Japanese positions at Ingywa were hit by a six-aircraft attack led by Flight Lieutenant Dewan on 22 December 1943, and on Christmas Eve Squadron Leader Prasad led

another attack, this time on the village of Kanyibyin. Nor did Christmas Day see any lessening of effort, Flight Lieutenant Berry leading seven Vengeances against supply dumps at Zadidaung at 0815. Eight bombs fell in the middle of the target.

The pattern continued. On 27 December six Vengeances took off at 1135 to bomb buildings at Kyaktaw, scoring direct hits, and next day came the squadron's first direct Army support mission, with Squadron Leader Prasad leading a six-plane box at 1605. The target was a Japanese forward position at Point 124. The weather was good, slightly hazy, and the leader and his vic attacked at 1710, as specified by the Army, in a north to south run and was then followed by the second vic on south to north-west steep dives from 10,000 ft down to 2500 ft at 310 mph. All their bombs fell in concentrations south of Chaung, eight bombs of the first vic bursting exactly on Point 124 and 16 bombs slightly north-west. This raid was considered very successful from reports received from the Army later. The success was however marred for the squadron by the fact that Sgt Rogers failed to return from a dive-bombing practice mission the same afternoon. It was later discovered that the aircraft had dived into the sea, killing both crew members. The body of the navigator, Flying Officer Woodmansey, was not recovered.

At 0700 on 29 December, another six-plane attack hit Kanzauk, scoring direct hits and starting fires, while on the last day of the year a similar attack was mounted against buildings at Kanwa and Linfu with dives from 11,000 ft down to 3000 ft. Again there were no casualties and all bombs hit the target area. No. 8 Squadron ended 1943 in very good mettle.

After completing their operational conversion training at Peshawar, 7 (Indian) Squadron had initially reorganised at Phaphamau, Allahabad. As with most Vengeance squadrons in India, No. 7 was termed a Mobile Squadron and was made as self-sufficient as possible. Like Harry Ramsden before him, Hem Choudhry and his opposite number in No. 8 Squadron,

The First and the Last at Northrop. First V-72 from Hawthorne in basic primer paint. *(Gerald H. Balzer)*

Niranjan Prasad (who had relieved the original RAF CO very early on), had to organise their own mechanical transport and equipment sections and train up on the Vultee the full support team, engine and airframe fitters, armourers etc., so they could be semi-independent of the Wing on which they were based. The officer establishment of 70 pilots, navigator/gunners, equipment, technical and administrative officers, threw a particular strain on the relatively new Indian Air Force units and they were forced to rely to a large extent on drafts from RAF and Commonwealth cadres for their back-up, and, ultimately, also for a large part of their aircrew establishment. Movement of such a large organisation around the vast sub-continent also presented special headaches, common of course also to the four British squadrons, but these latter had their earlier expertise to draw upon and smooth things out more readily.

Once No. 7 Squadron had collected their Vengeances they moved to Bairaganh, near Bhopal, to complete armament training, which included live bombing and gunnery. This took six weeks of intensive training and then No. 7 Squadron moved up to Combelpore on the North-West Frontier towards the end of the year. Here it awaited its orders to move east, but an uprising of local tribesmen gave them the chance to carry out combat missions earlier than expected. In December 1943, therefore, they were assigned to operate against these dissident tribesmen near Miranshah and Nowsherea.

This became known as the Waziristan Campaign and No. 7 Squadron was operating from the airfield at Miranshah, Quetta. Old Audax biplanes had been used to conduct recce flights and also carry out post-bombing assessments. Carrying two 500 lb bombs apiece, the Vengeances dive-bombed concentrations of the enemy at Sarkan and Chankani in January 1944, and precise hits were made on these villages, which caused much devastation. Flight Lieutenant Pinto, Flying Officer R. Singh and Flying Officer Goeal all distinguished themselves in this brief campaign.

No. 7 Squadron also found time to conduct exercises with the Army, in readiness, in conjunction with 84 Squadron, for the support of Wingate's Chindits. Like the Australian squadrons, the four British and two Indian Vengeance units thus stood poised, as 1943 gave way to 1944, for even larger-scale operations for which all these units were both now ready and eager.

The new penetration by Wingate's troops, codenamed Operation *Thursday*, had been mooted as far back as the Quebec Conference, which Wingate himself had secretly attended. Arthur Gill describes what this involved:

'We spent two months training and learning to co-operate with these jungle columns. It was in this period that we devised

121

our method of attack, after many arguments on the subject with Wingate himself.

Ultimately they got it right with Wingate, and when his column moved off in March 84 Squadron stood by to co-operate with his demands. They moved into Kumbhirgram airfield in Assam on 10 February 1944, in readiness. They were to relieve No. 45 Squadron initially, however, and they carried out their first dive-bombing attack proper on an enemy-occupied village a few days after their arrival in Assam.

No. 7 Squadron, IAF, had been conducting similar liaison work with Wingate up at Maharjpur. During this time it had suffered severe losses when three of its aircraft had crashed in bad weather conditions on 19 February, with the loss of two of the aircrew concerned. On 10 March it, too, concentrated down at Kumbhirgram.

In the interim, Nos 45 and 110 Squadrons had carried on their work indefatigably. This round of attacks opened on 17 January, with heavy strikes against the Japanese stronghold at Kyaukchaw. Twelve Vengeances of 110 Squadron hit this enemy position at 1518 and were followed 17 minutes later by another dozen from 45 Squadron. The same pattern could be seen the following day with the railway station at Wuntho as the target; 110 Squadron attacked with 12 planes at 1425, but the follow-up by 12 from 45 Squadron was aborted due to bad weather over the target. On 19 January 12 Vengeances from 45 attacked Mawku and on the 21st 11 from 45 and a dozen from 110 were sent against Pinebu. Next day the same target was hit hard by a further ten planes from 45 and eight from 110. On the 27th six planes from 45 dive-bombed Mawlaik.

This last operation was 45 Squadron's swan-song as a dive-bomber unit, unfortunately. On 24 January they had received orders to stand-by to move out to Yellahanka as from 1 February to convert to twin-engined de Havilland *Mosquito* aircraft. In respect of this conversion, orders were received from Air Command SEAC that Squadron Leader Traill was to report at once

to Delhi. This led to the first of two tragedies which marred the final days of 45's Vengeance operations. Anthony Traill and Flying Officer D. French took off at 0730 that day for Alipore in Vengeance AN656. Just under three hours later the stunned squadron received the news that this aircraft had crashed near the Ghagra River and both men had been killed. This was a heavy blow, and on 29 January Squadron Leader D. S. Edwards arrived from 189 Wing and later assumed command of the Squadron.

On the last mission on 27 January, only five of the six aircraft despatched returned. 'L', piloted by Pilot Officer H. C. Jewell with Pilot Officer K. Bottrill, was last identified overflying Kumbhirgram airfield and heading north-west; nobody knew why. Late the following night a report was received from Group that an aircraft, thought to be a Vengeance, had crashed at Nowgong at 1745 the previous evening. Jewell had been killed but Bottrill had baled out safely. Thus ended sadly a most successful tour of duty by this famous old squadron, and its association with the Vengeance. No. 110 carried on as before, as Bud McInnes recounts: 'Most of our trips involved one Flight, or six aircraft, but sometimes we went out as a complete squadron with twelve aircraft and have two Flights of six but only rarely did I take part in a really large raid which involved the whole Wing on a single target. In general, considering the whole tour of operations, we were lucky. As I mentioned before, the Japanese were short of aircraft, both bombers and fighters; the front was scattered over such a large area that very seldom did we ever run into even medium — and never did we encounter heavy — flak, so that ground fire on strafing runs and so on was the most we ever had to contend with. Thus we had very few casualties and to a large degree this was attributable to the sturdiness of the Vengeance aircraft. I did 66 operational trips in the six months we were at the front without a scratch.

'I think, like most people that fly in aircraft any length of time, if you love flying then you learn to love the aeroplane. She was slow, cruising at 180 mph, and we had no protection from underneath at all. One result of this however was the fact that our formation flying became so accurate even the Hurricane boys used to say they could not see how we could maintain such accurate formation, even during attacks when they would come right in. And we got pretty good at manoeuvring, especially if we only had a box of four. A box of six was not quite so manoeuvrable and, frankly, if I had ever had my say in the matter we would have flown boxes of four at all times, but the powers-that-be didn't see things that way. As to the manufacturing of the airplane, when one considers that Vultee only designed and built the aircraft after the *Stuka* had become so notorious in Europe, then I think they came up with a good product. It was no reflection on them that the *Cyclone* engine goofed up in the early stages.'

'Curly' Keech flew on another strike in Vengeance 'V' for Victor. Once more the dives were made accurately and direct hits were again registered, but there was some light flak hosing up to meet them this time. Keech's plane never pulled out of its dive and the distinctive oily burst of the Vengeance impacting later showed up clearly on the photographs of the strike, amidst the normal bomb explosions on the target. Both crew members were killed instantly, their loss being recorded as 'possibly due to AA fire from the ground . . .', although they would never be certain. Watkins had a small black and white mongrel called Snaggles with him, as he did on most missions.

Two dozen Vengeances, 12 from each squadron, went out on the 8 March 1944, and hit Sakhan. Next day, owing to the change in the tactical situation on 4 Corps' front, both 84 and 110 Squadrons were placed at the disposal of 23 ASC (Army Support Command). This brought forth a comment in the Wing's Record Book to the effect that 'It is hoped that the lessons learned when this Wing were last working for the ASC will be remembered, viz. that it is unfair for Vengeance pilots to be given pin-points in the jungle as targets without any photographs or smoke indication.'

Le-U was the target on the next combined attack by the Vengeance squadrons, both mounting two attacks each this day, with 22 machines from 110 Squadron and 23 from 84 Squadron. On the 11th the targets were more diverse, 84 Squadron striking at Gwengu and Nyaungintha, with six planes on each mission, while 110 was hitting Nanbon and Tanga with the same numbers of aircraft.

Bob Browning from Christchurch, New Zealand, described for me the training and the subsequent operations from a WOP/AG (Wireless Operator/Air Gunner's) point of view. 'I remember our first dive-bombing exercise. We climbed to 10,000 ft and the Controller then said, 'Yes — You may bomb;

The last Vengeance of the British order is wheeled out of Northrop's hangar. *(Gerald H. Balzer)*

You may bomb now.' A wing-over and down we went! Hugh was very intent on the hitting, lining up a yellow painted line on the engine cowling with the bullseye of the target. Facing forward myself this time I was able to see the target but was rather alarmed at the speed at which the altimeter was unwinding and the airspeed indicator was winding up! Then, suddenly, wham!, out went the dive brakes and 'Shiver my timbers' did she jar, but she still held together. 'Christ', Hugh said, 'I won't do that again.' The air brakes were like flaps with holes in them, they were extended at the time of the wing-over and held the

Northrop test pilot Dick Rinaldi in aircraft with USAAF pilot Major C. R. Douglas on wing.
*(Gerald H. Balzer)*

aircraft in a controlled dive around 300 mph. I would say the Vengeance was a very rugged plane and I myself do not recall any engine failures either in practice or on actual operations. A tribute to the marvellous and dedicated ground-crews of our squadrons, the unsung heroes behind the scenes who kept the aircraft always ready to strike'.

'On ops many incidents come to mind, even after all these years. Once, we were going in on a rare low-level attack, much more dangerous than a proper dive attack, kind of skip-bombing, with the three Vengeances going in to the target in waves, three abreast. On the final run-in I saw the aircraft on our right go in, slithering along the ground, saw the tail fin break off and then a big orange explosion. Something zipped past my helmeted head, our own plane lurched violently and a large, jagged hole appeared in the left wing. A man could have crawled through that hole but luckily it was outboard of the wing fuel tanks.

'A typical day's work in the life of a Vengeance Air Gunner/Navigator at this time would be something like this. The crews would be in the readiness hut or *Basha*, reading, dozing or eating, when the bell would summon us to the briefing hut, where Major Cottan would show the pilots the target positions on the map and inform us of the colour of the smoke and pattern of markers the Army would be using that day. You strapped on your seat pack and climbed up to your seat. After baking out on the strip for several hours the Vengeance would almost burn your fingers at a touch. When seated inside it was like being in an oven and streams of sweat would pour down your back, your legs and face, but it was good when the prop started up. You pulled your helmet off and stuck you head out to cool.

'Take-off and climb up to 10,-12,000 feet, then it was as cold as charity and the sweat was like ice on your body. One searched the sky constantly for enemy aircraft. Once the formation was over the target we circled around like a bunch of hawks until it was properly identified. Then a wing-over and down we would go. If you were the first in line, looking back you would see the rest of the flight strung out behind and above you in a straight line as they followed you down vertically. The pilot would be 'on the target' at about 4000 ft and bombs were released shortly after, it being pulled out of the belly on a fork that kept it clear of the propeller arc whilst the aircraft was still vertical.

'As we pulled up and away you could look back and see exactly where the bombs had hit. The flight then made a wide circle and formed up in loose formation before setting course for home. On the way back the pilots were told to open their bomb doors again and one plane swung out of formation under the rest while his gunner checked their bomb-bays for any 'hung-up' bombs. This rule was introduced in our squadron after one plane returned to base with a live 500 lb bomb loose in the bomb bay. The chief air armourer defused this as soon as it was revealed by the slowly opening bomb-bay doors. A close thing!'

# Chapter 9
# Confirmation

By April 1943, the Royal Australian Air Force was at last starting to receive numbers of Vultee Vengeances, which it classified as the A27. However, obtaining them and utilising them were two different matters, due both to shortage of trained aircrew and the serviceability problems. By the end of this month out of 108 Vultees delivered only 18 were serviceable and ready for operations; nine-tenths were still classified as temporarily unfit for operations.

At 4 OTU the training team being built was one of great expertise. Between October 1942, when it was set up, and May 1944, when it was disbanded, it trained a large number of dive-bomber crews. Although the composition of the team changed as instructors left to join units and were replaced, many of the original members carried on for much of this period, and were nicknamed 'The Vultures'. Many famous Australian dive-bomber pilots passed through their ranks: Doug Johnstone, Cyril McPherson and, of course, John Gerber. The latter recalls one of his companions, Flight Lieutenant H. Berry Newman, whose recent tragic demise left a huge gap in the RAAF's veterans' ranks.

'Flight Lieutenant Newman was already an experienced *Wirraway* and Fairey *Battle* pilot when he was transferred to Vengeance aircraft when they were first introduced into the RAAF Order of Battle. He remained in Vengeance squadrons and the OTU until the aircraft were withdrawn from service. During his service in Vengeance units Berry accumulated more hours in Vengeance

**Night working at Hawthorne. Engine testing under arc lamps on A-31 production line.** *(Gerald H. Balzer)*

The V-72 crating line for overseas despatch at Northrop's. *(Gerald H. Balzer)*

aircraft than almost any other pilot in the RAAF. In fact only Mac, as Cyril McPherson was known, flew more Vengeance hours, 603 as against Berry's 580 hours.'

Other 'Vultures' included Flight Lieutenant Keith Gulliver, Squadron Leader Douglas McKay, Squadron Leader Dick Wallace, Flight Lieutenant Pat Scandrett and the Chief Gunnery Officer, Flight Lieutenant Norman Collet. Training was of a high standard.

On the supply side things were not so well advanced. Great efforts were made by the Australian Minister for External Affairs, Dr Herbert V. Evatt, to wring more Vengeances out of 'Hap' Arnold, but he got short shrift at that time. In the event only an additional 34 Vengeances were thus acquired from the American 1943 allocations. By the end of the war, it is true, the RAAF was to receive 342 Vengeance Mks I, II and IV, out of the 400 it required. These were received as 15 in 1942, 227 in 1943 and 100 in 1944. Of those delivered, A27-400 to A27-422 were listed as — 'not suitable for operations'. A further 56 were later to be cancelled before shipment.

Northrop's crate test set-up, for V-72 shipments, left side. *(Gerald H. Balzer)*

Those received were assigned serials in the following ranges: A27-1/99; A27-200/321; A27-400/422; A27-500/549; A27-560/566 and A27-600/640.

Some American historians have attributed many of the accidents to inexperience or mishandling rather than to any basic fault in the power-plant itself. Certainly in India it was found that the unique 'dead-air' conditions there, similar to those found in certain parts of Australia, coupled with pilot caution, could lead to a high stall risk and may thus have contributed to the high accident rate experienced. This was spelt out by Vultee Rep. Spencer J. Leech in a memorandum dated 21 May 1943.

'It has come to notice that in at least two specific instances recently pilots have had difficulty in obtaining a satisfactory and safe initial climb after take-off. In both cases the trouble occurred in relatively dead air, towards the middle of the day when temperatures were high. It is felt that this condition is dangerous, that it results from a misunderstanding on the part of the pilot and that it can be remedied and/or avoided.

'In both cases the take-off was perfectly normal. After retracting the undercart (sic) the pilots throttled back to 30 inches of boost and 2300 and 2100 revs, respectively, endeavouring to climb at this power with an air speed of 110 to 120 miles per hour. Periodically they would try to increase the speed by dropping the nose, but would settle so rapidly that they immediately had to resume a climbing position to prevent crashing. They both complained that in this condition it took them twenty minutes to gain a thousand feet of altitude. Thereafter they were apparently able to achieve a normal climb.

'Both pilots arbitrarily reduced throttle after retracting the landing gear, regardless of land speed. Their commendable motive for doing so was to save wear and tear on the motor. Under normal conditions the airplane would behave satisfactorily, continuing to gain speed and to climb. It must be pointed

Another ground view of a No. 12 Squadron Vengeance at Cooktown in August 1943. This one is *Biddles* A27-211 (ex-AN543), which survived the war. *(Cyril McPherson)*

out, however, that 110 to 120 mph is a critical speed for this aircraft. It provides ample control in a gliding attitude and tests performed by this writer indicate that in an emergency the airplane may be climbed at this speed at FULL POWER for the purpose of clearing obstructions, etc. None the less at this speed in a climbing attitude and at REDUCED POWER the aircraft is dangerously close to a power stall. In these particular cases the air was hot and dead, and it is obvious that a partial power stall resulted. While these, and perhaps other pilots, have gotten away with it, it is at best an unpleasant experience and under other conditions, such as turbulent air or the necessity for turning, might result in a serious accident.

'If and when this condition recurs the correction is simple; merely put the propeller in full fine pitch and open the throttle fully, holding it there until the ship has gained *at least 140 mph* airspeed, at which time normal power may be resumed. Better still, when it is felt that this condition may be encountered due to air conditions, heavy load, etc, leave the throttle open during take-off until 140-150 mph is reached. It won't hurt the engine as much as an accident would!'

Leech concluded: 'The desire of a pilot to baby his engine along is a very fine idea, this writer is all for it. But there is apparently a tendency to overdo it as there have been shy and bashful hints that other chaps have had the same trouble. Also it might be pointed out that slow speed climbs are conducive to high head temperatures so the net gain in throttling back before a safe and proper speed is reached is nil. It takes only a few seconds more at full throttle to get 140 instead of 120 mph.'

Similar instructions were given with regard the other fault initially complained of, concerning the sticking of the Vengeance's undercarriage. George Limbrick with 23 Squadron noted this and his logbook contains the official remedies to this condition. There were three major faults identified.

(a) Failure of the warning devices when the throttle was closed: The solution here was to place the selector lever into the emergency position and engage the power valve. When

Good close-up detail of the above and below wing dive brakes extended, as RAF fitters of No. 84 Squadron set to work between sorties. *(Arthur Gill)*

the selector lever was seen to spring back into the normal 'down' position, when the legs overrode the locking-pins, this indicated that at least one leg of the landing gear was down and locked. The indicators would show if both were down. The selector was then moved to the emergency position.

(b) Indicators unserviceable and did not move forward when undercarriage 'down' was selected and hydraulic power control was pressed: The normal lowering procedure was

An aerial view showing the dive brakes extended prior to the attack dive, this being No. 12 Squadron RAAF. *(Cyril McPherson)*

An aerial shot of the legendary 'Ye Boss', one of the most famous of the Australian Vengeances, inscribed with the renowned YGOTIADKWIK. *(Douglas Johnstone)*

completed and the jolt of the undercarriage being released and the reduction in speed would indicate the wheels had gone down. If the undercarriage was not dropping from the locked position, due to fouling some part of the aircraft, or if the hooks were not releasing properly, all pressure in the hydraulic system could be released by unscrewing the emergency release cock. The aircraft was then rocked violently in the fore and aft and lateral planes. If this was successful in removing the obstruction the selector could be placed in the emergency position and tested for correct locking.

(c) If the selector lever could not be moved into the emergency position and the warning devices were indicating that the undercarriage was not locked down this indicated that the locking pins were damaged, a common fault, or that dirt had got in to prevent them operating: The undercarriage lowering procedure was repeated and endeavours would have to be made to force the lever into the emergency position, rocking the aircraft laterally while doing so. If it still did not clear then all that was left was a belly landing. George Limbrick survived it, others were not so fortunate.

For those squadrons that did equip with the Vengeance there was, initially, little action to enjoy. In April 1943 there was the first of several 'invasion' scares concerning the movements of the Japanese fleet. Plans were readied to counter-attack should full-scale landing take place in the vicinity of Darwin. The earlier massive Japanese carrier strike had not been forgotten and, like 84 Squadron, in Ceylon at this time, 12 Squadron RAAF, under Flight Lieutenant (later Squadron Leader) J. B. Hooper, was one of several units standing by on full-scale alert at Batchelor field, south-west of the city, but in the event were not called on as the threat remained only that of air raids.

Likewise, the only activity that disturbed the early days of Nos 23 and 24 Squadrons were the routine patrols over the coastline. Most exciting was the 'flap' described by George Limbrick concerning the attacks by a Japanese submarine on 4 June 1943. The following day had seen the placing on the alert of a striking force of two Vengeances of 23 Squadron and four of 24 Squadron but no further sightings were received of the enemy and they remained firmly on the deck. On 4 August 1943, a Vengeance of 12 Squadron

(AN 561) from Cairns engaged in anti-submarine patrol work had to make a forced-landing at Ruby Reef and its crew were rescued by a *Catalina* flying-boat.

In truth, with their short range and limited crew-members fully occupied with their own duties and not able to maintain a continual watch, the Vengeance was far from being the most suitable aircraft for these duties and only a shortage of other types led to their protracted use in this wasteful manner.

For all this, the Vultee Vengeance was far from being the 'outmoded and ungainly machine' claimed by one Australian historian, nor were all Douglas *Dauntless* pilots as scornful of its merits as the French flyers. For example, George Limbrick remembers how, 'In September 1943, the Squadron was visited by Major Robert Richard, US Marine Corps, who was a Douglas *Dauntless* dive-bomber pilot (he had served with VMSB on Gaudalcanal and had helped sink the Japanese battleship *Hiei* the previous year). Wing Commander Tom Philp took him up in a VV and gave him a display of aerobatics and dive-bombing that he thought was "incredible". He himself later flew a Vultee and told us he enjoyed it immensely and that his stay with us had been most enjoyable.'

This reflected earlier comments made during a trial flight at Nashville by Vultee test pilot, Harold Kincheloe, also a former US Navy pilot, 'She handles as well as a Pursuit' and by Lieutenant W. D. Carter, another Guadalcanal and *Dauntless* veteran, who said after a trial flight that the Vengeance was a much-better dive-bomber 'than anything the Navy currently is flying'.

Flight Lieutenant Cyril J. B. McPherson clocked up 603 hours of Vengeance flying time with 12 Squadron, 4 OTU and with a

No. 23 Squadron at the airstrip at Nazdab, New Guinea, in the special SWPA markings. Highly successful operations were conducted by No. 77 Wing from this hastily constructed system of airstrips before their abrupt termination due to some strange American policy decisions.
*(Australian Air Force Official via Chris Shores)*

An RAAF Vengeance Mk IV (A27-600) of No. 7 OTU at Tocumwal, NSW, April 1945. From this unusual angle the large nose of the Vultee is emphasised. *(Cyril McPherson)*

Target Towing and Communications Flight at Tocumwal, NSW. He is therefore able to speak with some authority on the Vengeance's true merit. He told me: 'As far as I am aware I had flown more hours on Vengeance than any other RAAF pilot, having flown them from their introduction into the RAAF until the end of the war, and I can boast of being the first pilot to bomb a Japanese target in the South-West Pacific theatre in a Vengeance. I also had considerable experience in instructing on the Vengeance, having been O/C of the Advanced Training Flight at Williamstown. In my opinion the Vengeance was an excellent, effective and reliable aircraft, but the media in Australia never gave it a fair go for some reason. Almost universally such comments are made by people who had never flown Vengeances or had any close association with them whatsoever. The reaction amongst most former Vengeance

pilots is very different, especially those who flew them in squadron service.'

'With *Kittyhawks* of No. 86 Squadron, RAAF, we did not lose one Vengeance, whereas in the same period the *Kittyhawk* unit lost, if my memory serves me, at least six aircraft — and none of these through enemy action. The *Kittyhawk* was a jolly fine aeroplane — but if the Vengeance is to be condemned on its accident record, which in my view was extremely good, so then must virtually all other types of aircraft in the RAAF during World War II.

'As a matter of interest, the Mark IV Vengeance was introduced to the RAAF after the Vengeance squadrons were withdrawn from operational areas, and consequently it did not see active service. This model was much lighter on the controls than its predecessor, and it did not fly in the nose-up attitude to which I have referred. However, I do not know whether its diving characteristics were as good as its older brother's because the dive brakes had been disconnected on those I flew at No. 7 OTU, Tocumwal, during 1944-45.'

Famous Fleet Air Arm test pilot Captain E. M. 'Winkle' Brown flew more different types of aircraft than any other pilot during the war, so his viewpoint deserves respect also. He confirmed to me that: 'True dive-bombers like the Ju 87, the *Dauntless* and the Vengeance were of course always superior in that role to fighters adapted for dive-bombing as a secondary role. The Vultee Vengeance I was a poor aircraft, which, by modification to become the Vengeance IV, eradicated all the original faults, until it was probably the nearest in efficiency to the Ju 87.'

The Royal Australian Air Force No. 24 Squadron, commanded by Squadron Leader Barton Henry moved into Tsili Tsili on 2 September and started operations from there one week later.

On 18 September 14 dive-bombers made attacks from 24 Squadron dived to 1400 ft and

500 lb bombs were used against gun positions, bunkers and occupied buildings at Finschafen. Kakakoo and Salankau were hit on 19 September 1943. A Japanese radio-location station on the islands of Kaial and Wonam in the Tami Group was hit six times, and completely demolished. During the Australian 9th Division's amphibious landing Satelberg, on 28 September 1943, a force of 12 Vengeances from 24 Squadron hit targets at Langemak Bay. On 1st October they were again in action here.

Between 6 and 9 October 1943, 24 Squadron was called on to make repeated dive-bombing attacks to halt Japanese attacks on the Australian 2/17th Battalion at Kumawa and, on the 18th and 19th, repeated bombing was needed to stop the enemy assault. 77 Wing was initially to go to Gasmata in Southern New Britain and, from there, attack the bypassed Japanese garrison there, but in January 1944 the main parties of Nos 21 and 23 Squadrons embarked aboard ship at Brisbane.

The wing began moving into Nadzab,

In a jungle-girt clearing on one of Nadzab's strips a white-tailed Vengeance sends up clouds of dust as she revs up in preparation for yet another sortie. *(Australian War Memorial)*

Classic pose of an early Vengeance under test entering the dive (in this case about 70 degree angle). Note navigator is facing forward. *(Smithsonian)*

Vengeance combat losses were minimal, in marked contrast to dire forebodings and predictions. One of the very few was No. 24 Squadron RAAF's A27-83, piloted by Hank Morgan. He was forced to force-land with engine trouble 22 miles up the Markham Valley close to Kiapit. He can be seen signalling to his circling companions by Aldis lamp. A Piper Cub was despatched to pick up him and his navigator and they were back in the mess at Nadzab by 1300 the same day. *(RAAF Official)*

Northern New Guinea, at Newton Field, in the Markham Valley.

Number 21 Squadron began to move from Lowood with No. 23 in December 1943 and into Nadzab in January 1944.

No. 24 *(City of Adelaide)* Squadron led by Squadron Leader B. Honey landed the 16th. Their future targets were enemy strongpoints and gun positions holding up the advance of the Australian 5th and 7th Divisions moving along the Huon Peninsula in New Guinea, meeting fanatical Japanese resistance from their 20th Division, against this fortress

position know as Shaggy Ridge that the RAAF Vengeances commenced their precision attacks with No. 24 Squadron on 17 January 1944. The Vengeances of 24 Squadron delivered some nine tons of bombs on this position, in their initial attacks. 12 aircraft under Wing Commander B. Honey, attacked a 5000 ft high ridge leading at right angles up to Kankiryo itself.

Some 22 500 lb bombs with 45-second delay fuses were deposited on the target, which enabled the 2/10 Battalion to clear the saddle.

Led by Wing Commander Honey, 11 of 24

Squadrons Vengeances took off at 0950 and delivered a further accurate consignment of bombs on 22 January. On the 23rd the squadron attacked targets near Kesawai. By evening of the same day the battle for Shaggy Ridge was over. On the 26th 11 Vengeances dive-bombed the village of Ngada.

On 29 January 11 aircraft dive-bombed enemy positions at Orgoruna.

On 31 January 1944, 24 Squadron made a strike on the Gori Bridge at Bogadjim.

They pressed in down to 800-400 ft made four direct hits, demolishing the bridge and two gun positions alongside.

At 0900 on 7 February, 24 Squadron's Vengeances attacked the Gori River bridge, but it was obscured by cloud.

On 11 February 1944 six planes from 24 Squadron, under Squadron Leader R. L. Lewis, and six more from 23 Squadron on their first combat mission, were led by Wing Commander T. R. Philp, DFC, attacked Yoga Yoga village. They scored several direct hits.

On 12 February 12 Vengeances of 23 Squadron and six from 24 squadron attacked the area between Bridges 13 and 14 on the Bogadjim road. Attacks were made the next day on the villages of Tarikngan, Gwarawan and Yoga Yoga, youth of Saidor. On Sunday 20 February, the dive-bombers' hit a Japanese supply dump at Aiyau, with eight bombs and destroyed it. On the 21st attacks were made on Saidor.

No. 21 Squadron had meantime arrived at Nadzab on 18 February, making its debut on 22 February 1944 when three of its aircraft joined with 23 and 24 Squadron machines in attacks on Japanese barges on the Wagol River, Madang. Saidor was attacked next day with 19 direct hits. On 24 February 23 and 24 Squadrons attacked Japanese anti-aircraft positions located at Hansa Bay, Cape Gloucester. Two Vengeances were lost to AA fire. Flying Officer N. G. Burnell's machine, with Captain W. P. Watson, Army Liaison Officer as passenger was hit by AA fire, and crashed into the sea. Flt Sgt F. G. McDonald, with Flying Officer C. McAllister as his observer, went down just off the coast and they were never heard of again.

Madang and Alexishhafen were hit on 27 February 1944 and on 28 February 24 Squadron attacked Madang strip while 21 and 23 Squadrons hit Alexishhafen. The next day all three squadrons bombed supply dumps at Madang.

# Chapter 10
# Vindication

Along the Indo-Burmese border in the spring of 1944 a whole series of intertwined battles were now under way, all of which required the specialised support of the five (once No. 45 Squadron had been withdrawn) remaining Vengeance squadrons. Engaged in the Arakan campaign were Nos 82 and 8 (Indian) Squadrons, as components of 224 Group under Air Commodore A. Gray. They were an essential part of 167 Wing as the Allied armies moved slowly towards Maungdaw and Buthidaung against fierce resistance. Nos 84 and 7 (Indian) Squadrons had been trained up to support Orde Wingate's Chindits but, as we have seen, they had also become sucked into the defensive fighting around the Imphal and Kohima 'boxes' as the Japanese launched a powerful invasion across the plain against the dug-in 14th Army under General Slim. With 110 Squadron they formed 168 Wing under 221 Group (Air Commodore H. V. Rowley) and were forced to divide their attentions between both forces, attack and defence. Between March and May 1944, therefore, dive-bombing missions all along this blazing front rose to a climax.

Uncovering a Vengeance of an Indian Air Force squadron, on a rain-sodden quagmire of a forward airstrip ready for another busy day. Vengeance units were flying up to four sorties a day during the long crisis of the Kohima and Imphal battles and maintained this impressive flying total despite deteriorating weather conditions. A far cry from early engine problems. *(Imperial War Museum)*

From 1 January to 3 February 1944, the two Vengeance squadrons in support of the 5th and 7th Divisions made 28 separate attacks, 552 sorties, against enemy positions in the Arakan, during which a total of 280 tons of bombs was dropped.

Twelve aircraft of 8 Squadron were despatched for A.S.C. targets on 11 and 12 February. On the latter date Flight Lieutenant Berry led them in at 0925 against buildings and enemy lines of communication at Lammadaw. The weather was fine and the target could easily be identified from a distance.

Twenty-four 500 lb TI bombs were dropped in stick covering the village; 18 burst on the target, four outside the village due to overshoots, and the whole target was covered with dust and smoke. They landed back at 10.55. Flying Officer Chukarbutty led a similar-strength mission the next day, against Schwechaing at 1000. The attack was

delivered in a steep dive and again 18 bombs fell on the target with four overshoots in a paddy-field. There was no flak and the aircraft returned at 1120. A second attack was mounted at 1615 with the same crews. The weather had closed in, obscuring the target, but the first box made pin-point bombing practice with nine bombs confirmed as bursting dead on the target and the rest adjacent. The pall of smoke from this attack made the work of the second box even more difficult and two aircraft did not bomb at all. However, a signal was received from the Army congratulating them on good results and confirmed they thought the attack was very successful. The 14th was a repetition, with Squadron Leader Prasad leading the first call at 1120 against enemy positions in 'Ring Contour 490417', and so it continued.

In the Arakan offensive three days of intensive 'softening up' was carried out by the Vengeances between 15 and 18 January 1944,

Sgt Das Copta and Aircraftman Enshain with another trailer load of 'cookies' for the Japanese besieging Kohima. Bombs were delivered to Indian Vengeance units at the height of the battle.
*(Imperial War Museum)*

Flying Officer Ibrahim and Sergeant Jagad, Indian Air Force, preparing for take-off in their Vengeance to give further close support to the Allied forces during the 'Battle of the Boxes' when a high sortie ratio became commonplace. *(Imperial War Museum)*

to the west of Kalapanzin. The 89th Brigade moved in at dusk and, after very fierce fighting, established a post overlooking the road east of Htindaw, but was unable to secure the centre and highest point of the feature until the 24th.

The initial advances soon ground to a halt and on 22 January both squadrons moved up to airfields in the Joari area to attack enemy positions at Razabil and Letwedet in the southern Arakan. The enemy were old hands at creating strong defences, often digging-in down to depths of 30 ft.

For the attack on Razabil by the 161st Brigade on 26 January 1944, Operation 'Wallop' was laid on. Twelve of 82 Squadron's Vengeances made the initial strike, with heavy and medium bombers following, and another 12 Vengeances from No. 8 Squadron followed this up. Despite this massive preparation and the delivery of 145,250 lb of high explosive the Army was only able to gain a minimum foothold there.

Accuracy figures make for an interesting comparison. The Indian Air Force later was to state that the B-24 *Liberator* heavy bombers scored 50 per cent hits, the B-25 *Mitchell* medium bombers 60 per cent. The much-derided Vengeances scored 100 per cent hits!

During the Japanese diversionary attack in the Arakan, the *Ha-Go* offensive which began on 3 February, some of the toughest fighting took place during the Battle of Ngakyedauk Pass, to the east of Wabyin and the Naf River. The two Vengeance squadrons flew no less than 269 sorties in just over a week in tactical support of the ground forces holding this position. Up to 50 sorties were mounted a day, with a maximum of two dozen aircraft on some targets. But most attacks were made by boxes of six diving from 8000 ft at 320 mph and pulling out around 2000 ft. No. 82 Squadron alone made 37 separate formation attacks against 28 different targets.

On 18 February No. 8 Squadron moved

into Mambur. Two aircraft were lost through collision on 9 March while in their attack dive, one cutting the tail off the other; both crashed, one crew baled out, the other was killed. The squadron kept up the pressure despite these losses. Squadron Leader Prasad was at an urgent conference on 13 March so a 12-plane attack delivered at 1645 was led by Flying Officer Dewan. 'Excellent results were observed with all bombs on target,' read the subsequent report. The squadron rested for the next two days but delivered a maximum

Typical of the terrain over which the Vultee dive-bombers operated in Burma. That unmistakeable shadow is etched on the jungle in a bend in a river during one of 110 (H) Squadron's many sorties, this one on 25 March 1944. *(Peter Latcham)*

effort on the 16th, flying four separate missions that day.

The first of these, led by Flight Lieutenant Berry with six aircraft, was launched at 0950 and bombed the Japanese at Chaung Junction, Kaladan. One aircraft failed to bomb but all returned safely at 1100. The second raid was led by Flight Lieutenant Chopra at 1015 and his six-plane box hit the village of Punkori. All the aircraft bombed the target and good concentrated shooting was made; again there were no casualties. At 1430 a third attack was launched, with Flight Lieutenant Berry again leading six Vengeances, and the majority of the bombs were seen to land on target, but there were also some overshoots of 100 yards.

At 1550 the fourth target came through and Flight Lieutenant Chopra took off and attacked at 1630, all bombs being seen to fall in close concentration on the eastern slope of the ridge. Photographic results analysed later showed perfect bombing. There was a brief lull due to bad weather and, on 18 March, seven Commonwealth crews posted to the squadron duly reported in.

The Indian squadrons, in particular, required additional influxes of aircrew in readiness for these great battles. As few Indian aircrew were yet available, further drafts from other Commonwealth nations were allocated to No. 8 Squadron, and included in this one was another young Canadian pilot, Hugh Seton.

'I flew with Warrant Officer Bob Browning of the Royal New Zealand Air Force. Thus thereafter we considered that we flew the most heavily armed Vengeance in the Arakan — four Brownings firing forward, and another Browning manning two flexible Brownings in the rear cockpit!'

'The Vengeance, while being a very heavy aircraft, was free from any bad flying characteristics, and quite simple to learn to fly. It had the typical American well-organised and roomy cockpit configuration. Training for solo flight consisted of a half-hour's dual familiarisation. The concept of sheer vertical dive-bombing was truly exhilarating. Due to the negative incidence to the wings, and the dive brake wing panels which could be operated for the dive, control of the aircraft while "hanging in the straps" at about 350 mph was excellent.

'We had some fifty hours of dives with practice bombing, and it was amazing the type of accuracy which could be attained. Ten to fifteen yards from a point was possible, with the average being in the range of forty yards. There was also considerable training in formation flying with particular reference to tactics for air-to-air defence. This involved a tight formation of four aircraft in a vee, with one in the box flying in a weaving pattern, both from side to side and up and down in a 'corkscrew' movement, designed to concentrate the gunners' firepower against attacks from astern or from the quarters.

'Upon completion of this training, our small (10) contingent of Canadians was posted to No. 8 Indian Air Force Squadron, which was stationed at Mambur, a dirt strip in the Arakan area of Bengal, just south of Cox's Bazaar, and very close to the line of ground fighting by the British, South Africans and Gurkhas from Nepal.

'The flying complement of the squadron was made up almost totally of RAF and Dominion Air Force crews, initially (March 1944) under the command of Squadron Leader Prasad.

Meanwhile, on 19 March 1944, the squadron was informed that 'special targets are expected of the highest priority'. At 1000 the first of these was identified as enemy artillery batteries on Hill 1301, which were holding up the advance of the Allied troops who were within 200 yards of the target, 'hence precision bombing was required to destroy this strong gun position'. The mission was led by Squadron Leader Prasad with six aircraft. They attacked at 1130 in a steep dive from 9000 ft down to 2000 ft with 6000 lb of GPTI bombs. Direct hits on the guns were scored by Prasad himself and Warrant Officer Lamb. The remaining bombs burst in close concentration within 30 yards all round. Photographs later showed this to be one of the best groupings of bombs on a pinpoint target the squadron had achieved. At 1215 news

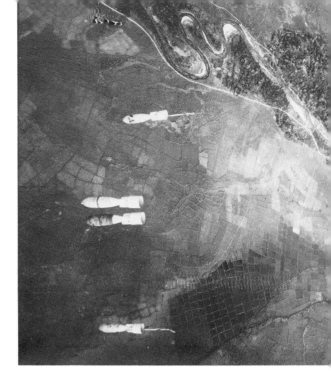

Typical of the mixed bomb loads being delivered onto Japanese targets during the fighting of 1943/44. Two 500 lb and two 250 lb general purpose bombs head towards the target with the tail-fuse streamers tailing behind them in an attack on 29 March 1944. *(Arthur Gill)*

came through that the Army had taken the position and a signal was received from them, congratulating 8 Squadron for 'Excellent support,' and adding, 'gun position completely destroyed'.

Almost totally negative press descriptions were belied by the actual Army reports of the time however, all of which were unequivocal in their praise of the Vengeance squadrons' support and the accuracy and effectiveness of their delivery. Far from standing well back, dive-bombing attacks were being delivered regularly within 200 yards of the enemy targets, and, while fighter-bombers, medium bombers and heavy bombers were unable to score direct hits, the Vengeances were doing so consistently. Even the newspapers were forced to concede elsewhere that the Vengeance (described as an 'American-built light bomber used exclusively by the RAF', a descriptive sentence that contains two completely false statements in eight words), 'proved most effective as a dive-bomber against tactical targets'. Which, considering that is what it was built for, is hardly surprising!

A second attack, led by Flying Officer Curtis, was a dummy dive delivered on PT 1301 at 1215, followed up with a real attack on PT 162. Unfortunately Curtis had to abort the mission due to engine problems and Flying Officer Dhillon led the actual attacks.

The third mission this day saw all 12 aircraft, led by Squadron Leader Prasad and Curtis in two boxes, attacking PT 162 once more. Prasad again made a perfect approach and dived from 8000 ft, the rest following him down. Bombing was tight and on target. However, on the way home Flying Officer Chuckarbutty broke off from the formation with smoke and oil pouring from his engine. The Vengeance began losing power and height but he managed to get down safely at the 'Lyons' emergency strip. On landing the undercarriage collapsed and a crash-landing was made in a paddy-field at the end of the strip, both crew members surviving this without injury.

On 20 March 1944, 82 Squadron moved over to assist the operations from Kumbhirgram with 16 aircraft, leaving 8 Squadron to continue operations on the Arakan front alone.

Flight Lieutenant Chopra led one six-plane box at 1030 against gun positions and a second at 1458 against the stubborn hill 162. In both raids bombing was reported as excellent. A direct hit was again scored on a Japanese gun position, which was busily firing on a landing strip and causing a complete hold-up in clearing casualties from Kaladan. With this threat promptly removed further congratulatory signals flowed in from the Army.

Next day, 21 March, even more spectacular shooting was made. On the second attack another enemy artillery battery at Point 935594 was hit by five Vengeances as three guns were destroyed by 'excellent bombing'. A two-day lull followed, again due to weather, but operations resumed on 24 March. The success achieved by the squadron had been notable in this period, which made it

all the more of a shock when news came through that Squadron Leader Prasad was being sent to AHQ and that a British CO was to take over the squadron.

'This came as a surprise to all ranks, and all Indian officers and other ranks took it as real sad news. One could see a gloomy atmosphere all round the camp. It was evident that everyone will feel the absence of Squadron Leader Prasad who has been with the squadron ever since it was formed, and who raised the squadron and in such a short time brought it to operational standard. Crews felt that they are losing a good leader and others felt the loss of a good commanding officer. Prasad handed over to Squadron Leader Sutherland on 27 March. The new pilots were less affected by the general gloom than the old hands, as Hugh Seton recalls:

'Shortly after our arrival Squadron Leader Ira "Sag" Sutherland took over command. He had come from No. 82 Squadron, which also flew the Vengeance and which operated from another strip close by. 8 Squadron had been a subject of ridicule in the area, and the new CO was determined to change this image. His mandate was obviously to improve performance, for he insisted on firm discipline both on the ground and in the air on flying operations.'

Australian Don Ritchie also recalls: 'I served in 82 Squadron with Frank Sutherland, he was unfortunately to be killed later, in 1945. If it was the case that 8 Squadron needed a jolt, then Frank was the man to shake any unit up!'

Ritchie had resumed operational duties after recovery from his earlier flying accident, not with his old unit, 110 Squadron, but with 82 Squadron on 30 April 1944, following Gibbs' departure. After his accident he had lost his rank while in hospital and had then served on the Vengeance Flight with 153 OTU at Peshawar from November 1943, then he joined 21 APC for a brief period. He flew a variety of aircraft with these units, but mainly the Vultee Vengeance on local flying instruction, drogue tests, formation and dive-bombing training, Army co-operation exercises and calibration flights.

In April, 8 Squadron continued to be heavily committed, making 277 sorties with 1500 lb bomb loads. Another new tactic was employed against deep enemy bunkers at Buthidaung. Wave after wave of Vengeances, six at a time, from 8 and 82 Squadrons, delivered their bombs onto the target, until the last wave. These aircraft dived as before but did not actually release their bombs at the end of the dive. The infantry moved forward smartly in conjunction with this ruse and were able to reach the enemy bunkers before the defenders emerged. Another idea was the use of delayed-action bombs on a grand scale, with a good mixture of 11-second, six-hour and 12-hour fuses.

'We went on operations immediately,' said Hugh Seton with 8 Squadron, 'these trips being concurrent with squadron practice in bombing and formation flying, all under the CO's leadership. In this way he was able to assess the performance of each crew and point out any shortcomings in flying procedures. Very shortly, the performance of the squadron improved dramatically, both in results on operations and in *esprit de corps.*

'We Canadians flew on virtually every mission, and usually totalled two per day. As we were located close to the ground fighting line, and our role was principally in army support, each mission was from 1.15 to 1.35 hour's duration. We were over enemy-held territory very shortly after take-off. The squadron took off in formation pairs, and formed up in three sections of four aircraft each in the vee-plus box configuration. Once over the target area each section formed into echelon, bomb-bay doors were opened, and each aircraft in succession executed a half-roll into the vertical dive position and deployed the wing dive brake panels. Adjustment during the dive to line up properly with the target consisted of rolling the aircraft in its now vertical position, or shallowing the dive angle. The ideal dive was vertical in order to achieve maximum accuracy. Great care had to be exercised in avoiding any yaw or side-slipping at the release of bombs, as such action would result in bombs being flung sideways and off the target. We carried four

A No. 84 Squadron Vengeance releases two 500 lb general purpose bombs, one 250 lb general purpose bomb and four 30 lb incendiary bombs in an attack on 31 March 1944. *(Arthur Gill)*

500 lb bombs in the body bomb bay, with each bomb on a yoke assembly which moved outward so that the bomb cleared the propeller arc after its release.

'Dives were usually commenced at ten to twelve thousand feet above the target, with release of bombs and immediate pull-out usually made at about thirty-five hundred feet. Thus a very quick identification of the target had to be made at the start of the dive. I do not recall any situations where we missed targets sufficiently to endanger our own ground forces, even though they were frequently only several hundred yards from the target.

Bombs bursting on the Japanese-held village of Inawnkang during at attack by 110 (H) Squadron, 28 March 1944. *(Peter Latcham)*

'In April 1944, ground fighting in the Arakan was concentrated along a line between Maungdaw and Buthidaung in densely forested, jungle-type terrain. Our role was frequently to bomb dug-in troops' positions, which were sometimes difficult to identify. At times, all growth was blasted from suspected fox hole positions in order to assist the Army in making progress. Enemy supply routes and centres were also bombed, often with good visual results. Usually, intelligence reports came back rapidly after each mission, and return strikes were made.'

'On 16 April 1944 the squadron lost another aircraft, when a pilot failed to pull out of an attack dive over the target. On 22 May they moved to Chirignga, while in June a detachment operated for a few days from Cox's Bazaar. Weather, however, was beginning to affect dive-bombing operations and more shallow-dive operations with delayed-action bombs to enable the aircraft to get clear of the explosions, were utilised. These of course were not so accurate and were soon abandoned.

'Our squadron did not experience any air-to-air contact with the enemy. There was evidence of ground-to-air action by the enemy, principally in the form of organised small-arms fire. We lost one aircraft in 8 Squadron's 1944 campaign, which was believed to be due to such enemy action. Some bombing and strafing actions were carried out at low level, using ten-second delay fuses to the bombs. Enemy return fire was recorded. This form of attack was presumably found to be relatively ineffective, as only a few such sorties were carried out.'

On the Imphal front the Vengeance attacks steadily gained in momentum as the crisis worsened. Plans were made for the dive-bomber Wing's strength to be built up to four squadrons, with the addition of 7 Squadron Indian Air Force and 82 Squadron from the Arakan front. On 13 March Tonmahe was attacked at 1235 by six Vengeances of 110 Squadron under Squadron Leader L. F. Penny, DFC, and 12 from 84 Squadron led by Squadron Leader Arthur Gill, DFC. Four sorties were undertaken the next day, six Vengeances hitting Sunle at 0910; 12 Vengeances from 110 attacking enemy positions at RP146127 at 1107; five from 84 attacking position RP668634 at 1426 and six from 110 against RP667627 at 1521. There were no losses. On 15 March both 84 and 110 flew—three missions, 16 sorties each, hitting targets at Malu, Pyingaing, and Zibyugon among others.

Three full squadrons were again flung in on 24 March, 82 Squadron launching two 12-plane strikes at Tamanthi and Ketta; 110 Squadron putting up six and 11 Vengeances against Manpa and Kongyi respectively; and

84 putting in two 12-plane attacks on both Homalin and Dolaibung. Thus the pace was maintained. In April 1944, 82 Squadron undertook 400 sorties, 344 of them on 4 Corps' front in just 16 days. No. 110 Squadron mounted 55 strikes, totalling 542 sorties, and dropped 2319 bombs weighing 703,000 lb. In fact, such were the demands on the units and the intensity of the sortie rate that there was a temporary shortage of 250 lb bombs. In May operations continued at the same high rate against the enemy units dug in around Imphal.

Most historians have given the impression that the Vengeance units only ventured out with fighter cover from the Mohawk and Spitfire squadrons, some stating indeed that they operated *'always* with fighter cover', but like so much else written about this aircraft this is entirely incorrect. Examination of the logbooks of six different squadrons and the ORPs and Record Books of the Wing reveal a vastly different picture. Arthur Gill was questioned on this very point. Asked 'Did you always have fighter escort?', his reply was:

'No, no. Very seldom, because the fighters

No lack of action for this scantily-clad Miss! She adorned an 84 Squadron Vengeance flown by an Australian pilot. She was named *'The Troll'* (for Trollop) and as she could boast of 141 'actions' at this time, she was not mis-named! *(Arthur Gill)*

didn't have the range. The few occasions we had fighter cover are listed in my logbook, they would be Hurricanes with long-range drop-tanks. Even when our targets were Japanese airfields themselves, where fighter cover might be expected to be an essential item, we very seldom had it. On these missions, in the main, we were not bombing the aircraft but the supply dumps and such around the strips, as this would immobilise whole units and not just destroy individual aircraft, often dummies. It required just as much precision to do this but the results were more far-reaching.'

One of the rare times fighter cover was given on this type of mission was the strike against the Japanese-held airfield of Tamu. Gill led 36 Vengeances from 84, 110 and 7 Squadrons against this target on 4 April, the second mission carried out that day. He was flying one of the new Vengeance IIIs (FB 964) instead of his usual Mark II (AN 824); 48,000 lb of general-purpose bombs were dropped on this raid and 4440 lb of incendiaries. The attack was very successful and top cover was provided by Spitfires of 136 Squadron.

The strangest event however occurred to an Australian rear-seat man, Pilot Officer Ron Gabrielson.

Let Ron Gabrielson continue the story, as he told it to me: 'It was my nineteenth sortie and we were on our way to a Japanese-occupied village called Tonathe. Our flight (B) broke formation in heavy cloud. My pilot set course for base and we then ran into a terrific thunderstorm. As we were nearing the target I had swivelled round to man the twin Browning machine-guns which were located behind the back seat. However, as we were now heading for home, I had to face forward again so that I could operate the radio and attend to navigation.

'I had swivelled halfway, when the pilot lost complete control and the plane was thrown violently upward and then we started down in a very tight spin. My sliding roof was open and, although my safety-belt held me in my seat, my head and shoulders were forced into the slipstream and away went my helmet.

'When flying later missions I made

absolutely sure that the chin-strap of my helmet was secured. Anyway, not being able to see nor speak to the pilot, and being aware that the aircraft was out of control and on the way down, I decided to bale out. I hit the quick-release buckle of my safety belt, and, because of the spin we were in, I did not have to climb out — I was thrown out!

'I landed in thick jungle in the Naga hills, which run north to south, and I had to travel west. After cutting my way down to the ground with my machete, with which we were issued and which fitted in a pocket down the right thigh of our khaki flying overalls, I made my way down to the fast-flowing river—at the bottom of a ravine. The machete was a godsend. When not in use the blade folded back into the handle.

'When I reached the river I could see, on the opposite side, a sandy beach and a track running up the mountain. I crossed the river with some difficulty, went back to the beach and started climbing the track which I was sure would lead me to a village. All Naga villages were located on ridges. The Japanese lines of supply were very long, and they used to raid villages for food. I was hoping that they were not in the village I was headed for. I had taken a chance, because, without the assistance of the locals, I knew that I would never get back to my squadron.

'When I finally reached the village there was no one in sight, but I could sense their presence. The natives were hidden behind trees and in their huts, and they came out when they realised that I was not a Jap. From there on I was passed from village to village and finished up at the railway line which was under the control of the Army. I flagged down a train after a lengthy wait and got off at Silchar where an Army unit contacted Kumbhirgram for me. A truck eventually arrived and took me home.

Don Ritchie flew missions with 82 Squadron from the beginning of May 1944. On the 2nd they flew from Jumchar to hit Pimples (Point 121) with 12 aircraft in the morning and struck at Inbauk with six in the afternoon. On the 3rd another two missions were flown; an enemy supply dump was smashed near Seinnyinya village twice, and this time the Vengeances went in low to conduct strafing runs as well. Still working from Jumchar, 82 Squadron hit Atet, Ngetthe and Buhidaung with a dozen aircraft at a time on the 6th and attacked enemy field guns at Kyacikhtayan on 10 May. On the 11th Labawa was the target with 13 aircraft but the following day a mission against the road to the west of that village was recalled, then sent out again later. The third sortie that day was against a hill feature at the same spot and on the 15th the road junction at Hill 305 was hit. Strafing again featured in an attack on the Japanese Signals Centre at Zedidaung, which was bombed on the 15th. Ritchie's mount on all these operations was AN703 while his navigators included Pilot Officers Harrower, Webb and Keefe.

'We saw very few Japanese aircraft,' he told me, 'and the flak was nothing like that over Holland earlier in the war. Nor of course were we such a sitting duck as in a Blenheim, because by going down almost vertically and rotating around the tail as we went, we could present a very difficult target and surprise was usually achieved.'

Back with 110 Squadron, Bud McInnes's experiences were similar. 'By far the majority of our trips involved one flight of six aircraft. Some of the time we would go as a complete squadron and have two flights of six aircraft each but occasionally I did take part in larger raids when the whole Wing went in at one target, 36 Vengeances.'

No. 7 Squadron, under Squadron Leader Hem Chaudhry, had hit hard at the Japanese from 28 March onward, striking from the narrow Kutcha strip in Uderbund and conducting 34 attacks within three days. During April they struck, with great accuracy, Japanese concentrations at Sittaung and Thaungdut before the shift to Kumbhirgram to support 33 Corps. Despite the handicap of restricted flying from the waterlogged Uderbund airstrip that month, the squadron achieved a maximum effort of 630 hours' operations, undertaking 344 sorties, which was the most of any squadron in 221 Group that month. Pilot Officers P. C. Lal and E. W. Pinot made outstanding contributions to this impressive total. Each morning, before dawn, the squadron's personnel had to travel a distance of 20 kilometres over the rutted *kucha* roads, often ankle-deep in mud, to reach the Uderbund airstrip before they could even begin flying operations.

In May the squadron's sortie total was 353 or 611 operational flying hours, an average of 16 sorties per day. Perhaps one of the major achievements of No. 7 Squadron was the bombing of the Manipur Bridge, a key link in the Japanese lines of communication for the armies attacking Imphal above the Tiddim road. On 25 May 1944, the Vengeances made their attack dives through thick cloud. A direct hit was scored on the eastern end of the bridge, completely demolishing it. This effectively stopped the Japanese from entering Manipur. Despite completely overcast conditions, 7 Squadron's targets ranged from Myothit to Thaugdut, bombing supply camps in the Chindwin river, Imphal, Kalewa and Fort White areas. Japanese targets destroyed included those at Thaungora, Ingywa, Kayaktan, Kanzawk and Pankoi and supply dumps at Langonag, Pauktan, Kangyibin, Zaidaung and Ktinpan.

In May repeated attempts were made by the squadron to destroy two further bridges on the Manipur river but the monsoon rains weathered many of these strikes out. It was a foretaste of what was to come.

# Chapter 11
# Cancellation

In New Guinea the continuing round-the-clock pounding of the enemy airfields had been maintained by the three RAAF Vengeance squadrons, 21, 23 and 24. They formed Number 77 Wing, which had moved into Nadzab in December 1943. This was part of a major attempt to keep the Japanese airstrips neutralised pending General Douglas MacArthur's assault on the Admiralty Islands, planned for 29 February.

Commencing on the 26th of the month the RAAF dive-bombers therefore launched an all-out effort. A dozen Vengeances from 21 and 23 Squadrons hit No. 1 Strip at Alexishafen this day, while another 12 from 24 Squadron bombed Madang strip. They repeated the same dosage the next day against the same targets. On 28 February 33 Vengeances from the Wing were despatched and dive-bombed both airstrips at Alexishafen and the one at Madang again, although the damage caused by the previous two days' attacks still appeared unrepaired. No. 24 Squadron's Vengeances lingered for 20 minutes over Madang itself, strafing any likely target with impunity.

Operations at this intensity were continued thereafter.

Climax of the Vengeance missions came on the morning of 8 March 1944, with an attack by 36 dive-bombers from all three Australian squadrons on the enemy-held village of Rempi ten miles to the north of Alexishafen.

As a seemingly back-handed reward for all their efforts on his behalf MacArthur's HQ signalled that same day that 77 Wing was to cease all operations forthwith and return to Australia. Air Commodore F. R. W. Scherger, commander of 10 Group, was unfortunately absent in Australia when this order came through. His second-in-command, Group Captain C. W. Pearce, duly notified him of what had taken place, but when Scherger tried to see Major-General

At Nazdab, New Guinea. Flying Officer Eric Nicholls awaits take-off with bomb doors open in readiness to load up for another sortie to add to the impressive total recorded under his cockpit.
*(George Limbrick)*

Ennis C. Whitehead of the US 5th Air Force, to find out the reason for this decision, he was told that Whitehead had left instructions 'not to be disturbed'.

John Gerber told me how this abrupt change of policy affected the OTUs at this time: 'The last OTU course carried out the usual dive-bombing exercise against Bird Island, according to my logbook, on 8 April 1944, Flight Lieutenant Cyril McPherson being the formation leader and I was his Nav BW. This flight was notable for one reason. Mac was a very capable and keen pilot, eager to get all the hours he could. About this time he had broken a small bone in his left hand and had to wear a plaster cast. With the co-operation of the Medical Officer he had a cast built which allowed him to operate the undercarriage lever. This selector had a complicated three-way action, in which the pilot had to squeeze, lift and pull to get the undercarriage up.

'Initially all went well. Mac got the undercarriage retracted without any troubles whatsoever and led the squadron attack on Bird Island. In the dive I was sitting backwards watching the other aircraft doing vertical aileron turns to get on the target, and watching their bombs leave the aircraft. It was a spectacular sight. Pilots never saw this aspect of an attack.

'The mission completed, the formation returned to Williamstown to land but there was a design fault in the manufacture of the cast! Mac could not get the gear down. Although the cast allowed him to select the gear up, a different set of actions was necessary to get the undercarriage down.

'An embarrassed formation leader had to watch his formation while he circled the airfield, bashing his plaster cast against the longerons to enable him to operate the U/C lever. When we got down it was a case of Mac taking his cast (or its remains) back to the drawing board for a re-work. This was done and the MK. II design allowed him to get the wheels up and down.

'At this stage, April 1944, the OTU stopped training Vengeance crews and most of the personnel were posted out. Thus March 1944

was the last "recruiting" tour. There was no need to train more crews. The squadrons in PNG were withdrawn to Australia, later to be re-equipped with Liberators. The OTU was organised to train Beaufighter and Mosquito crews: these aircraft were beginning to come off the production lines in increasing numbers. The Vengeance staff was dispersed. I was posted to No. 21 Squadron, which had been re-deployed to Camden, NSW. A month later I was posted to No. 8 EFTS for pilot training.'

In this abrupt fashion the Vengeance ended its hitherto highly successful six-week combat period, and within a short time the dumbfounded squadrons had shorn themselves of their Vultees in readiness for re-forming as Liberator squadrons. There was one more loss to 23 Squadron, for when the Wing returned to Higgins Field (Jacky-Jacky) on the northern tip of Cape Yorke, on 12 April 1944, Flying Officer Syd Porter (a pre-war instructor from South Australia) tried to stretch his glide to the beach (after engine-failure) but crashed into the sea in the Princess Marianne Strait and both crewmen were killed.

John Gerber told me: 'The Vultee Vengeance aircraft suffered from a number of problems. It is understood that the aircraft was of British design built in the United States of America. Some time late in 1942 the first few aircraft arrived in Australia. Then, apparently, a bulk shipment to Australia was lost at sea and this put the project behind schedule. Had they arrived earlier the story of their employment in the RAAF may have been different.

'Their serviceability never reached a high standard. Many years later I heard that the cylinders were not properly finished, scraper rings placed in grooves incorrectly and other faults contributed to general unserviceability.

'There was a spectacular accident in Melbourne during a flying display to raise funds for the war effort. One of the Vengeances went in during a roll, fortunately missing all the spectators. The pilot's name was Vial. Other members of his unit were of the opinion that, while shoving the stick over

A classic sequence of photos showing a typical 'Full Wing' Vengeance attack. Three squadrons, 36 dive-bombers in total, led by 84 Squadron, make an attack against Japanese troops dug-in at the northern end of the village of Potsangbam (in the Imphal plain) on 7 May 1944. Each Vengeance was carrying a 1500 lb bomb-load which meant a total of 54,000 lb of bombs on the enemy positions. The Allied troops held the southern end of the village so the attack had to be precise. It was!

This sequence shows the leading squadron forming up at the commencement of the one hour, ten minute mission in 'Vics' of three and crossing the mountain ranges of the frontier. A perfect photograph shows the complete sequence of the Vengeance attack dive as practised by the RAF squadrons. The bombs are shown exploding exactly on the target zone after the first attack, and smoke spreads as each subsequent flight adds its quota of high-explosive. The final photograph shows the scene from ground-level, with British Sherman tanks waiting to follow up and clear the village.

*(Arthur Gill)*

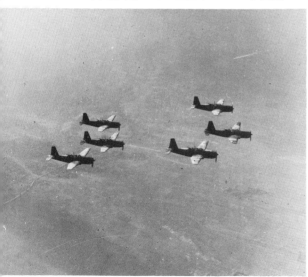

to the left to initiate the climbing roll, his sleeve caught the catch of the lap strap and undid it. Then at the *moment critique* he fell out of the seat, lost control and crashed. A theory which may or may not be true.'

The withdrawal of 77 Wing left only No. 25 *(City of Perth)* Squadron, which had re-equipped with the Vengeance at Freemantle, Western Australia, earlier. They were utilised on coastal patrol work from mid-1943 onward, and being the last operational Vengeance unit, became the only one to re-equip with the much superior Vengeance IV.

It saw little or no combat but it was to be involved with another of the Australian invasion scares. On 7 March 1944, some credence was given to these fears by the report by an American submarine of two Japanese heavy units, which it was assumed were battleships, steering south from Singapore. Next day, therefore, forces in Western Australia were placed on the alert. These purely precautionary measures leaked to the media and resulted in wholesale rumours of an imminent invasion, which was reinforced

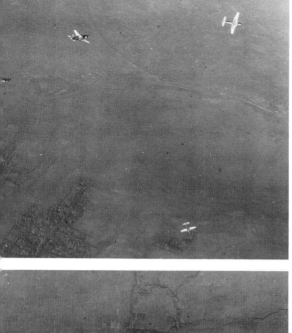

by the CO of a fighter squadron telling his men that a 'Japanese naval task force was loose in the Indian Ocean headed in the general direction of the Perth area'. Squadrons were concentrated at Guildford, north-east of Perth, and 25 Squadron's Vengeance dive-bombers were instructed to carry out attacks when this force came within 200 miles of the coast. It seemed like their hour had come indeed, especially when a radar sighting led to the air-raid sirens being sounded in Perth and Freemantle on 10 March 1944. But it was all an illusion; no Japanese invasion fleet ever came within 1500 miles of Perth!

John Gerber recalled the effect this caused: 'It appeared that Japanese carriers in the Indian Ocean might make an attack on Perth, WA. All available aircraft were concentrated in the Perth area. There were half a dozen Vultees available at Bankstown but yet unassembled. Six crews were sent from No. 4 OTU, Williamstown, to Bankstown to fly these aircraft to Perth and be ready for operations.

'The aircraft took some time to assemble and, as the need was urgent, the aircraft were despatched to Perth in ones and twos as soon as they were test-flown and accepted. The officer in charge of the detachment was Flying Officer J. See and I was his Nav BW. Our

151

aircraft was the last to leave Bankstown but the first to arrive at Perth. All the other aircraft experienced unserviceabilities *en route,* and some engine changes were necessary.

'In retrospect we were lucky, particularly as the pilot picked up a couple of passengers at Adelaide, SA. The aircraft, A27-505, was a Mk. IV with the rear seat permanently facing backwards. The two passengers sat on the floor, also facing backwards, their feet dangling in the well. Due to crowding one of them had to operate the canopy opening handle, usually squashing my face against the gun trips in the process!'

Thus 25 Squadron continued to operate its Vengeances on routine patrol duties until it too became earmarked for Liberator conversion in January 1945. However, this was not quite the end for the Vultee Vengeance in Australian service, as we shall see.

Back in the Arakan, 8 Squadron was continuing to operate as well. On 4 July 1944, Hugh Seton was flying a low-level bombing mission against heavily wooded hill positions near the Buthidaung area. His subsequent log entry read, 'Shot up on bombing run — OK'. Hugh amplified this for me: 'Several smallish holes were registered near the trailing edge of the starboard wing adjacent to the fuselage. We guessed it was light flak. There was no structural damage. The mission was completed OK, but I do not recall the intelligence reports covering the effects of our strike, which was against troop positions.

'Maintenance of the aircraft was carried out mainly by RAF personnel, and was of a very high standard. We were always able to field the standard twelve aircraft for a mission, and there were no engine failures. There were sometimes some minor mechanical difficulties resulting in a return, but we always had a standby aircraft, with crew in place and engine running, ready to take-off and bring the squadron up to full strength.

'The weather during the winter and spring was warm and dry, and very suitable for flying operations. However, towards the end of June the annual monsoon rains would commence, rendering flying conditions of the type we were set for virtually impossible. At the height of the monsoon season, rainfall was so extremely heavy and continuous that the Army's ground operations were almost at a standstill.

'At the first signs of the monsoon rains, we moved off the dirt strip at Mambur and located at an all-weather strip at Cox's Bazaar. We attempted to carry out some operations but without much luck. Our Group commander, Group Captain Chater, RAF, seemed particularly partial to our small, rather wild contingent of Canadians. Knowing of my intense desire to fly at all times, he placed his personal Hurricane IIC (complete with its twelve guns!) for weather recce trips or whatever I chose. He always insisted that I go and fire the guns. This I did on several occasions after first making sure of the enemy positions. We called Group Captain Chater the "War Lord of the Arakan"!'

No. 8 Squadron actually made its last Vengeance sortie on 7 July 1944, after which they pulled back to Samungli and later were re-equipped with Spitfire VIIIs.

'During my training and operational flying with 8 Squadron I totalled 191 hours on the Vengeance and carried out a tour of 45 operational missions. In all that time, and under a variety of conditions, the aircraft performed extremely well and I did not have any mechanical problems whatsoever. This speaks so well for the performance of the RAF erks who looked after the aircraft. We reckoned that they were the best in the world. Also, of course, the basic design and construction of the aircraft itself could not be faulted, as it could perform so well in a 90-degree vertical dive position!'

On 8 August 1944, a search was flown for a Vengeance from No. 8 Squadron which was lost flying into Quetta several days after the main body of the squadron's arrival there.

The squadron never forgot their true traditions, however, as was recorded in the Squadron Record Book over a year later when, during the final Japanese rout, they made some bombing attacks on fleeing enemy columns between 4 and 9 August 1945: '. . . these good results can be attributed to the tradition of this Squadron being originally a DIVE-BOMBER Squadron — the spirit of VENGEANCE still lingers!'

Arthur Gill was now leading the main Wing strikes against the targets.

No. 82 Squadron flew its last sorties on 19 May 1942 and then withdrew to Kolar to re-equip with Mosquitoes.

No. 110 Squadron, despite the fact that it began re-equipping with modern Vengeance IIIs and IVs, and despite the fact that Imphal was still besieged, was also pulled out of the front line. It was still at Kumbhirgram on 1 June 1944, but was reported as having ceased operations and was awaiting a train to move ground personnel out. It finally moved to Kalyan. A detachment of ten aircrews, equipped with Mark IVs, was then detailed to ship out to West Africa in order to conduct a series of anti-malaria mosquito spraying tests. The rest of the squadron meanwhile moved first to Yelahanka, then to Kolar. On 1 June, 24 Vengeance sorties were flown by 7 and 84 Squadrons but all were aborted due to bad weather conditions, and low cloud kept them grounded on 2 June also. Next day, and on 4 June also, 12 Vengeances were airborne from 84 Squadron but again had to abort their missions. Not until the 5th did the clouds lift sufficiently for 60 Vengeance sorties to be made by the two squadrons. Also on this day, Squadron Leader Aiwan took over administrative control of 7 Squadron, although Squadron Leader Choudry continued in charge of operations.

No missions took place on 6 June (D-Day in Europe), but 7 and 84 put up 24 Vengeances the day after, around Imphal itself. No. 7 Squadron became the fourth Vengeance unit to be withdrawn from battle, after flying its last sortie on 11 June 1944. According to the Official Indian statement on the operations, 'The units had displayed a high degree of skill, the Vengeance having proved itself to be the most accurate form of "artillery" for attacking targets in mountain and jungle-

shrouded country.' It flew to Ranchi and then to Chara to begin conversion to Hawker Hurricane IV fighter-bombers.

Due in large measure to their contribution, the tide had been turned in this most bitter of campaigns and the Japanese threat to the encircled Allied garrisons was defeated. The Vengeances now began to harass the fleeing enemy as he began to withdraw. However, the onset of the monsoon season began to limit their effectiveness as did the lack of suitable close-range airstrips. In addition most had almost completed their normal tours and the decision had already been taken in England to re-equip them all anyway.

Only Arthur Gill's battle-hardened 84 Squadron continued to soldier on indefatigably on this front, and when 8 Squadron pulled out this unit became the last to fly the Vengeance in combat operations against the fleeing Japanese enemy.

The final attack by 84 Squadron, indeed the final combat mission flown by the Vultee Vengeance, took place on 16 July 1944. Arthur Gill flew a Vengeance III (FB981) on this historic mission with Flight Lieutenant Blackburn as navigator. Twelve Vengeances flew against the ammunition dumps at Le-U to carry out a low-level attack. Ten-tenths cloud persisted for most of the flight and covered the mountains in a grim pall, but they found their target and the strike was put in. 'Accurate bombing,' Gill noted in his log. An overall mission time of two hours five minutes was recorded.

That was the swan-song of the Vengeance in the RAF's combat line for, like its Australian and Indian counterparts, its success failed to save it from pre-conceived prejudice. It is another irony in the Vengeance's story that, while it was at the peak of its achievements in combat, decisions had already been taken to withdraw it from service. Around the world in Washington D.C., February 1944, saw the initiation of the final moves to kill off production once and for all. On the 14th of that month Brigadier-General M. E. Gross, Assistant Chief of the Air Staff (ACAS), Operations, Commitments and Requirements, Requirements Division, informed the ACAS, Materiel, Maintenance and Distribution, that there had actually been no American military requirement for the A-35 airplane for approximately one year, and that production for the Army Air Force should therefore be stopped immediately. Materiel Command was requested to submit its recommendations.

Colonel W. M. Morgan, Chief, Production Engineering Section, duly presented his report on 22 February, in which he suggested the desirability of maintaining employee morale at Convair's Nashville plant, and of ensuring an adequate supply of trained personnel for the coming P-38 programme. On 25 February, General Meyers advised the Chief of Staff that an additional cancellation of 300 A-35s had been made, which would result in the stopping of production in April 1944. Wright Field advised the contractor of the action on 1 March 1944, adding the statement, 'The situation with respect to loss of personnel is regretted.' The cancellation was accepted in June.

There remained the question of spares to keep the existing machines running, the 'life-of-the-type' factor. On 19 May 1944, representatives of Convair and of Air Service Command found that the 829th Specialised Depot at Gadsden, Alabama, had spare parts for the A-35 far in excess of USAAF needs in this respect. As these spares were then urgently required overseas for the RAF, RAAF and North African French, steps were taken to release them for this purpose. On 15 June 1944, Colonel W. D. Dana, Deputy Chief, Supply Division, Patterson Field, wrote that he was fully aware of the large inventory of A-35 maintenance spare parts at Gadsden and that certain items had already been used to fill United Nations' requirements. Cessation of Allied use of the plane, other than in secondary roles, overtook this re-allocation also.

The USAAF's final summary of production of the V-72 and A-31 contracts and allocation of production indicated that of 900 under contract with Vultee for the British, all of which contracts were completed, 164 constituted the net allocation to the USAAF.

Northrop's production of 400 V-72s all went to the British. Of the grand total of 2730 A-35s contracted for, 2035 had been cancelled in May 1943. Of these, 250 were later reinstated and then there was a final cancellation of 300. Thus, of the total of 645 A-35s produced, the USAAF initial allocation had been 382. As well as allocations to the North African French, and since the USAAF had no requirements for the plane, production was diverted, as far as possible, to foreign governments. In March 1944 the British indicated that they wanted no more and Air Vice-Marshal Jones ordered the cancellation of the assignment and delivery of the final 56 of the Australian order in the same month. For the rest, of the last 82 to be disposed of, 50 were allocated to Brazil on 2 June 1944.

The improved Mark IVs were just about reaching the squadrons in numbers when the decision to terminate front-line use was made and thus large numbers of this upgraded Vengeance were on hand to be utilised in whatever role could be found for them. These proved to be many and varied.

Ten Mark IV's from 110 Squadron, it will be recalled, had been shipped out to Takoradi, in the British colony of Gold Coast (now Ghana). Here in the malaria-stricken jungles of 'The White Man's Grave' exhaustive test flights were made in spraying the swampy breeding grounds of this pest with DDT from the special tanks fitted to the Vengeances. This humanitarian work continued until December 1944, when the crews were posted home. Their aircraft were handed over to a maintenance unit and put in store.

A similar but much more military use was made of sprays fitted to Vengeances by No. 1340 Flight, RAF, officially established at Cannanare on 1 December 1944. Vengeance IIIs were fitted with tanks under their wings and experiments were conducted with the use of poison gas. Later, detailed tests were also made by this unit on the application of aerial smoke-screens for use in the planned combined operations for the invasion of Malaya, Operation *Zipper*. Bud McInnes from 110 Squadron was in charge of this Flight and provided me with very interesting details of its work, which *almost* resulted in a combat use for the Vengeance after all.

'I went to the Malibar coast of southern India in November 1944. I was posted to a Flight called the Chemical Defence Research Establishment and the idea was that we were going to duplicate a lot of tests with poison gas that had been conducted in England and western Canada. We were going to do them under tropical conditions and they were going to be assessed accordingly. When I got there the place was a madhouse, the airfield was still under construction, half mud, half grass and the aircraft were going to be Vengeances.

'I was to be CO of the unit so they promoted me to Flight Lieutenant and the first aircraft to come in were Mark IVs, which differed considerably from those I had been flying up at the front. These were FD225, FD240 and FD275. The Mark IVs were more sophisticated in that they had a more powerful engine, but it was still a Wright *Cyclone,* and more electronics, even the trim-tabs were electric. It had a higher carrying capacity in that it was supposed to be able to carry four 500 lb bombs. As for the machine-guns, we had four instead of six, but they were .5s. The aircraft was also heavily protected with armour plating.

'When I found out what my job was going to be, I discovered it was to involve a lot of low flying. In fact it had to be very accurate, flying for the most part at heights of only 30 ft. This was a far from enviable job in the Vengeance because of the high angle of attack, especially at lower speeds. So as soon as I was able to fly off the airstrip I started a programme of low flying to be able to lay a screen that again was measurable from the ground in the size of the molecules that dropped. We practised until we became quite proficient. They supplied me with three aircraft and aircrew who had never been on operations, but we succeeded in developing a pretty good unit.'

Exercises and tests had commenced on 19 November 1944, and continued through to the end of January 1945. In February the Flight started work out to Santa Cruz, Sambre, Deolali and Kalyan with Vengeance IIIs (FD240, FD955, FD966 and FD955). The reason for the switch was explained by Red McInnes thus: 'The Army, however, were still miles behind us in the preparations and my people were becoming pretty bored so I volunteered our services for other purposes as there was great preparation taking place at the time in readiness for the planned seaborne invasions of Burma and Malaya. Thus we took part in exercises that required the laying

Working to keep the sortie rate going under a camouflage net at a forward airstrip. Vengeance W of 84 Squadron undergoing field maintenance. The high sortie rate maintained throughout the winter of 1943/44 and the following spring made a mockery of the earlier unreliability of the Vengeance and proved what could be done given dedicated and determined ground crew. *(Arthur Gill)*

of aerial smoke-screens as the landing-craft approached the shore.

'These exercises broke the monotony for my men and myself and were quite interesting. And we had quite a few amusing incidents because the Army with whom we were working were, for the most part, in the lower stages of training and had no idea what to expect and they were blundering away. I in turn had to learn all the procedures of laying smoke-screens, signalling between the attacking forces, which were invariably late, and so on, and so we had a lot of fun doing it.

'The last one I did was the most interesting of the lot. It took place just north of Bombay. I had my three aircraft there and this was to be the final rehearsal for the landing before they left and landed in Rangoon. My aircraft were again called on for laying smoke. Two aircraft were to lay a screen along the beach, but one aircraft had to lay the perimeters; in other words, each side of an area about 400 yards from the shore had to have a marker dropped to guide in the ships and the landing craft from the sea.

'Well, as CO, all this fell on my shoulders and when I went and had a look at the type of marker I was quite apprehensive. It was a float marker of course and it was perfectly spherical, about the size of an ordinary sea mine about 28-30 inches in diameter. I had to hook one under each wing and drop them in turn, not only accurately but again from not more than 35 ft. Well, there was no means of practising, no means of knowing how the aircraft was going to handle after one was dropped and naturally they had to be dropped at two different times, one at each side of the landing area.

'So I briefed my men on the straight smoke-screen and armed up my aircraft with the smoke-floats. An amusing aspect of it too was that, just as I was going in to lay the first one, off my starboard side was a small island which was supposed to simulate an island that was just alive with artillery and ack-ack and it was to be bombed with Hurricanes armed with napalm bombs. I had never seen napalm at this point and I was just getting nicely lined up to go in and drop my own smoke marker and

concentrating hard, when suddenly the complete island erupted in flame. I can still remember what a terrible fright it was for me, because I didn't know whether it was going to have any repercussions on my own aircraft or not. But the napalm, having such a low explosive factor, didn't affect my Vengeance at all. So I got rid of my first marker and was pleasantly surprised to feel very little difference in lowering and dropping the second marker. Again, it is a tribute to the solidness of the Vengeance that you could do this sort of thing and get away with it. This exercise was conducted on 27 March 1945. Two days later I returned to my own base where there was a signal saying that I must report to Bombay for repatriation, so I never flew a Vengeance again.'

The United States also considered the use of the Vultee as a gas-spraying aircraft. On 12 September 1942, Production Engineering at Wright Field wrote to the Commanding Officer of the Proving Ground at Eglin Field, Florida, informing him that a prototype A-35-B was to be sent to Eglin Field for extensive dive-bombing and gunnery tests, 'and some missions with M-10 chemical tanks'. Comments on tests were requested asap, in order that the contractor might be notified concerning future production.

Quite a large number of Vengeances, especially of the later marks, turned up in the skies over the United Kingdom between 1942 and 1945, but never in a combat role. Apart from the large numbers of test and trial aircraft, many were used as 'hacks' by a whole variety of forces. A good number were turned over to the US 8th Air Force by the RAF for use in this role, some being repainted overall, but retaining their original US Army serials on their tails, others just having the national insignia, with the bars either side of the white star, painted up.

Others were acquired by the American forces in other ways, as Richard L. Smith was to remember. He was a pilot with the First Scouting Force in England, flying B-17s and P-51s; he also flew fighter cover with Mustangs. His Group or Squadron

Commander heard of a V-72 in Northern Ireland which he thought he could use for tow-target practice, so he went over and flew it back. As he was going to land, he found he couldn't get the landing gear down (that old problem) so he circled the field until someone on the ground could locate a V-72 manual on emergency gear procedures. None could be found so he finished up making a belly landing, but the Vengeance was worthless after that.

Other more exotic 'hacks' appeared in the strangest garbs and in the strangest places as the war went on. For example, Mike Bowyer was based at Cambridge, which was as remote from the events in the real world in 1944 as it is today. Yet at such an out-of-way airfield Vengeance sightings were to be had; for example, A-31 target-tugs in USAAF markings and olive drab/grey finish but sometimes with RAF serials, sometimes not.

On 27 May 1944, he noted a British Vengeance with the code letters 'LJ-H' painted in Navy-style, drab green and grey with dark grey undersurface. It was logged as FJ859 and belonged to the RN. A Ferry Command pilot, Hugh Bergel, recalls flying two Vengeances, HB307 from South Marston to Weston Zoyland on 13 October 1944, and HB531 on exactly the same trip on 27 October 1944.

'I seem to remember it was rather a large aeroplane with an unusual wing arrangement, the centre section sloping quite steeply down and the rest of the wing turning quite sharply up'.

Of course, by far the bulk of the Vengeances in British skies during 1944-46 were the target-towing conversions. Indeed, it was in this role that the Vultee Vengeance was most widely and consistently utilised in the final years of its complex life.

# Chapter 12
# Conclusion

Production finally ceased at Nashville on 2 June 1944, when the last Vengeance (A-35) was towed out of the final assembly line. Work then commenced on preparing it for the P-38 line which was scheduled to follow it.

What it meant to the Nashville workforce was spelt out in *The Volunteer* of 10 March 1944: 'Arrangements have been made by Convair for those employees who are temporarily terminating because of the cutback in A-35 production to continue their life, hospitalization and medical fee insurance for the entire period of the lay-off, C. N. Crocker, Nashville Treasurer, announced . . .'

Apart from a few (like AN610) used by the Bombing Development Unit at Feltwell as late as August 1945, the majority of the Mark IV-1s and -2s that reached England were converted for drogue target-towing duties by the firm of Cunliffe-Owen Aircraft after feasibility studies had shown that the Vengeance was quite suitable in this role. They were used thus extensively both at home and overseas. Those in British hands were fitted with the Type B Mk IIB winch on the port side of the fuselage. This was wind-driven when feathered. As such they equipped Nos 288, 289, 567, 577, 587, 595, 631, 667, 691 and 695 Squadrons, RAF.

A very detailed account of Vengeance target-towing with the Anti-Aircraft Co-operation Unit at Katni, 200 miles north-west of Allahabad, was provided for me by Flight Sgt L. R. M. Tibble.

'The aircraft stood out in the weather,

Other small-scale, but vital, war work continued to be performed by the Vengeance, however. No. 1340 Flight was formed in India to test poison-gas trials under tropical conditions. Later it conducted a series of smoke-laying exercises with the Army and Royal Navy designed to screen the landing fleet for the proposed Operation 'Zipper', the invasion of Malaya. Here Bud McInnes takes off with his Vengeance awkwardly laden with one of the bulky spherical smoke-floats under her wing. *(Bud McInnes)*

mostly dry and very hot. If left standing for three months in monsoon weather I understand the cadmium of the metal fuselage would oxidize sufficiently for the airframe to be useless. In monsoon weather the *Cyclone* engine of the Vengeance, with its eighteen cylinders with two plugs per cylinder, each night would have its plugs taken out and placed in a carrier similar to a bingo-ball holder and transported in this tray to the mess kitchen where they were kept dry overnight. Just imagine the nightmare of the engine fitters.

'However, it ensured full power on take-off and the Vengeance needed everything to get its 16,000 lb to a reasonably safe height of 1000 ft (at least). Here I pay tribute to the ground-staff engineers. Spare parts were impossible but none of us in two years needed to complain about loss of power on take-offs or indeed engine failure. Mind you, if it had happened, the pilot would probably not have been around to discuss it!

'Our flying duties consisted of either using the aircraft as a target for live firing work, the drogue being towed on a long wire of 3,000 ft. This was run out by the LAC in the rear seat and retrieved by the side propeller which efficiently operated the wire drum by turning in the slip-stream.

'The alternative was a low-flying course to allow Bofors guns to gain experience. This occurred at 1000 ft with either a 1500 ft drogue or practice at the same height. Generally we flew 2 1/2 hours at 10,000 ft, perhaps every two or three days and together with the 1500 ft run for Bofors gun firing at 2000 ft.

'These flights were along a six to eight mile run. At the completion of these runs the Army liked the low beat-up for special practice but were not too happy one day when, at 100 ft or so, I beat up the camp with 1000 ft of wire still strung out behind the aircraft! Only on a squadron does one have one's own personal aircraft, most of the aircraft that I flew were flown by all the members available on the Flight, from the CO down to the newest Sgt Pilot. My last flight in a Vengeance was on 19 January 1945, AN881, twenty-five minutes of air and engine tests.

'I flew the Vengeance mostly for these two years, giving an overall total on the Vultee of approximately 300. The Vengeance was a splendid aircraft, it flew very well, very smoothly and with no vices or inherent instability. It was, of course, heavy, and without any power dropped like a stone. For its weight it was perhaps somewhat underpowered for combat purposes. For aerobatics (with sufficient height) it was quite superb for its size. The later two and three-

Vultee-built Vengeance IVs Stateside awaiting shipment to Australia. Far superior to the early models used in combat, the Mark IVs unfortunately arrived too late to see active service, the decision not to allow the Australian dive-bombers to be used directly against the enemy having been taken by the American Air Commander in New Guinea, despite their proven success rate. However, No. 25 Squadron did equip with these later marks and used them for anti-submarine patrols during the last years of the war. *(Smithsonian)*

thousand horse-power engines towards the end of the war would have given it a formidable turn of speed for the type.

'It must be realised of course that I have never flown a brand-new Vengeance. All aircraft at OTUs, and more so as towing aircraft, were ex-squadron aircraft and mostly not good enough for further operational use. Even so, I never had, in those three hundred hours, any cause to worry about engine cuts, rough running, oil misting up the screen, etc. I often felt that if I had had to put it down on the nearest field, with its sturdiness and its quick responses, I would have done so with reasonable confidence of getting away with it. One could land the aircraft in a glide approach with no more difficulty than if one were flying a Harvard.'

The Royal Navy also acquired the Vengeance for the same duties, equipping 721, 791 and 733 Squadrons, Fleet Air Arm. The Navy had modified exhaust stacks fitted to most of their Vengeances. No. 721 Squadron was established at Belfast on 1 March 1945, under the command of Lieutenant-Commander (Air) F. A. Simpson, RNVR, with 12 Vengeance TT.IVs, some of which were from RAAF conversion allocations. Six of these were initially used at Belfast for pilot familiarisation, while the other flight was prepared for ferrying on the escort carrier *Begum*. The squadron embarked aboard her on 17 April and she arrived in India on 28 May 1945, the aircraft disembarking at Ponam. FRU duties were then undertaken by the squadron, as well as air-to-air target-towing and acting as targets for·the local MONAB No. 4. The Vengeances were then grounded and some, under Lieutenant R. D. Head, DSC, RN, re-embarked on the escort carrier *Speaker* on 28 December and took passage aboard her to Hong Kong, being disembarked at Kai Tak airfield. Here they remained in use until May 1947. The squadron finally disbanded on 27 November of the same year.

No. 733 Squadron was formed as a Fleet Requirements Squadron at Minneriya on 1 January 1944, but it didn't include Vengeances on its strength until July 1945,

when it was operating from China Bay (Trincomalee) and commanded by Lieutenant-Commander (Air) J. A. Ansell, RNVR. He was later relieved by Lieutenant-Commander (Air) I. O. Robertson, RNVR, but although some sources state that the Vengeance had been phased out by September 1945, it was still being flown by that unit nine months later than this date.

Jack Bryant, at that time a young Telegraphist/Air Gunner (TAG) in the Fleet Air Arm, gave me this graphic and detailed account of another Royal Navy Vengeance unit in the Far East at this time.

'791 Squadron formed up at RNAS China Bay (Trincomalee) on 1 November, 1945, as a Fleet Requirements Unit, its personnel being drawn mainly from other stations in SEAC. The C.O. was Lieutenant Commander Hallewell, R.N., the senior pilot Lieutenant Shilcock, R.N.

'When we arrived at RNAS China Bay there were no aircraft on the strength and, in order to learn the ropes of what was required of a Fleet Replacement Unit TAG I spent my time with the resident FRU, namely 733 Squadron, flying Boulton Paul Defiants towing drogues, plus 16 feet and 32 feet winged targets. There were certainly no Vengeance on the strength of 733 up until after we left China Bay about five days before Christmas 1945.

'During the early weeks of December our pilots were flown up to Cochin to pick up our aircraft, six Corsairs, two Havards and six Vultee Vengeance. The latter had their wings removed and the squadron boarded the Escort Carrier H.M.S. *Smiter* for passage to Singapore. The aircraft were pushed onto lighters and taken out to the carrier and manhandled aboard by using derricks. Other aircraft taking passage were a number of Photo Reconnaisance Hellcats of 888 Squadron who were doing a photo-survey of the Far East, plus three Sea Otters of 1700 Squadron, which were eventually to go to the RAF at Changi.

'We landed at Singapore on Boxing Day, 1945, and moved to RNAS Sembawang on the following day, the aircraft of course being man-handled off *Smiter* by use of the derricks. These aircraft (which included FD409 and HB462), were camouflaged in dark green and dark earth on upper surfaces and sides; the undersides were overall yellow, with black stripes and prominent serial numbers, and had an 18-inch pale blue band in front of the tail. A further six Vengeance arrived from Australia and during my time at Sembawang only one ever flew! (A27-520 piloted by Sub-Lieutenant Edwards on 27 March, 1946). These aircraft were overall dark earth with cream undersides.

'While our aircraft were being re-assembled I had a bit of a shock to see how few bolts were used to fix the mainplanes onto the centre-section. I seem to recall that they were held on by just four 5/8-inch bolts! My mind returned to our Aircraft Recognition classes at Nova Scotia, when an Instructor had told us the story that the peculiar wing form on the Vengeance was due to the centre of gravity going astray during its early days in construction, but I have never heard of this from any other source.

'Taking off from a small grass airfield like ours was had its problems — with a large, somewhat under-powered aircraft such as the Vengeance — and to add to the problem the field was for the most part surrounded by a fringe of trees. Eventually, and after experimenting with varying degrees of flap, we would taxi to the extremity of the airfield and the pilot would stand on the brakes and rev up until the tail was in the flying position. The brakes were then released and we would bump over a gravel perimeter road and head for the trees on the other side of the field. It took what seemed like an age to unstick, and then, with any Roman Catholics on board beginning to finger their rosaries, and others wishing they hadn't joined, we were off the ground and the trees were flashing past just underneath our wings. I don't know what it was like for the pilot seeing the trees getting closer, but it was a bit hairy for us in the back!

'When we were about to commence drogue towing we would tie a drogue to the end of the towing cable and release the brake. Poised on our knees over a panel cut out of the fuselage

Target-towing became the principal duty of the Vengeance TT IVs which were converted in both Britain and Australia in 1944, and this improved model was never given the chance to prove itself in proper combat. Here is A27-9 an early RAAF Vengeance, converted to this role with the winch on the starboard side of the fuselage instead of the more normal port side as featured by those converted by the firm of Cunliffe-Owen in the UK. *(RAAF Officaial via Chris Shores)*

A spectacular underside view of A27-9 of No. 4 OTU, working as a target-tower, as she banks away to reveal the orange and black diagonal striped markings of these units. Despite this, and the unique Vengeance silhouette, some Australian Army AA gunners *still* had difficulty in distinguishing a Vengeance from a Boomerang on occasion! *(RAAF Official via Chris Shores)*

floor (from memory about 18-inches long by 2-inches wide) the pilot would throttle back, put the aircraft's nose down and we would throw out the folded-up drogue, ensuring that it would not be forced back into the fuselage by the slip-stream and also that it cleared the tailplane.

'The drogues would then be streamed to a distance of, say 4,000 or 6,500 ft and care would be taken by operating the brake to ensure that it didn't race away and possibly snap the cable off at the drum. A cable guide runner used to traverse from side-to-side in order that the cable was evenly distributed on the cable drum. The next bit was just simply to fly on a steady course, backwards and

forwards to allow the warships to fire at the target. This was fine when passing alongside, but the further away you flew, the target's relative position closed up to the aircraft's visual position and you hoped that the firing would cease before it got too close!

'After a shoot, the windmill on the outside of the aircraft would be turned a little into wind, the brake released and the cable would be wound back in. Again care had to be taken because if the windmill was too far into wind the cable would be wound in too quickly; if the brake was applied more fiercely it would smoke. The last yard or two of cable needed very gentle winding in order to get the end of the cable into position under the cut-out in the cockpit floor.

162

'Having achieved this, the object of the exercise was to get the drogue into an area outside the squadron office that was marked out in a ring of blancoed stones. The aircraft would fly low over the airfield and the TAG have a sharp knife in hand ready for the pilot to say 'Stand by, one, two, three — Cut!' The cord would be cut and if the drop was successful, the drogue would flutter down into the circle of stones, If it was missed, then you were in for a lot of leg-pulling in the crewroom. Cutting the drogue wasn't as easy as it sounds. You were on your knees but your arm was dangling in the slip-stream a couple of feet beneath the aircraft.'

During the spring of 1946 Jack Bryant's logbook shows many such runs in which he was TAG on various of the Squadron's Vengeances. Typical of these was on 28 March, 1946, when, with Sub-Lieutenant Edwards as pilot and Petty Officer Wilkins also up, Bryant was TAG aboard Vengeance HB462. They took off at 1245 and, in a two hour 40 minute flight, they streamed three drogues for the destroyers H.M.S. *Cavendish* and *Cavalier* (The latter, incidentally, nowadays the only surviving genuine British destroyer left afloat and preserved as a floating Museum at Chatham).

One Navy flyer from that period was Peter R. Dallosso and he gave me this information on the Vengeances of this unit. 'For a few months in 1946, I served in 733 Squadron at Trincomalee and ferried two Vengeance aircraft from Cochin to Trincomalee. From my logbooks I can confirm that the first trip took place on 24 May 1946 and was in HB 335, a Vengeance IV, and it was my first solo. I carried out familiarisation tests and stalls for forty minutes and noted that I found it a "pleasant aircraft". The following day the engine failed in the same aircraft. I put her down safely on the non-duty runway. Next day the carb was still cutting out but on the 27th I had her in the air for twenty minutes and the carburettor accelerator pump was finally OK. On 28 May I flew this machine to Trincomalee with Sub-Lieutenant Geoghegan as my navigator but had to turn back due to bad weather. We were airborne an hour and a half. I finally delivered this machine on the 28th after a flight of two hours ten minutes.

'My second ferry mission in the Vengeance took place on 3 June 1946, with Petty Officer Radio Mechanic Watson as my back-seat man. This was in FD 417, also a Mark IV. We led four Corsair fighters to Trincomalee from Cochin but again suffered engine failure. This was due to someone else's error — a misalignment of the fuel selectors. Fortunately it only caused alarm when I was almost at Trinco! We had to land downwind but we survived it.'

The USAAF used A-35Bs, converted for the job in the same way as the RAF and the French Air Force, as we have already noted. As early as 16 July 1942, the feasibility of installing C-5A target-towing equipment in

Another Vengeance converted for target-towing. This is the RAAF's A27-14 over East Sale, Victoria, November 1944. *(Cyril McPherson)*

A-31 was being studied and it was estimated that 150 man hours per ship would probably be required for the necessary modification work involved. The effect this equipment would have on the aircraft's centre of gravity was also being considered.

By 16 January 1943 Engineering Division at Wright Field informed AC/S (E) Washington that shop work on a A-31 equipped with the tow-target installation had been completed and plane and engine flights made. Repairs to electrical system, and final flight-test of the installation were to be made asap.

In a letter dated 13 August 1943, Colonel Orval R. Cook told Vultee that permission was secured from BAC to modify 100 A-35 (B) for the tow-target installation at Chicago and Southern Modification Center, thereby alleviating the shortage of storage space at the contractor's plant.

As well as target towing, glider tug possibilities were studied. However, by 5 August 1942 Engineering Division at Wright Field was reporting that first studies had indicated that the A-31 and A-35 were not suitable as tow airplanes for troop gliders.

Another fascination sidelight was revealed in a memo of 8 May 1943. An examination of a Vultee report on the use of jets to decrease the Vengeance's over-long take-off distance was made by Aircraft Lab at Wright Field. It was decided that the value of jet propulsion on this particular plane would be 'very questionable'.

The RAAF also utilised the Vengeance for special duties with 1 APU at Laverton, Victoria, during the 1943-44 period, as Australia's leading test pilot of the war, D. R. 'Gel' Cuming, told me. 'These tests at Laverton were carried out on behalf of the USAAF. Our Flight was called the Aircraft Performance Unit. We only used the Vengeance as a platform for dropping experimental bombs and thus were interested only in the performance of the bombs, not the aircraft. The bombs we dropped were mainly 250 lb experimental anti-personnel bombs for use in New Guinea and we carried them under the wings, not in the bomb bay. The Vengeance worked well enough in this role as a "hack" and was easy to fly.'

The RAAF of course also used them, with the winch mounted on the *starboard* side of the fuselage, with No. 7 OTU based at Tocumwal, NSW. They also passed some of their allocations of target-tug conversions direct to the Royal Navy in England before they had themselves taken delivery. The eight aircraft transferred thus to the Royal Navy were: A27-619 on 6 September 1945: A27-539 and 545 on 9 September; A27-520, 547, 549 and 502 on 7 October; and A27-529 on 22 October 1945. Of these aircraft the original US serial numbers had been: 41-31300, 41-31420, 41-31425, 41-31430, 41-31431, 41-31438, 42-94379 and 43-31436.

Postwar, they also transferred some of their own Vengeances to the Royal Australian Navy, mainly worn-out hulks for use by fire-fighting teams. The following 12 were given as free-transfers to the RAN in this manner: A27-402, 403, 404 and 563 on 2 March 1949; A27-530 on 5 February 1951; A27-4 on 6 February 1951; A27-9 on 27 February 1951; A27-14, 506 and 526 on 15 March 1951; A27-617 on 1 May 1951 and A27-600 on 11 May 1951.

Others were used as 'hacks' and target tugs with Nos 1, 5 and 6 Communications Units. George Limbrick joined 3 CU at Mascot field on 1 November 1944, where he found himself flying the Vengeance once more, mainly as a target-tug for the Army and the RAAF but also for the Royal Navy, who were working up two carrier task forces in Australia to join the Americans for the final stages of the Pacific War.

'All drogues were streamed from the back cockpit by WAGs (Wireless-Operator and Gunner) who operated an electric winch. Firstly the Army. They used drogues at 10-12,000 ft for heavy AA streamed at 300-400 yards, and shoots took place with us flying a set course about one-and-a-half miles off the coast. Their base was near to the old Long Bay Range, twelve miles south of Sydney harbour. Speed with drogues had to be kept to, or below, 160 mph, so we flew in a very

Head-on view of the V-72 climbing shows to advantage the deep fuselage and the marked dihedral of the other wing section. *(Smithsonian)*

tail-down configuration. At higher speeds the drogues would tear and split and disintegrate. Drogues were rarely shot down by the Army. Their other method was to fire shells to explode at a height of 10,000 ft and have an aircraft flying at 12,500 ft and this was called a "Short Shoot". I cannot remember doing any light AA work with the Army.'

This was done mainly off Cemetery Point at Newcastle, NSW, Bluefish Point and Magic Point near Wollongong.

Target-towing for the Navy was both surface-to-air and air-to-air, as George described to me. 'A lot of our work with the Navy consisted of flying a set course, while they checked radar, compass and, as I understand it, also checked the operation and sighting devices of their AA armaments. Our co-operation with the Fleet Air Arm was with Fairey Fireflies, Grumman Hellcats and

Vought Corsairs mainly. While the carriers were in dock or harbour their air complements were flown off ashore. As each carrier left to join the fleet off Okinawa we would give them air-to-air gunnery practice with drogues streamed at 250-300 ft. This was short, but they were very accurate and warships usually disposed of drogues every few minutes, then we would wind-in and tie a new one on and put it out smartly. I think about two minutes was the average for this. On completion of these aerial shoots the aircraft would rejoin their ships.'

These flights took place from early December 1944, onwards. 'Among the first warships I towed for were the escort carriers *Arbiter* and *Chaser*, US minesweeper, *Alchemy*, an American landing ship, *Fort Wrangle*, which had been damaged and after repairs had a go at the drogue with her new guns. On 13 January 1945, there was a most impressive display by the battleship *Howe,* the New Zealand-manned light cruiser *Achilles* and three Australian-manned destroyers, *Quadrant, Quality* and *Queenborough.* The ships steamed out of Sydney and the cruiser and destroyers were like chicks flocking round a hen. Off the coast we followed our orders, which had been conveyed to us on board the previous day. When the multiple pom-poms and other light AA opened up, our drogues disappeared in ribbons before we could, literally, take a deep breath. We finished up streaming them at only 200 ft to save time, but we soon ran out of drogues. Six I think, or it could have been eight, and the cable near the drogue was badly damaged. Pilot Officer Knapp had a rare busy time. The ships were a magnificent sight as they steamed away from us at speed.'

In June 1945 Limbrick was posted to 5 CU at Garbutt, where work was very spasmodic. Vengeances A27-2, 4, 407, 447, 483, and 608 were on hand with this unit. 'The Vultees were mainly used for ferrying VIPs on buildings, stores and equipment inspections. The rear cockpit and bomb bay had been converted to seat three people. The only events that occurred in this period were a search for a Mustang which went down in the sea off Magnetic Island and, on 7 September, an electrical failure which caused our return to Cloncurry. The rail line made a very good direction indicator.

'May I say that I enjoyed flying the Vultee and would say that it was a very reliable aircraft with an aerobatic quality which belied its weight. Its biggest trouble was if it ran out of noise — then the descent was very sudden! Its flying attitude and high tail made it almost impossible to jump from the rear cockpit. One WAG of 25 Squadron at Pearce, West Australia, tried it and was gravely injured.'

Motion-picture film of the Vultee dive-bomber was not restricted to 110's training production in India. Another 'starring' role for the Vengeances of No. 21 Squadron, RAAF, was their employment as make-believe *Stukas,* with totally unconvincing *Swastikas* painted on their still all-white South-West Pacific Area tails and crosses on the fuselages and made-up *Luftwaffe* serials.

The Fleet Air Arm of the Royal Navy utilised RAAF Vengeance target tugs to work up the AA gunners of the British Pacific Fleet in readiness to tackle the Kamikazes off Okinawa and Japan in 1945. Later they acquired some ex-RAAF and RAF Vengeance target tugs for themselves and equipped two squadrons with them for use on Eastern Stations at China Bay, Trincomalee and at Hong Kong, post-war. This is HB335, a Vengeance II converted to a TT IV target tug and delivered to the Royal Naval Air Station near Belfast. *(R. C. Sturtivant)*

Thus they were flown by their crews for the benefits of the movie cameras at Bankstown, NSW, in May 1944, for the film *Rats of Tobruk*. A final humiliation for the aircraft conceived in the image of the Ju 87, designed to outclass it in every way, but in the end destined to play second-fiddle to its much more famous, if technically less efficient, cousin.

No. 84 Squadron's magazine for Christmas 1943 provides a fitting epitaph to an aircraft that was much-acclaimed for its achievements in battle, much-loved by the combat pilots who flew it but much-abused by everyone else.

Ode to a Pranged Vengi
or (somewhat unkindly)
Gray's Other Elegy

You always were an ugly brute,
A fact that's quite beyond dispute;
Indeed, for grace and elegance,
A horde of angry elephants
Would take the biscuit every time
From you, you Vultee pantomime.
This much I'll say, to justify
Your place amongst the Things that Fly;
-Touch wood-you'd always yield the boost
To bring me safely home to roost.
Although you ne'er acquired a bent
For dazzling accomplishment,

Each of your horses proved a steed
Unfailing in the hour of need.
(And on that score alone, I find
I've really got no room to bind!)
And so I mourn your Waterloo
The graveyard of an R.S.U.
Is your Last Happy Hunting Ground . . .
But here's the moral to be found
In your unfortunate demise;
If any more of you VVs
*Must* pick up some unoffending kite,
On which to expedite your spite,
For Pete's sake chose a Tiger Moth
To be the victim of your wrath;
Don't tackle with impunity
The first thing that you chance to see:
And take a tip from 'W' —
A Wimpey's much too big for you!

Do any Vultee Vengeances survive? Well yes, there is one almost whole one preserved in a museum in Australia, several mounted engines on display at civilian airports in the same country and a large collection of parts and pieces, which it is hoped will one day be reassembled for a second Vengeance, again in Australia. Twenty years ago there were persistent hints of an almost complete Vengeance somewhere either in India or in what is now Pakistan, but to date I have been unable to substantiate this.

Frank Purser, Curator of the Air Force Memorial Estate at Bull Creek, Western Australia, provided the following useful details on what remains of approximately 30 Vengeances which were sold, like all the other survivors, by the Commonwealth Disposable Commission, in 1951.

1. A collection of damaged and vandalised airframe assemblies which constitute the major part of A27-247, an ex-RAAF Vengeance. This is minus the bomb-bay doors and a few other pieces.

2. The engine and nose cowl from the above aircraft which has been restored to display condition and completed with carburettor, magnetos and all accessories, together with a propeller, the blades of which are of doubtful authenticity.

3. Several major fuselage assemblies, very badly damaged, rescued from a scrap yard.

4. Three *Cyclone* GR2600 engines, two of them stripped of all accessories, one of them complete with nose and side cowls, gill flaps, oil cooler and mountings back to the fire wall.

'All these are in the possession of the RAFA Aviation Museum with the restored engine on display. There are no immediate plans to undertake the task of restoring the airframe. There are no decipherable serial numbers on any of the engines or airframe assemblies but A27-247 can be read on the fuselage.'

After post-war service the bulk of all Vengeances were quickly sold off for scrap at knock-down prices. Very few managed to survive for very long. Here the shattered remnants of A27-247 arrive at the RAAF Museum at Bull Creek aboard a road transporter. Happily, attempts are now being made to piece together this heartbreaking jigsaw into the second surviving Vultee dive-bomber. *(Frank Purser)*

David A. Saunders brings the story of A27-247 up to date:

'Many of us have long thought it is such a shame that the Vultee has been labelled a bad aircraft by a lot of people. With your book and help from people such as myself maybe we ought finally put the record straight.

'The Vultee I have is in very bad condition. The Australian Registration A27-247, and the original registration is AF929. These registration marks are only on the tail of the aircraft but the major part of the fuselage up front does bear 14 bombing runs mark-ups from the war. She obviously saw active service. I'd like to find out more about this particular part of the aircraft as I'd like to name the whole aircraft after this section. The only identifying marks I have found on her is, while removing the outside skin, one of the skins, (you know the fuselage section is double-skinned), the inside skin has written in pencil 'Ship 223'. I'm under the impression that the Americans used to call their aircraft 'Ships'. If this is the case it probably could be AF233 we are talking about.

'Unfortunately with the skin rebuild I do have in front of me I do have to have all the technical information I can get hold of. You see what has actually happened is they've actually cut the fuselage with an angle grinder right through. Investigating the area, which is in the area of the rear gunner, I found that the fuselage here is actually joined together by bolting it. This must be a factory join as you have to do a fair bit of riveting to achieve this. What I plan to do is to make the actual split there. Rebuild the actual fuselage forward of that station as completely as I can. Then rebuild the whole tail section again. That is the biggest job I have ahead of me because there's virtually nothing left of it.

'One side of the tail section is there but the other side there is virtually nothing there it's been completely cut off there is nothing there at all. Plus a series of bullet holes and just vandals attacking this section. On the tail section the vertical fin has been hacked off at the top. I'm rather lucky to have come across the leading section of that vertical fin, the complete section, so with the drawings and

168

everything else I should be able to rebuild that section quite well. The rest of the fuselage is going to be a headache. I'm looking forward to this challenge, should be rather interesting!

'In my travels around obtaining parts I've obviously got more than I need of the Vultee. I hope to approach the Museum after I've completed the task of rebuilding her and see if I can obtain all the rest of the Vultee parts as I'm sure somewhere around the world these days there has to be another Vultee still remaining or a complete fuselage anyway and I'm sure I can be of assistance to somebody who does find that aircraft with all the parts I do have here.'

The only '233' serial I have traced so far is the RAF Serial 'FD233', A Vengeance IV-2 built by Vultee themselves under Lend-Lease. But I cannot trace this through to the RAAF. American Serials consisted of year of manufacture and a five or six figure appendage (E.G.:- 41-30848 or 42-101236). The RAAF took delivery of some of its Vengeances via the RAF (Hence they would have original serials, AF, AN, HD etc etc) and some straight from the USA which would have USA Serials. Of these the only possibility would be A27-420 which was ex 41-31223. This particular aircraft was delivered to the RAAF on 19 August 1943 and was 'Converted to Components' on 29 November 1946. I have no details of any action service, or that she was issued to an active squadron.

On the other hand A27-247, the tail, was delivered to the RAAF on 24 April 1943 at No. 1 Aircraft Depot at Laverton and issued to Point Cook on 28 May 1943. She was a Northrop-built Mk II, ex-AF.929, and she still bore this serial on delivery. She was then returned to No. 1 AD on 7 July 1943 and two days later she was issued to No. 25 (City of Perth) Squadron at Pearce RAAF Base. She crashed there on 19 September 1943, but was repaired and had certain conversions done to her by No. 17 Repair and Salvage Unit. On 19 August 1944, she was re-issued to No. 17 RSU for a 240 hour overhaul and inspection, returning to No. 25 Squadron on 1 October. She served well and was finally passed to DAF on 22 June 1948. She probably saw all her service at Pearce RAAF base and at Guildford but only on anti-submarine duties.

On 2 January 1945, she was issued to No. 4 Aircraft depot, and on 22 March 1946 was stored category 'E' at Boulder, W.A. CMU. This Vengeance was offered for disposal through the Commonwealth Disposals Commission on the 10 April, 1946, and was authorised for write off from the RAAF's

Close-up of the reconstructed rear cockpit of the Narellan Vengeance with single .5 inch calibre gun.
*(Wayne Brown)*

Giving an excellent detailed view of the re-built *Cyclone* engine *in situ* on the Narellan Vengeance and the ease of access, with removal of side panels by the serving Australian mechanic who is restoring her to a taxying condition. *(Wayne Brown)*

records on 16 May 1946. She was one of 31 Vengeances sold at Boulder on 22 June 1948 nineteen of which were brought by Perth scrap metal dealer Bill Thomas for £5 each, and he cut off the engines and removed the undercarriages and transported these back to Perth, burning the rest of the aircraft on site. The other dozen were mostly sold to local residents, who purchased the aircraft as playthings for their children. These machines being towed to various locations around Kalgoorlie, some surviving until the 1960s. A decade later most had gone for scrap.

In the late 1960s John Bell obtained various Vengeance components from this area which he hoped to assembly at his Albany property as a tourist attraction. He even obtained a Wright *Cyclone* engine through the Midland Technical School but eventually this proposed rebuild fell through.

The Aviation Historical Group contacted Mr Bell in early 1971 and, after correspondence, the aircraft was donated to the Group. On 4 December 1971, the Group visited Albany and photographed the machine which had many parts missing. Early the next year Bill Thomas at his Bentley scrapyard, donated a number of Vultee undercarriages to the Group and on 3 June 1972, these were finally assembled at the AFA for storage. Other Vengeance parts were obtained from the Kalgoorlie area in July 1971 and October 1972 and stored at the home of Fred Cherry at Perth. When the theme of the establishment of an aviation museum came up in a Television Documentary on Channel 2's *This Day Tonight* programme on 31 October 1978 the Vengeance parts featured prominently. Now David Saunders is carrying on the good work at his own home at Coolbelling.

Another GR2600 engine is on display at Perth International Airport, without accessories but with nose cowl and propeller. Two of the blades are fibreglass mouldings and there is no serial number.

H. G. Jacob, Duty Terminal Manager at Perth International Airport, gave the

Carrier-borne Vengeance! Extremely rare photograph of Vultee Vengeances aboard an aircraft-carrier. These are from No. 791 Squadron, Fleet Air Arm, taking passage from China Bay to Singapore aboard the Escort Carrier HMS *Smiter* in December, 1945. *(Jack Bryant)*

following information about the engine displayed at the Terminal Building. 'This particular engine was fitted to one of nineteen Vultee Vengeance aircraft disposed of at Boulder, Western Australia, in 1947, for the sum of ten Australian dollars each (!). The aircraft were purchased for their scrap metal value. The engine was later acquired by the Sport Aircraft Association of Australia, Western Australia Division, for 40 Australian dollars and subsequently donated to the Department of Aviation Historical Society for restoration. This restoration was accomplished with the kind co-operation and assistance of the Sport Aircraft Association and of Ansett Airlines of Australia, Universal Plastics, CIBA-GEIGY Australia Ltd, the

Air Force Association Aviation Museum and the Department of Aviation Regional Workshops.'

The most complete specimen is that held at the Camden Museum of Aviation, located at 11 Stewart Street, Narellan, NSW. This is a privately owned museum with no state funding and was founded, and is still run and maintained, by Harold, Verna and Alan Thomas. Harold was a former apprentice with Australian National Airways. All restoration work there is done by the family themselves and a couple of interested volunteers. One of these, who has specialised on the Vengeance, is LAC Wayne Brown from 77 Squadron Engine Section at RAAF Base Williamstown. He very kindly provided details of the work conducted there on this aircraft.

'This aircraft was the last Mk 1A Vengeance built by Northrop aircraft. It did not see active service with the RAAF and spent most of her career being sent from one storage depot to another, and as such has very few flying hours under wing. The markings EZ999 now carries are fictitious and the code NH-Y represents the code carried by an aircraft of 12 Squadron RAAF, in late 1943.

'After being disposed of by the RAAF she was used by the Sydney Technical College for many years, for training aircraft tradesmen, and it is only through this that she survived being scrapped. Eventually, she was obtained by Harold Thomas who stored her in his back yard before restoring her to display condition and putting her on display to the public at his museum at Camden airport. In 1979 the museum was forced to move from the airport and is now situated a short distance away at Narellan.'

The RAAF Historical Section at the Air Force Office, Canberra, kindly provided the author with a copy of this aircraft's detail sheet. EZ999 was given Australian serial A27-99 and was received on 20 June 1943 from the United States by 2AD. On 30 October she was moved into their store, and on 30 August 1945 allotted to 2CRD for further storage; this took place on 28 November. On 13 February 1946 she was allocated to 2AD Store and on 22 was ordered to be stored *in situ*. On 27 April 1948 it was approved for her to be moved to the RANS, but this move was cancelled on 11 June 1948 and she was passed to the DAP on the 24th.

It is to be hoped that this unfunded work, both at Narellan and Bull Creek, will receive more support, both physical and monetary, and that both airframes can be fully restored as tangible reminders of the 'Forgotten Dive-Bomber', the Vultee Vengeance.

# Appendix 1

## Operational Squadrons Utilising the Vultee Vengeance
(V-72, A-31, A-35, A27, VENGEANCE I, II, III, IV, TT)

### Royal Air Force

No. 45 Squadron
No. 82 Squadron
No. 84 Squadron
No. 110 (*Nizam of Hyderabad*) Squadron
No. 288 Squadron
No. 289 Squadron
No. 567 Squadron
No. 577 Squadron
No. 595 Squadron
No. 631 Squadron
No. 667 Squadron
No. 691 Squadron
No. 695 Squadron

### Fleet Air Arm

No. 721 Squadron
No. 733 Squadron
No. 791 Squadron

### Royal Australian Air Force

No. 12 Squadron
No. 21 (*City of Melbourne*) Squadron
No. 23 (*City of Brisbane*) Squadron
No. 24 (*City of Adelaide*) Squadron
No. 25 (*City of Perth*) Squadron

### Indian Air Force

No. 7 Squadron
No. 8 Squadron

### United States Army Air Force

55th Bombardment Squadron (Dive)
56th Bombardment Squadron (Dive)
57th Bombardment Squadron (Dive)
88th Bombardment Squadron (Dive)
309th Bombardment Squadron (Dive)
311th Bombardment Squadron (Dive)
312th Bombardment Squadron (Dive)
623rd Bombardment Squadron (Dive)
628th Bombardment Squadron (Dive)
629th Bombardment Squadron (Dive)
630th Bombardment Squadron (Dive)
631st Bombardment Squadron (Dive)

### French Air Force

GBI/32 *Bourgogne*
GBI/17 *Picardie*
GBII/15 *Anjon*

### Brazilian Air Force

1st Dive-Bombing Squadron
2nd Dive-Bombing Squadron

# Appendix 2

## Wright *Cyclone* GR2600.A.S.B. Radial Engine
14 Cylinder Double-row Air-cooled 1193 kW (1600 hp) Manufactured by
Wright Aeronautical Corporation, New Jersey USA

### Brief Specification

Bore: 155.6 mm
Stroke: 160.2 mm
Displacement: 42.7 litres
Compression: 6.3 : 1
Propeller reduction gear ratio: 16.9
Rated rpm of crankshaft: 2300 rpm

Max cruising rpm of crankshaft: 1900 rpm
Fuel Grade: 90 octane
Fuel consumption: 795 litres/hours at max rpm
Oil circulation: 63.5 kg/minute at rated rpm
Oil consumption: 23 litres/hour at max rpm

**Engine:**

Diameter: 1378 mm
Length: 1647 mm
Weight including accessories: 898 kg
Firing order: 1, 10, 5, 14, 9, 4, 13, 8, 3, 12, 7, 2, 11, 6

**Notes on engine problems**

By far the most serious reason for the delay, operational limitations and final rejection of the Vengeance was initially the unreliability of its power-plant. The *Cyclone* has been called a 'totally reliable' engine by one American magazine writer but the following excerpts from official USAAF documents tell a somewhat different tale.

1. 27 June 1942: Capt A. A. Watson, Asst AF Sec, ASC Wright Field to Chief Aero Equip Br Prod Wright Field: Spare R–2600 model engines were requested for the 100 V-72 (A-31) airplanes being diverted to AAF from contract A-557. Difficulties with engine necessitated high percentage of spares to avoid grounding of airplanes.

2. 13 March 1943. Telex from Major Thorpe at Vultee to Colonel S. R. Brentnall, Wright Field. Concern with failures of R-2600 engines in A35. Test on an engine at Nashville was expected to prove whether rust was the principal trouble, as Wright Aeronautical contended, or whether ring set-up and barrel material were responsible, as Power Plant Lab had maintained. An additional problem had been created by Ferry Command's refusal to handle the plane but Air Corps rep was directed to continue acceptance.

3. 19 March 1943: Major General H. L. George, ATC Washington to Materiel Command, Washington. George recommended all A35s be grounded until engine difficulties had been corrected. Numerous instances of forced landings because of excessive oil consumption and various other factors were cited. Fourteen A-35s had been delivered from Nashville

by Ferry Division pilots. Two made forced landings en route, one at Waycross, Georgia, the other at Birmingham, Alabama. The other 12 reached their destinations but all 14 were grounded because of excessive oil consumption. 'Inspection disclosed one or more of the following conditions: Fouled spark-plugs, badly worn piston-rings, warped piston-rings, pitted piston-rings, pitted and worn cylinder walls and warped cylinder walls. In the case of the airplane forced down at Waycross Lieutenant West, Vultee Factory Resident Representative test pilot, stated that, due to the extreme heat of the engine, the piston-rings had become welded to the cylinder walls.'

4. 1 April 1943: Colonel J. F. Phillips, Chief Development Engineering Branch Materiel Division OAC/AS MM&D Washington to ATC Washington. Phillips stated all available technical skill of AAF Wright Aeronautical and 'outside help' were being employed to solve the problem of R-2600 engine failures. In meantime instructions were given to airplane factories to limit power output of all engines for first ten hours of flight.

5. 4 April 1943: Sessums to ATC. Sessums questioned advisability of grounding all A35s in view of the fact that A-35-B and some As had engines which were performing satisfactorily. Grounding order would also interfere with flight delivery of airplanes allocated to foreign governments. He recommended that restricted flying be continued.

6. 5 July 1944: Colonel M. D. Burnside, Air Inspector Materiel Command to Technical Executive, Materiel Command. Excessive rust in R-2600 in A-35s had resulted in a number of crashes, one of which was fatal. Investigation seemed to show that the difficulty was due to use of ordinary compressed air instead of dehydrated air in treating the engines, and further investigation was to be made on this line.

# Appendix 3

## Serial Numbers

### 1. British

AF745-AF944 Vengeance II (Vultee-built, British contract)

AN538-AN837 (Vultee-built, British contract)

AN838-AN999 Vengeance 1 (Northrop built, British contract)

AP001-AP137 Vengeance 1 (Northrop-built, British contract)

EZ800-EZ999 Vengeance 1A (Northrop built, Lend-Lease) US Serials 41-30848 to 41–31047

FB918-FD117 Vengeance III (Vultee-built, USAAF Contract for Lend-Lease) US Serials 41-31048 to 41-31147

FD118-FD221 Vengeance IV-1 (Vultee-built, Lend-Lease)

FD222-FD417 Vengeance IV-2 (Vultee-built, Lend-Lease)

FP686 (Vultee-built, British contract; replacement for AN679 which crashed before delivery)

HB300-HB550 Vengeance IV-2 (Vultee-built, Lend-Lease)

KG810-KG820 Vengeance IV-2 (Vultee-built, Lend-Lease)

### 2. Australian

A27-1 to A27-5 (ex-AN853 to AN857)

A27-6 to A27-10 (ex-AN872, 874, 875, 876, 878)

A27-11 to A27-15 (ex-AN892, 894, 896, 897, 898)

A27-16 to A27-24 (ex-EZ880 to EZ888; US Serials 41-30928 to 41-30936)

A27-25 to A27-57 (ex EZ905 to EZ911, EZ913 to EZ915, EZ919 to EZ925, EZ930 to EZ945)

A27-58 (ex-EZ912)

A27-59 to A27-61 (ex-EZ916 to EZ918)

A27-62 to A27-65 (ex-EZ926 to EZ929)

A27-66 to A27-72 (ex-EZ946 to EZ952)

A27-73 (ex-EZ954)

A27-74 (ex-EZ953)

A27-75 to A27-94 (ex-EZ955 to EZ974)

A27-95 to A27-99 (ex-EZ995 to EZ999)

A27-200 (ex-AN550)

A27-201 (ex-AN556)

A27-202 (ex-AN559)

A27-203 (ex-AN579)

A27-204 (ex-AN558)

A27-205 (ex-AF943)

A27-206 (ex-AN539)

A27-207 (ex-AF941)

A27-208 (ex-AN574)

A27-209 (ex-AN540)

A27-210 (ex-AN565)

A27-211 (ex-AN543)

A27-212 (ex-AF926)

A27-213 (ex-AN544)

A27-214 (ex-AN548)

A27-215 (ex-AN570)

A27-216 (ex-AF934)

A27-217 to A27-218 (ex-AF940 and AF942)

A27-219 to A27-220 (ex-AN973 and AN576)

A27-221 (ex-AN549)

A27-222 to A27-224 (ex-AN569, AN571 and AN578)

A27-225 to A27-226 (ex-AN553 and AN564)

A27-227 to A27-238 (ex-AN546 to AN547, AN551 to AN552, AN554 to AN555, AN557, AN560-AN561, AN567 to AN568 and AN580)

A27-239 (ex-AF861)

A27-240 to A27-251 (ex-AF893, AF901, AF909, AF911, AF924 to AF925, AF927, AF929, AF932, AF935 to AF936, and AF939)

A27-252 to A27-256 (ex-AN541, AN562 to AN563, AN572 and AN577)

A27-257 to A27-260 (ex-AF896, AF906, AF916 and AF938)

A27-261 (ex-AN538)
A27-262 to A27-263 (ex-AF821 and AF838)
A27-264 (ex-AF944)
A27-265 (ex-AF913)
A27-266 to A27-268 (ex-AF905, AF907 and AF920)
A27-269 to A27-272 (ex-AF870, AF874, AF878 and AF912)
A27-273 (ex-AN542)
A27-274 to A27-283 (ex-AF796, AF810, AF841, AF854 to AF855, AF858, AF871, AF889, AF895 and AF914)
A27-284 to A27-293 (ex-AF793, AF803, AF809, AF836, AF842, AF884, AF891, AF917, AF921 and AF933)
A27-294 to AF296 (ex-AF778, AF 800 and AF849)
A27-297 (ex-AF758)
A27-298 (ex-AF763)
A27-299 to A27-311 (ex-AF763, AF781, AF797, AF814, AF820, AF828, AF840, AF859, AF860, AF862, AF869, AF888, AF918, AF931)
A27-312 to A27-313 (ex-AF767 and AF886)
A27-314 to A27-317 (ex-AF805, 881, 902 and 908)
A27-318 to A27-321 (ex-AF774, 818 and 877)
A27-400 to A27-404 (ex-41-31230, 41-31232, 41-31235, 41-31237 and 41-31238)
A27-405 to A27-408 (ex-41-31152, 41-31168, 41-31175 and 41-31196)
A27-409 to A27-419 (ex-41-31231, 31233 to 31234, 31236,31239, 31240 to 31242, 31244 to 31246)
A27-420 to A27-422 (ex-41-31223, 31229 and 31243)
A27-500 to A27-504 (ex-41-31264, 31299 to 31300, 31302 and 31309)
A27-505 to A27-507 (ex-41-31303, 31305 and 31306)
A27-508 to A27-518 (ex-41-31304, 31307, 31310, 31313, 31316 to 31317, 31319, 31326, 31329, 31333 to 31334)
A27-519 to A27-523 (ex-41-31422, 31436 and 32437, 31439, 31347)
A27-524 to A27-527 (ex-41-31308, 31440, 31445 and 31446)
A27-528 to A27-531 (ex-41-31418, 31430, 311435, 31443)

A27-532 to A27-535 (ex-41-31427, 31441 to 31443)
A27-536 to A27-539 (ex-41-31412, 31424, 31428, 31431)
A27-540 to A27-549 (ex-41-31301, 31411, 31414 to 31415, 31420 to 31421, 31423, 31425, 31432, 31438)
A27-560 to A27-563 (ex-42-94188, 94199, 94200, 94222)
A27-564 to A27-565 (ex-42-94171 and 42-94194)
A27-566 (ex-42-94180)
A27-600 to A27-602 (ex-42-94458, 94469 and 94488)
A27-603 to A27-606 (ex-42-94386, 94390, 94391, 94395)
A27-607 to A27-620 (ex-42-94350, 94352, 94355, 94359 to 94362, 94364, 94368, 94370 to 94371, 94378 to 94379, 94384)
A27-621 (ex-42-94407)
A27-622 to A27-630 (ex-42-94393, 94399 to 94402, 94405, 94409, 94413, 94419)
A27-631 to A27-640 (ex-42-94201, 94394, 94397 to 94398, 94403, 94406, 94410, 94412, 94415, 94417)

## 3. USA

41-30848 to 41-31047 (Northrop-built, Lend-Lease A-31-Nos)
41-31048 to 41-31147 (Vultee-built, Lend-Lease A31-VNs, including six for XA-31 and YA-31 projects)
41-31148 to 41-31246 (Vultee-built A35As)
41-31247 to 41-31447 (Vultee-built A35Bs)
42-94149 to 42-94548 (Vultee-built A35Bs)
42-101236 to 42-101465 (Vultee-built A35Bs)

## 4. French

Known American Serials used:
*July 1943 delivery*
41-31193
41-31200 (Lost in US hands before delivery)
41-31201
41-31202 (later fitted with A5B5 engine)
41-31203 (later fitted with A5B5 engine)
41-31204 (later fitted with A5B5 engine)
41-31209
41-31207

41-31211
41-31212
41-31213
41-31214
41-31216
41-31217
41-31219
41-31221
41-31220
41-31222
41-31224
41-31225
41-31226
41-31227
41-31228
41-31231

*December 1943 delivery*
41-31266
41-31269
41-31275
41-31276

41-31277
41-31283
41-31289
41-31292
41-31294
41-31296
41-31297
41-31298

**5. Brazil**
*February 1943 delivery*
6000-6011 AN581-AN592 (V-72s)
6012-6025 AN593-AN608 (R-V-72s) (AN608
lost *en route*)

*September 1944 delivery*
6056 41-101412 (A35B-15-VN)
6057 41-101421 (A35B-15-VN)
6058 41-101422 (A35B-15-VN)
6059 41-101426 (A35B-15-VN)
6060 41-101435 (A35B-15-VN)

# Appendix 4

## A Note on the Vengeance Wing Structure

Many and various have been the explanations of the unique wing form of the Vultee Vengeance, that special cranked inner wing and straight leading edge. I have quoted a selection from various 'experts' in the text. The truth however follows none of their theorising but is contained within the almost incomprehensible jargon of the U.S. Patent, 2,370,801, appertaining to that filed on 14 May 1941 by Alfred J. Klose, of Inglewood, California, assignor, by mesne assignments, to Consolidated Vultee Aircraft Corporation of Delaware. The Application Serial Number 393,322 and the Patent registered on 6 March, 1945, contain a total of 19 separate claims relating to Airplane Wing Structure. All but the really pedantic can dismiss most of this but the following points are a layman's guide to more pertinent points. I owe a debt of gratitude to Gerald H. Balzer for guidance in this field.

The key feature of the whole V-72 design was the desired objective of not having the primary (i.e. the heavy, bulky construction) structure penetrating into or through the crew compartment and bomb-bay of the aircraft. The one overriding criteria to anybody building dive-bombers was structural strength. The plane had to stand up to high 'G' forces and be sound enough, especially in the wing construction, to withstand to stresses undergone, not once or twice, but regularly, as part and parcel of the aircraft's total operational life. Bear in mind that the Vengeance was *specifically* designed to dive at 90 degrees, a true vertical attack not a compromise like most other dive-bombers, whose attack dives could vary from 50 to 75 degrees.

The 'Vultee Method' for construction resulted in an enormously powerful wing structure, testified to in the text by many operational pilots. It was a very tough airplane indeed. This reflected on its performance but it was built as a bomber, not a fighter, and, furthermore, it was built as a

177

dive-bomber, not as a jack-of-all-trades. With these essential points in mind the design of the Vengeance was a great success.

The following brief extracts from the Patent are particularly relevant in describing the resultant wing form.

1. "By having the inboard part of the wing structure that is the fuselage enclosed parts of the primary load carrying elements disposed within the fuselage at a point in front of the center of gravity and arranging the inner portions of the leading margins of the side parts of the wing structure so that they extend or sweep rearwards the side parts serve as the proper or desired load supporting media while at the same time it is possible to obtain, as far as the fuselage of the airplane is concerned, a most favorable disposition of the useful load with respect to the center of gravity without increasing the height of the fuselage."

2. "The central portion of the fuselage is of minimum height and is shaped to form a compartment for the pilot and other personnel of the airplane as well as the useful load."

3. "The leading edge of the section extends or sweeps rearwards at approximately an angle of 74 degrees with respect to the adjacent side portion of the fuselage "

4. "By forming the inner section of the wing structure so that the leading edge and the main or primary load carrying elements sweep rearwards at an acute angle with respect to the fuselage it is possible to position the inboard section in front of the center of gravity of the airplane. By so positioning the inboard section of the wing structure the compartment or useful load may be positioned most advantageously so far as the center of gravity is concerned while at the same time employing a fuselage of minimum height."

5. "The leading edge of the outer section is straight and is substantially truly normal to the fuselage and the line of flight of the airplane with the result that any tendency on the part of the wing structure as a whole to tip-stall is eliminated."

6. "The herein described wing structure effectively and efficiently fulfills its intended purpose and is characterized by the fact that the rearward sweep of the leading portions of the inner sections makes it possible to position the inboard section sufficiently in front of the center of gravity of the airplane to permit of the most favorable disposition of the useful load without necessitating any undue increase in the height of the fuselage."

# Appendix 5

Cockpit Layout —Vultee Vengeance dive-bomber, *(Designed by L. R. M. Tibble, drawn by Catherine Parker especially for the author)*

**BLIND FLYING INSTRUMENT PANEL**
**1–6, (SPERRY)**

1  Airspeed Indicator
2  Artificial Horizon
3  Climb/Descent Rate
4  Altimeter
5  Gyro Compass
6  Turn and Bank Indicator

7  Cylinder Head Temperature Gauge
8  R.P.M. Meter Gauge
9  Generator Meter Gauge
10 Trap Tank Fuel Switch
11 Ignition, Switch, Magneto
12 Oil Pressure Gauge (Engine)
13 Wheel Up/Down Indicator
14 Boost Gauge
15 Air Temperature Gauge
16 Engine Operation Instructions
17 Permissible Diving Speed Instructions
18 Parking Lever
19 Tail Wheel Lock Lever
20 Bomb Bay Switch

21 Fuse Bomb Switch
22 Bomb Release Button (Column)
23 Trap Tank Pump
24 Fuel Pressure Warning Light and Button
25 Six Fuel Tank Switches

**STARTER SWITCHES 26—27**

26 Energize Switch
27 Engage Switch

28 Cockpit Light Dimmers
29 Pilot Light Switch
30 Primer Switch
31 Pitot Head Heater Switch
32 Instrument Light Switch
33 Port Light
34 Taxy Light
35 Starboard Light
36 Gun Safety Switch
37 Dimmer Gun Sight
38 Fuel Gauge
39 Gun Sight
40 Dimmer Fuel Gauge Light

41 Destructor Switch and Lever
42 Gun Firing Trigger and Control Column
43 Nacelle Gills Lever
44 Flap Decrease Control
45 Flap Operating Lever
46 Undercarriage Selector
47 Aileron Trim Tab
48 Control Column and Rudder Bar Lock/Release
49 Compass
50 Supercharge Lever (Blower)
51 Throttle Lever
52 Mixture Lever
53 Pitch Lever
54 2-Speed Supercharger Operating Instruction Plate
55 Dive Brakes Lever
56 Elevator Trimming Tab
57 Rudder Trimming Tab
58 Cockpit Light Switch
59 Cockpit Light
60 Cockpit Light
61 Swing Up Sighting Ring
62 Rudder Pedals

179

# Notes on sources

My main sources are of course the interviews, tapes and written material obtained from the former designers, constructors, test pilots, air and ground crews who knew the Vengeance intimately. However, the use of much hitherto unpublished documentation added much to the story. Published material has been examined in relation to the above, but little consulted was of much value, most being repetitive and largely inaccurate. There were a few exceptions which, although incomplete, are the more worthwhile studies.

**Main Sources**

1. *Contract* as of 3 July 1940, between His Majesty's Government in the United Kingdom and Vultee Aircraft, Inc. (Copy in author's collection)

2. *Supplementary Letter to Contract* from British Purchasing Commission to Vultee Aircraft, Inc., dated 30 September 1940. (Copy in author's collection)

3. *Supplementary Letter to Contract* from British Purchasing Commission to Northrop Aircraft, Inc., dated 1 October 1940. (Copy in author's collection).

4. *Letter of Authorisation* from Viscount Halifax for Sir Henry Self, Director General British Air Commission, Washington, dated 3 February 1941. (Copy in author's collection)

5. *Contract* between His Majesty's Government in the United Kingdom and Northrop Aircraft, Inc., dated 25 February 1941. (Copy in author's collection)

6. *Letter of Amendment* No. 35, to Northrop Aircraft, Inc., from British Air Commission, dated 12 March 1942. (Copy in author's collection)

7. *Letter of Amendment* No. 43, to Northrop Aircraft, Inc., from British Air Commission, dated 29 May 1942. (Copy in author's collection)

8. *Telegram* to General Manager La Motte Cohu, Northrop Aircraft, Hawthorne, from C. R. Fairey, Director General, British Air Commission, dated 22 August 1943. (Original loaned to author by Ted Coleman)

9. *The Vultee Vengeance Specification – Model and Description A-31,* Northrop Aircraft Report No. 572-EN, dated 29 July 1942. (Copy in author's collection)

10. *Erection and Maintenance Instructions for Army Model RA-35B,* Manual AN 01–50AE-2, dated 15 March 1944, revised 15 November 1944. (Copy in author's collection)

11. *Pilot's Flight Operating Instructions for Army Model RA-35B-10,-15,* Manual AN 01–50AE-1, dated 5 June 1944. (Copy in author's collection)

12. *Parts Catalog for RA-35A Airplanes,* Restricted Manual AN 01-50AD-4, dated 1 July 1944. (Copy in author's collection)

13. *Erection and Maintenance Instructions* for *Army Model RA-35B,* Manual AN 01–50AE-2, dated 15 March 1944. (Copy in author's collection)

14. *A27 – Vultee Vengeance,* Detailed History List. (Copy prepared for author by RAAF Historical Section)

15. *Summary of the A-35 Airplane Project,* USAAF Document No 202 1-3, dated September 1944. (Copy in author's collection)

16. *Letter* from Consolidated Vultee Representative William H. Jones, to Morris Tombler, Field Service Dept, Consolidated Vultee, Nashville, dated 8 November 1943. USAAF Document 142 16-23.

17. *Dive-Bomber Requirements and Production*, (D.O.R. Folder), I D/5/334 (AIR 8/430)

18. *Dive-Bomber Aircraft – Introduction into 221 Group*, II J 51/48/03/22 (AIR 23/4361)

19. *Allied Air Tactics – Dive-Bombing* (AHQ India), II J 51/40/6/417 (AIR 23/5287–8)

20. *AAEE (Boscombe Down) RPT. No. 797 – Vengeance Aircraft: Trials, etc.,* IV/A/86/2. (Min. of Tech.)

21. *Tactical Memo No. 35 (RAF INDIA) Vengeance Ops. in Arakan*, II/M/A16/1/E. (AIR 24/803)

22. *Tactical Memo No.1 and No.5 (SEAC) Employment of Vengeance Aircraft*, II M/A44/1 S (AIR 24/1376)

23. *Delivery of Dive-Bombers and Characteristics*, CAS 1960 (AIR 8/631)

24. *Squadron Histories*, Monographs prepared by the USAAF Historical Section, Maxwell AFB. Various Bombardment Squadron (Dive) histories, copies in author's collection.

25. *Vengeance Bombers in the IAF*, Memorandum for the author, prepared by the Indian Air Force.

26. *Vultee A-31 Vengeance Marks I and II*, Memorandum for the author, prepared by the Indian Air Force.

27. *Operational Details of Vultee Vengeance Aircraft*, Memorandum for the Author, prepared by the Indian Air Force

28. *Operational Records Book*, No. 168 Wing, RAF India. (AIR 26/246; 71965)

29. *Operational Records Book*, No. 8 (Indian Air Force) Squadron (AIR 27/123; 71942)

30. *Flying Logbooks* of the following Vengeance pilots: Arthur M. Gill, RAF,; Donald J. J. Ritchie, RAAF; V. B. 'Red' McInnes, RCAF; George A. Limbrick, RAAF; Hugh W. Seton, RCAF; Freddie F. Lambert, RAF; Peter Latcham, RAF; L. R. M. Tibble, RAF.

**Secondary (Published) Sources**

31. *AVCO Corporation – History of Changes*, AVCO Information Sheet, 1965.

32. *The AVCO Story in Nashville*, AVCO Information Sheet.

33. *General Dynamics Convair Division Unpublished History* circa 1955

34. *'Vultee: Up From Nowhere'*, article in *Fortune*, September 1941.

35. *Vultee Volunteer*, various issues from 25 July 1941 to 9 June 1944.

36. *The Norcrafter*, various issues from May 1941 to December 1941.

37. *The Northrop News*, various editions from 5 May 1942 to 22 June 1943.

38. *'Those Versatile Vultees'*, article in *Air Enthusiast*, July 1972.

39. *The Historical Aviation Album*, Vol XVI, Produced by Paul R. Matt, Temple City, 1980.

40. *'Vengeance Diary'* posthumous excerpts from the Diary of Squadron Leader R. L. Lewis, edited by Frank F. Smith, published in *Journal of the Aviation Historical Society of Australia*, Vol 21, No 3, 1982.

41. *'Diving Vengeance'*, article by Christopher Shores and Frank F. Smith in *Air Enthusiast Five*, November 1977.

42. *'The Vultee Vengeance in the RAAF'*, by Keith Meggs, article published in *Aviation Historical Society Journal*, August 1965.

43. *Impact!: the Dive-Bomber Pilots Speak* by Peter C. Smith, Kimber, London, 1981.

44. *Dive Bomber!*, by Peter C. Smith, Moorland, Ashbourne, 1982.

45. *Beaverbrook,* by A. J. P. Taylor, FBA, Hamish Hamilton, London, 1972.

46. *'How Vultee Vengeance Crews Are Trained,* article by Adele Shelton Smith in *The Australian Woman's Weekly,* 19 February 1944.

47. *'Hitting with a Vengeance',* article by Flt Lt S. H. Swaffer, *Flight* magazine, 12 July 1945.

48. *'Vengeance'* article in *Model Airplane News* (USA), September 1943.

49. *'Vultee Vengeance',* article by Maurice F. Allward in *A.T.C. Gazette,* January 1945.

50. *'RAAF Vultee Vengeance Dive-Bombers Blast Tojo's Front Line',* by F/O N. Bartlett, Department of Air, Press Release, RAAF, Bulletin No. 3378, 1944. (Copy provided for the author by RAAF Historical Section)

51. *'Le General Jacquin':* Obit. by Andre Leuba, *Les Ailes Tricolores,* 19 May 1951.

52. *'Souvenirs de Marrakech',* extract from the Periodical *Forces Aeriennes Francaises,* No. 199, January 1964.

53. *'Vengeance! The Dive Bomber That Bombed Out!',* by Peter M. Bowers, article in *Wings,* vol 15, No.5, September 1985.

54. *'Vultee Vengeance. The Dive Bomber That Didn't/Finally Did!;* article by Peter M. Bowers in *Wings,* Vol. 15, No 5, October 1985.

55. *'Waiting for D-Day',* article by Mike Bowyer in *Aviation News,* 15-28 June 1984.

56. *'Dive-Bombing the Japs',* article in *The Sunday Statesman,* New Delhi, 28 May 1944.

57. *'Dive-Bombing the Japs',* article in *Indian Information,* August 1943.

58. *'Nizam-Backed Squadron Includes Toronto Flyers',* article in *The Globe and Mail,* 27 October 1944.

59. *Air War Against Japan 1943-1945,* by George Odgers, Australian War Memorial, 1968.

60. *The War Against Japan,* Vol 3, by S. W. Kirby, HMSO, London, 1962.

61. *Wings of the Phoenix,* HMSO, London 1949.

62. *History of the Indian Air Force,* by Air Marshal M. S. Chaturvedi, Vikas Publishing House, New Delhi, 1978.

63. *Aircraft of the Royal Air Force since 1918,* by Owen Thetford, Putnam, London, 1979.

64. *Australian Air Force Since 1911* by N. M. Parnell and C. A. Lynch, A. H. and A. W. Reed, Sydney.

65. *US Military Aircraft since 1909,* by Frederick G. Swanborough and Peter M. Bowers, Putnam, London, 1963.

66. *Encyclopaedia of Military Aircraft (1914-1980),* by Rand NcNally (USA edition), 1981.

67. *US Army Aircraft 1908-1946,* by J. C. Fahey (US edition).

# Index